GLOBAL RESOURCES AND
INTERNATIONAL CONFLICT

Global Resources and International Conflict

Environmental Factors in Strategic Policy and Action

Edited by
ARTHUR H. WESTING

sipri

Stockholm International Peace Research Institute

United Nations Environment Programme

Oxford · New York
OXFORD UNIVERSITY PRESS
1986

Oxford University Press, Walton Street, Oxford OX2 6DP
Oxford New York Toronto
Delhi Bombay Calcutta Madras Karachi
Kuala Lumpur Singapore Hong Kong Tokyo
Nairobi Dar es Salaam Cape Town
Melbourne Auckland
and associated companies in
Beirut Berlin Ibadan Nicosia

Oxford is a trade mark of Oxford University Press

Published in the United States
by Oxford University Press, New York

British Library Cataloguing in Publication Data
Global resources and international conflict:
environmental factors in strategic policy
and action.
1. Natural resources   2. World politics
—1975–1985
I. Westing, Arthur H.   II. Stockholm
International Peace Research Institute
III. United Nations. Environment Programme
333.7   HC55
ISBN 0–19–829104–3

Library of Congress Cataloging in Publication Data
Global resources and international conflict.
'Stockholm International Peace Research Institute,
United Nations Environment Programme.'
Bibliography: p.
Includes index.
1. Military policy.   2. Natural resources—Law and
legislation.   3. World War III.   I. Westing, Arthur H.
II. Stockholm International Peace Research Institute.
III. United Nations Environment Programme.
UA11.G57 1986   355'.023   86–5216
ISBN 0–19–829104–3

Set by Wyvern Typesetting Ltd.
Printed and bound in
Great Britain by Biddles Ltd,
Guildford and King's Lynn

Global Resources and International Conflict: Environmental Factors in Strategic Policy and Action has been prepared by SIPRI as a project within the SIPRI/UNEP programme on 'Military activities and the human environment'. The present volume is an outgrowth of a select symposium convened by the Stockholm International Peace Research Institute (SIPRI) in co-operation with the United Nations Environment Programme (UNEP) in Stockholm, 8–11 October 1985.

Any findings, opinions, conclusions, or recommendations expressed in this book are those of the authors and do not necessarily reflect the views of either SIPRI or UNEP.

SIPRI and the authors dedicate this book to the celebration of both World Environment Day, 5 June 1986, and the 1986 United Nations Year of Peace.

1. *Environmental Warfare: a Technical, Legal and Policy Appraisal* (edited by A. H. Westing; Taylor & Francis, London, 108 pp., 1984);
2. *Herbicides in War: the Long-Term Ecological and Human Consequences* (edited by A. H. Westing; Taylor & Francis, London, 210 pp., 1984); and
3. *Explosive Remnants of War: Mitigating the Environmental Effects* (edited by A. H. Westing; Taylor & Francis, London, 141 pp., 1985).

Preface

This book is the fourth in a major series on military activities and the human environment, resulting from a research programme jointly financed by SIPRI and the United Nations Environment Programme (UNEP). The programme is directed by Dr Arthur H. Westing (Adjunct Professor of Ecology at Hampshire College in Massachusetts, USA), an authority on the ecological impact of war.

The study considers the extent to which such factors as the geographical distribution, availability, scarcity, and degradation of the world's natural resources, both renewable and non-renewable, influence the international security perceptions that govern strategic policies and the use of military force. Singled out for detailed analysis are oil, minerals, fresh waters, ocean fisheries, food crops, and the human population. Differential population growth and the uneven distribution and degradation of natural resources combine to produce shifts in the distribution of power and influence. It thus becomes a major challenge to the world to ensure access to global resources in a way that will avoid international conflict. In recognition of this challenge, the study concludes with an expanded, environmentally based concept of international security.

Frank T. Blackaby
Director
SIPRI

Mostafa K. Tolba
Executive Director
UNEP

April 1986

Acknowledgements

The editor is pleased to acknowledge the very able research assistance of Carol Stoltenberg-Hansen, editorial assistance of Billie Bielckus, and secretarial assistance of Cynthia Loo.

Contents

Glossary and units of measure

I. Glossary

barrel, oil: *circa* 159 litres (see section II below).

basin, river: the area within which rainfall drains into a given stream; a catchment area (British usage) or watershed (US usage).

Capitalist state: Market economy (United Nations usage).

CMEA: Council for Mutual Economic Assistance (Moscow); COMECON; established in 1949; members as of January 1986: Bulgaria, Cuba, Czechoslovakia, German Democratic Republic (East Germany), Hungary, Mongolia, Poland, Romania, the USSR, and Viet Nam.

EEC: European Economic Community (Brussels); the 'Common Market'; established in 1958; members as of January 1986: Belgium, Denmark (not including Greenland), France, FR Germany (West Germany), Greece, Ireland, Italy, Luxembourg, the Netherlands, Portugal, Spain, and the United Kingdom.

FAO: Food and Agriculture Organization of the United Nations (Rome); established in 1945.

IUCN: International Union for Conservation of Nature and Natural Resources (Gland, Switzerland); established in 1948.

mile, nautical: 1.852 kilometres (see section II below).

NATO: North Atlantic Treaty Organization (Brussels); established in 1949; members as of January 1986: Belgium, Canada, Denmark, France (with reservations), FR Germany (West Germany), Greece, Iceland, Italy, Luxembourg, the Netherlands, Norway, Portugal, Spain, Turkey, the United Kingdom, and the USA.

OAPEC: Organization of Arab Petroleum Exporting Countries (Kuwait City); established in 1968; members as of January 1986: Algeria, Bahrain, Egypt (in suspension), Iraq, Kuwait, Libya, Qatar, Saudi Arabia, Syria, Tunisia, and the United Arab Emirates.

OECD: Organisation for Economic Co-operation and Development (Paris); established in 1961; members as of January 1986:

Australia, Austria, Belgium, Canada, Denmark, Finland, France, FR Germany (West Germany), Greece, Iceland, Ireland, Italy, Japan, Luxembourg, the Netherlands, New Zealand, Norway, Portugal, Spain, Sweden, Switzerland, Turkey, the United Kingdom, the USA, and Yugoslavia (with a special status).

OPEC: Organization of Petroleum Exporting Countries (Vienna); established in 1960; members as of January 1986: Algeria, Ecuador, Gabon, Indonesia, Iran, Iraq, Kuwait, Libya, Nigeria, Qatar, Saudi Arabia, the United Arab Emirates, and Venezuela.

Persian Gulf: Arabian Gulf; Gulf between Iran and Saudi Arabia (United Nations usage).

UNCLOS-III: Third United Nations Conference on the Law of the Sea, 1973–82; mandated by UN General Assembly Resolution No. 3067 (XXVIII) of 16 November 1973.

SIPRI: Stockholm International Peace Research Institute; established in 1966.

Socialist state: Centrally planned economy (United Nations usage).

UNEP: United Nations Environment Programme (Nairobi); established in 1972.

II. Units of Measure

The units of measure and prefixes (and the abbreviations) employed in the text are in accordance with the international system (SI) of units (Goldman & Bell, 1981). Standard conversion factors are used (Weast & Astle, 1979–1980, pages F307–29).

gram (g) = 10^{-3} kilogram = $2.204\ 62 \times 10^{-3}$ pound
hertz (Hz) = frequency per second
joule (J) = 0.238 846 calorie
kilo- (k-) = $10^{3} \times$
kilogram (kg) = 2.204 62 pounds
kilometre (km) = 10^{3} metres = 0.621 371 statute mile = 0.539 957 nautical mile
kilometre, square (km^2) = 10^{6} square metres = 100 hectares = 247.105 acres = 0.386 102 square statute mile = 0.291 553 square nautical mile
litre (L) = $10^{-3}\ m^3$ = 0.264 172 US gallon = 0.219 969 British gallon = $6.289\ 81 \times 10^{-3}$ US oil barrel

metre (m) = 3.280 84 feet

metre, cubic (m^3) = 10^3 litres = 264.172 US gallons = 219.969
   British gallons = 6.289 81 US oil barrels

second (s) = unit of time (see Goldman & Bell, 1981, page 3)

tonne (t) = 10^3 kilograms = 1.102 31 US (short) tons = 0.984 207
   British (long) ton

References

Goldman, D. T. & Bell, R. J. (eds). 1981. *International system of units (SI)*. Washington: US National Bureau of Standards, Special Publication No. 330, 48 pp.

Weast, R. C. & Astle, M. J. (eds). 1979–1980. *CRC handbook of chemistry and physics*. 60th ed. Boca Raton, Florida: CRC Press, [2447] pp.

Introduction

Global deficiencies and degradation of natural resources, both renewable and non-renewable, coupled with the uneven distribution of these raw materials, can lead to unlikely—and thus unstable—alliances, to national rivalries, and, of course, to war.

This multi-authored volume begins with an overview of raw-material and other global environmental factors in strategic policy and action (chapter 1). This survey is followed by in-depth analyses of a selection of key components of the environment, those especially likely to lead to future interstate disputes and conflicts: oil and natural gas (chapters 2 and 3) and other minerals (chapter 4); fresh waters (chapter 5); and ocean fisheries (chapter 6) and food crops (chapter 7). Next examined is the role of human population in exacerbating environmental problems as they relate to international conflict (chapter 8). The book concludes with policy recommendations within the framework of an expanded concept of international security, one that takes natural-resource and other environmental factors into consideration (chapter 9).

The text of the volume is complemented by a selection of apropos background references (appendix 1), an annotated compilation of wars and skirmishes from this century that have involved natural resources (appendix 2), and copies of the most relevant multilateral treaties (appendices 3–7).

The present volume is an outgrowth of a select symposium convened by SIPRI in co-operation with UNEP in Stockholm, 8–11 October 1985. The authors of this book are:

Dr *Alexander A. Arbatov* (Institute for Systems Studies; 117312 Moscow B–312; USSR), an authority on mineral geology;

Prof. *Malin Falkenmark* (Committee for Hydrology; Swedish Natural Science Research Council; S–113 85 Stockholm; Sweden), an authority on global hydrology;

Prof. *Helge Hveem* (Institute of Political Science; University of Oslo; N–0317 Oslo 3; Norway), an authority on international relations and economics;

Prof. *Marcel Leroy* (Department of Social Sciences; University

College of Cape Breton; Sydney, Nova Scotia B1P 6L2; Canada),
an authority on international relations and demography;

Dr *Susan B. Peterson* (Institute for Employment Policy; Boston
University; Boston, MA 02215; USA), an authority on marine
fisheries development and policy;

Mr *Antony F. G. Scanlan* (British Institute of Energy Economics;
London SW1Y 4LE; UK), an authority on the oil industry;

Dr *Erik Solem* (Political & Strategic Analysis Division; Policy
Development Bureau; Canadian Department of External
Affairs; Ottawa, Ontario K1A 0G2; Canada), an authority on
global resource planning and forecasting;

Dr *John M. Teal* (Woods Hole Oceanographic Institution; Woods
Hole, MA 02543; USA), an authority on biological ocean-
ography and marine ecology;

Prof. *Peter Wallensteen* (Department of Peace & Conflict Research;
Uppsala University; S–751 05 Uppsala; Sweden), an authority on
peace studies; and

Prof. *Arthur H. Westing* (Stockholm International Peace Research
Institute; S–171 73 Solna; Sweden), an authority on environmental impact of military activities.

The authors are pleased to acknowledge thoughtful suggestions
by Mr Frank T. Blackaby (SIPRI), Mr Michael Brzoska (SIPRI),
Mr Jozef Goldblat (SIPRI), Mr Haroldo M. de Lemos (UNEP),
and Dr Norman Myers (IUCN) during the symposium.

1. Environmental factors in strategic policy and action: an overview

Arthur H. Westing
Stockholm International Peace Research Institute

I. Introduction

Humans depend for their well-being and very survival on the resources they derive from the environment. Warfare—a prominent human activity—is one of the means by which access to these resources is achieved. Thus, explored here is the extent to which natural resources lead to interstate rivalries, disputes, and war. Only those natural resources which are in short supply, either globally or regionally, are of relevance to this analysis. Such natural resources can be conveniently divided into two categories, non-living and living.

Of special interest among the non-living resources—many of which also fall into the category of non-renewable resources—are the land itself, fresh waters, and minerals, the last encompassing both those from which energy is derived (the fuels) and those used as materials (the non-fuel minerals). Of special interest among the living, or renewable (and thus manageable), resources are staple food crops and ocean fisheries.

The universe from which natural resources are obtained can be split into two broad categories: (*a*) national territories, including territorial seas and possessions (e.g., colonies); and (*b*) extra-national territories, including the ocean beyond national jurisdiction (and the sea-bed beneath it), perhaps Antarctica, and celestial bodies such as the moon. A natural resource can, of course, overlap two or more national territories or national and extra-national territories.

A natural resource is in short supply for any particular country, or for the earth as a whole, when demand—or, more accurately, need—exceeds availability, that is to say, when the human carrying capacity of the unit of area under consideration is exceeded. This dilemma of natural-resource insufficiency can come about for one or both of two broad reasons: (a) when either population numbers or human aspirations grow too rapidly or are otherwise too large; and (b) when the natural resource becomes degraded through misuse, for example, by practices that lead to soil erosion or by the harvesting of renewable resources beyond their capacity to regenerate themselves. Population has become excessive when its growth rate is more rapid than the ability to: (a) extract or harvest an essential natural resource; (b) obtain this resource from beyond its borders; (c) substitute for it; (d) curb the per-capita demand for it; or (e) live in balance with the other living things on earth.

Of special interest is the extent to which states resort to military action, or the threat of such action, to ensure continuing access to what they deem to be an adequate supply of natural resources, the major subject of this chapter. Of equal, if not greater, importance is the extent to which the global natural resources can be managed and exploited in a way that: (a) will be in harmony with nature; (b) will avoid interstate conflict; and (c) will, in the case of the renewable ones, assure their long-term integrity. These matters are the subject of the final chapter (chapter 9).

This chapter builds upon prior work by the author (Westing, 1980, chapter 8; 1981e) and also draws upon the subsequent chapters in this book (chapters 2–8). Dealt with below, following the presentation of some basic relationships, are questions relating to both non-living resources and living resources. An annotated selection of wars and skirmishes of this century that have been fought at least in part over natural resources is provided elsewhere (see appendix 2), as are selected references to studies by others related to this subject (see appendix 1).

II. Basic relationships

The racial, ethnic, religious, and political groupings that comprise the human species have come to organize themselves into some 170 sovereign nations that together account for all or most of the global land area. These many countries vary remarkably in size, in climate and other natural endowments, in demography, in stage of development, and in internal uniformity and stability. The demographic differences include population numbers, population density, and population growth rate.

Human beings and the nations they constitute must have continuous access to natural resources in order to sustain themselves and, in many instances, in order to improve their standards of living. Each nation requires a continuing supply of staple foods—which, in turn, requires sufficient arable land and water to grow these foods—as well as a continuing supply of fuels and other raw materials for clothing, shelter, heating, transportation, and further necessities and cultural amenities.

Few, if any, nations are fully self-sufficient in all of the natural resources that they need or desire, and some are hardly so. Thus, essentially all nations depend upon external sources of at least some natural resources for their continued development, and even for their survival. The external sources of the demanded natural resources are either other nations (i.e., via international trade) or such extra-territorial areas as the oceans beyond national jurisdiction or the sea-bed beneath it. Moreover, given the finite and now presumably more or less fixed size of each country, some means must be achieved to keep up with any increases in population, if a country is not to regress in its capability to sustain itself and perhaps to continue its development to a higher level.

The nations of the world interact with each other in their pursuit of external natural resources—as in all other endeavours—via governmental and non-governmental avenues in a bewildering variety of bilateral and multilateral ways. These international interactions change with time, ranging from cordial and synergistic to antagonistic and destructive. For example, one of the several explicitly enunciated national-security objectives of the USA is to 'protect U.S. economic interests worldwide by maintaining steady access to energy supplies, other critical resources, and foreign markets' (Weinberger, 1985, page 25). The relations among subdivisions or portions of a nation similarly range in changing patterns from the harmonious to the discordant. At the negative extreme of these spectra of international and domestic interaction are found overt threats of aggression and, of course, the actual pursuit of war.

The resort to war by a nation, a group of nations, or a portion of a nation has been—and remains—a common approach to achieving a policy objective (Eckhardt, 1985; Goose, 1983). The half-dozen or more significant wars currently in progress represent a routine human activity that appears not to have changed significantly in recent decades or centuries in either frequency or—with some notable exceptions—in intensity (Westing, 1981b; 1982; 1984). Indeed, clear evidence for organized warfare dates back more than nine thousand years, to the early Neolithic Age (Ferrill, 1985, page 20; Roper, 1975, page 304).

What the ultimate cause or causes of war might be defies simple explanation and is, at any rate, far beyond the scope of this analysis. What is, however, attempted here is an examination of the extent to which one factor—the global or regional shortage, or perceived shortage, of one or more natural resources—contributes to belligerent political behaviour and the onset of war.

The relationship in a country between a sufficiency of natural resources and the size of its population is an obvious one, but must nevertheless be stressed. The human population has grown remarkably through the millennia (Westing, 1981d) and the continuously expanding need for land and other natural resources has in recent centuries been met in a variety of ways, important among them: (*a*) improvement in agricultural and extractive techniques; (*b*) exploitation of extra-territorial areas such as the ocean; (*c*) trade with other nations possessing surpluses; and (*d*) wars of plunder or expansion.

In modern history, resort to war to satisfy a demand for natural resources has sometimes involved the forced annexation of neighbouring land areas (i.e., of adjacent countries or portions of them) and sometimes the conquering of distant lands—typically those inhabited by 'primitive' or 'uncivilized' peoples—and converting them into so-called colonies. The various colonial empires have now largely collapsed, mostly during the past four decades. The numerous wars during the past two centuries of colonial conquest, of colonial retention, and of unsuccessful colonial retention (i.e., of national liberation) must for the most part be categorized as wars over natural resources.

The ever-growing world-wide demand for natural resources is the result of: (*a*) a global population that is growing at the compound growth rate of 1.7 per cent per year (UN, 1985, page 11), a rate of increase that will lead to a doubling of the global population in only four decades; (*b*) increasing standards of living in the developed nations; and (*c*) the growing aspirations of the many developing nations, most of whose inhabitants live in abject poverty. The rapidly growing demands for natural resources have a number of important consequences: (*a*) the more or less rapid depletion of non-renewable resources and the greater difficulties associated with extracting more diffuse or inaccessible deposits; (*b*) the exploitation of renewable resources at rates that exceed their natural ability to renew themselves; and (*c*) expansion into the remaining wild or semi-wild areas of the world for living space, agricultural lands, range (grazing) lands, and other natural resources. Such expansion into the dwindling natural areas of the world is ill-advised not only because these areas are often submarginal for the intended purposes, but because it is at the inevitable direct expense of the world's remaining natural vegetation and wildlife (Westing, 1981c; 1981e).

III. Non-living resources

The land

The basic non-living resource is the land itself—land on which to live and build one's cities, to farm and graze one's livestock, to log, to mine and quarry, to hunt and fish, and to recreate. As human populations grow the global land area in effect shrinks. At the turn of the century there were nine hectares per person, at the end of World War II six, and today (1986) three; by the year 2000 there will be but two (UN, 1985, table A-1; Westing, 1980, page 20; 1981d). Humans have accommodated to the dilemma of a functionally shrinking global land area by concentrating into cities, by increasing the efficiency of their agriculture, by more heavily exploiting the ocean resources, by encroaching on the remaining areas of wild nature, and by conquering (about which more below). Today, the biomass of humans plus that of their livestock represents—that is, has displaced—more than 20 per cent of the terrestrial animal biomass (Westing, 1981c; 1981e). Within about four decades from now humans plus their entourage of livestock will have substituted for fully 40 per cent of the total terrestrial animal biomass.

As human populations and human aspirations have grown in a global land area that has long been fully divided among the nations of the world, one of the time-honoured approaches to alleviating the problem of land shortage has been a resort to wars of conquest. The land needs of expanding populations have been met in this fashion since the wars of conquest by Alexander the Great (336–323 BC) (Colinvaux, 1980) and almost certainly even earlier (Carneiro, 1970). Indeed, it has been forcefully argued that population press-

ures—that is, shortages of land—have been at the root of all wars of
aggrandizement throughout human history (Colinvaux, 1980).
However, it is prudent to qualify such a sweeping generalization by
suggesting that population pressures alone cannot explain the
multifarious antecedents to a war of conquest, even though such
pressures can often be identified as one of the crucial contributing
factors (Choucri, 1983; North, 1984). Indeed, the complexity of the
interactions among demographic factors, the exploitation of natural
resources, and the international behaviour of states is described in
some detail by Leroy (see chapter 8).

In modern times, it has been persuasively argued that perhaps the
most important underlying cause of World War I was the pressure
of population, that is, a need for land, in central Europe (see
appendix 2, war 1). Several decades later, one of the justifications
given by Germany for its aggression in World War II was a need for
added living space (*Lebensraum*) (see appendix 2, war 3). The
invasion in 1969 of sparsely populated Honduras by densely
populated and fast-growing El Salvador can be attributed in large
measure to the latter's shortage of land (see appendix 2, war 8).

Population growth in a country can lead to less land per capita
than simple arithmetic would suggest owing to overly intense
agricultural, range, and tree-cutting practices that result in
accelerated erosion and other forms of land degradation. Increases
in population density in concert with lowered carrying capacity of
the land have been the cause of substantial population displace-
ments in a growing number of instances in Africa (as well as in Asia
and elsewhere) (see chapter 8, section VI). These so-called
environmental refugees cause domestic strife and result in considerable political friction when they cross international borders (Timberlake & Tinker, 1984, pages 21–26). The Somali–Ethiopian War
of 1977–78 (Hodson *et al.*, 1978) has been speculated to have had its
origin in such population movements (Myers, 1985).

Fresh waters

Aside from land, no limited natural resource is more important than
fresh waters. Its central role in sustaining all life on earth is felt
especially keenly in the many more or less arid and overpopulated
regions of the world. Scores of major bodies of water—rivers, lakes,
aquifers—are shared by two or more countries (see chapter 5, tables

5.1 and 5.2). The competition for limited supplies of fresh water between such neighbouring countries leads to severe political tensions and even to war (see chapter 5, section III). An important cause of the Third Arab–Israeli War of 1967 was the struggle over the waters of the Jordan and other rivers in the area (see appendix 2, war 6). Acrimonious dispute over the waters of the Río Lauca is of long standing and has in the past led Bolivia to sever its diplomatic relations with Chile (Glassner, 1970). A number of recent international conflicts attributed in part to competition over fresh waters have been outlined elsewhere (Timberlake & Tinker, 1984, pages 54–66).

The potential for future conflict over scarce fresh waters is growing in various regions of the world, as is clearly demonstrated by Falkenmark (see chapter 5; see also Beaumont, 1978). Special problem areas involve upstream/downstream water competition in arid and other regions of rapidly increasing population.

Non-fuel minerals

Global deficiencies of non-fuel minerals, coupled with their uneven distribution throughout the world, can lead to unlikely—and thus unstable—alliances, to national rivalries, and, of course, to war (see chapter 4). Indeed, mineral wars may date back to the Bronze Age. It has been suggested that the Greeks initiated the Trojan War (*circa* 1200 BC) in order to assure their access to a source of tin, necessary in the manufacture of the then all-important bronze (Ager, 1985).

The Lorraine region just south of Luxembourg, one of the rare iron-rich regions of Europe, provides a modern example of the military significance of non-fuel minerals. A part of France since 1766, Lorraine was ceded to Germany as one outcome of the Franco-Prussian War of 1870–71. It reverted to France as a result of World War I (see appendix 2, war 1). The region was re-acquired by Germany early in World War II (see appendix 2, war 3), only to be re-annexed by France at the end of that war, this status having been maintained since then. Both Germany and Japan pursued World War II in significant measure in order to attain control over natural resources. During that war, the USSR in 1944 annexed from Finland the Petsamo (now Pechenga) territory on the Barents Sea, motivated in part by the rich local deposits of nickel.

More recently, the Congo Civil War of 1960–64 was to a major extent a struggle over control of the copper and other mineral resources of Katanga (now Shaba) Province in what is now Zaire (see appendix 2, war 5). The Western Sahara Revolt that began in 1976 has been pursued through the years by Morocco in large part because the latter is reluctant to relinquish the rich phosphate deposits in the contested region (see appendix 2, war 11).

Today, the mineral often assumed to be most likely to lead to conflict is chromium, an element essential to modern industry. Chromium has various highly useful applications, but—most importantly—seems to be indispensable as an alloy for stainless and other high-grade steels, this additive making the steel harder, less subject to corrosion, and more resistant to heat (Morning *et al.*, 1980; Papp, 1983). Most chromium in the world is now produced in (and exported by) the USSR, South Africa, and Albania; and known global reserves are largely restricted to South Africa, and to a lesser extent, Zimbabwe (see chapter 4, table 4.2). The USA imports most of its chromium (table 4.1) and is strategically more vulnerable to a chromium embargo than to that of any other mineral, whether non-fuel or fuel (Bullis, 1981, page 136). Japan imports virtually all of its chromium (Wu, 1983); and France (Sondermayer, 1983), FR Germany (Rabchevsky, 1983), and the United Kingdom (table 4.1) import all of theirs.

Despite the limited distribution of some important non-fuel minerals, it is generally agreed that access to these natural resources is not likely to be a primary cause of wars in the coming years, at least not among developed nations (Arad & Arad, 1979; Legvold, 1981; Maull, 1984; McCartan, 1985; Shafer, 1982; Tilton & Landsberg, 1983). This is so because a disruption of supply could be overcome in one or more of a variety of non-hostile ways: turning to alternate suppliers, exploiting previously uneconomic domestic sources, substituting other materials, making do with less, prolonging use, recycling, dipping into domestic stockpiles, and so forth. Nevertheless, the importance of chromium and its politically capricious pattern of distribution combine to at least suggest the possibility of future military action (Russett, 1981–1982), action that could be aimed either at assuring sustained access to, or denial of, chromium.

Finally it must be stressed in regard to possible future conflict involving non-fuel minerals that southern Africa occupies a prominent position in the strategic thinking of the major powers, a point well developed by Hveem (see chapter 4). The strategic importance of this politically volatile region derives from its vast reserves of such strategic minerals as chromium, cobalt, uranium, manganese, platinum, vanadium, gold, and diamonds.

Fuels

Of the mineral fuels—coal, oil, natural gas, and uranium—the ones most often considered as possible causes of future wars are oil and uranium. Uranium is used largely as a fuel and to a comparatively very small extent (and by a very limited number of nations) as a military explosive. The current major producers of uranium are Canada, South Africa, and the USA (see chapter 4, table 4.2); other important producers are France, Niger, and the USSR (Brigg, 1985, page 24). The USA consumes considerably more uranium than any other nation (almost one-third of the world total); other important consumers are France, FR Germany, Japan, and the USSR (Brigg, 1985, page 24). Major known global uranium deposits are located in Australia, Canada, South Africa, and the USA; further deposits are in various countries of Africa, Asia, Europe, and South America (Brigg, 1985, page 25; see also chapter 4, table 4.2). Although definitive information is lacking, China and the USSR are thought to possess large reserves as well. There is, of course, some modest potential for conflict arising over access to uranium (see chapter 4), but owing to the relative abundance and wide distribution of this mineral, such a possibility seems remote.

The world has become dependent upon continuing supplies of huge quantities of oil, especially so the industrialized nations. Many nations must depend upon imports to satisfy their demand for this commodity. Among the major powers, the USSR, China, and the United Kingdom are self-sufficient (and, indeed, exporters); the USA is at present importing about one-third of its consumption; and France, FR Germany, and Japan must import virtually all of theirs (Brigg, 1985, pages 4, 7; see also chapter 3, table 3.1). The major exporting nations at present are Saudi Arabia, Iran, the USSR, and Mexico; and the overwhelmingly major exporting region is, of course, the Middle East (Brigg, 1985, pages 4, 7, 16–17). Known global reserves of oil are highly concentrated: one-quarter of these are in Saudi Arabia alone and more than half in the Middle East as a whole (Brigg, 1985, page 2).

A number of wars in this century have been fought over oil. For example, in the Chaco War of 1932–35, Paraguay annexed a region of Bolivia in the mistaken belief that it contained oil deposits (see appendix 2, war 2). France was reluctant to lose Algeria in the latter's war of independence of 1954–62 partly because of Algeria's oil deposits, but was unable to prevail (see appendix 2, war 4). Similarly, Nigeria was reluctant to lose Biafra in the latter's bid for independence in 1967–70 in large part owing to the local oil deposits, and was able to thwart Biafra's attempt at seccession (see appendix 2, war 7). The Paracel (Hsi-sha) Island Clash of 1974, in which China routed Viet Nam in re-establishing its claim to this island group in the South China Sea, was apparently motivated chiefly by the presumed offshore oil deposits (see appendix 2, war 10). A number of additional oil-related conflicts are presented elsewhere (see chapter 2, section IV).

The military significance of oil is clearly enormous (Christman & Clark, 1978; Heinebäck, 1974; Kemp, 1977–1978; Meyerhoff, 1976; Russett, 1981–1982; see also chapters 2 and 3). One plausible scenario for how war might spread to Europe has its origins in oil-related conflict in the Middle East (Nincic, 1985). The security of the Middle East has become a major concern of the USA and this has had a strong influence on US foreign and related military policies (McNaugher, 1985; see also chapter 2, section IV). It appears also to have had a significant influence on Soviet foreign and related military policies (Bokhari, 1985).

The economic and strategic importance of oil and other mineral fuels is obvious, as is the political sensitivity associated with some of the major sources of these natural resources. Nonetheless, Arbatov has cogently argued that the desire of the major oil-importing nations to maintain the stability of oil production mitigates against their armed intervention in oil-exporting nations to achieve control of the oil resources (see chapter 2). Indeed, it has been persuasively argued by Solem & Scanlan that a desirable long-term global energy strategy—one beneficial to the developed and developing nations alike—will require co-operation between the oil and natural gas consumer and supplier nations (see chapter 3).

IV. Living (renewable) resources

The most important living (renewable) resources are agricultural crops, both edible and industrial; wood for fuel, construction, and paper; grass for livestock forage; and ocean fish, mostly for human consumption. Of these, staple food crops and ocean fish are singled out here in regard to their potential for causing international conflict.

Staple food crops

Grains (cereals) are the staple food crops of primary interest in the present context. About 1.7 thousand million tonnes of grain—wheat, maize (corn), rice, barley, oats, etc.—are produced annually around the world (UN, 1982, table 76). About 90 per cent of this grain is consumed in the countries in which it is grown. Most countries produce enough, or else make do with what they produce, and thus import little or no grain. A very limited number of countries produce a large enough surplus to export significant amounts of grain, altogether about 175 million tonnes (see chapter 7, table 7.1). In 1983–84, the USA accounted for fully half of all such grain exports; indeed, only five countries—the USA, followed by Canada, France, Argentina, and Australia—accounted for about 90 per cent of them. The USSR, the world's largest grain importer, purchased about 17 per cent of what was traded on the world market, followed by Japan which purchased some 12 per cent and China 6 per cent. The remainder was divided among many countries.

In order to produce its staple food crops a country must satisfy a number of conditions, among them: (*a*) have sufficient arable land and appropriate climate; (*b*) receive sufficient rainfall or other source of fresh water; (*c*) manufacture or import sufficient amounts of fertilizer; and (*d*) produce or import enough oil and other fuels. To the extent that these and various other prerequisites are not satisfied, the food deficit must be taken care of by imports (which, in turn, generally require some form of exports of comparable value).

As discussed in prior sections, countries have resorted to war in order to alleviate perceived shortcomings in land, fresh water, and oil. Moreover, in time of war itself, belligerents frequently attempt to subdue an enemy by destroying its croplands and food supplies or by preventing external supplies of food from reaching it (Westing, 1981a).

Countries that depend upon imports for a significant fraction of their staple foods might well be vulnerable to a food embargo or blockade. However, of the three major importers referred to above, China's imports represent only about 3 per cent of its total consumption and those of the USSR about 15 per cent. Japan's by contrast represent about 60 per cent, making it highly vulnerable to such coercion. Bangladesh, Egypt, Iceland, the Republic of [South] Korea, and Singapore come to mind as other countries potentially vulnerable in this regard.

Looked at from the standpoint of the grain supplier nations, the USA would appear to be in the best position to exert at least economic or political influence by withholding food, or threatening to do so. Indeed, the USA has a history of providing or withholding food in support of its foreign relations (Hathaway, 1983; Wallerstein, 1980). However, it appears on the basis of such past experience that the peacetime use of food for coercive purposes might be feasible only in a limited number of situations. Such action would generally be of only marginal utility, or even ineffective if not counter-productive (Galdi *et al.*, 1977; Hathaway, 1983; LeCuyer, 1977; see also chapter 7, section III).

Fertilizers—especially of nitrogen, phosphorus, and potassium— are crucial to the agriculture of today. Without them the global production of grain would drop by perhaps one-third (Brown, 1985). Nitrogen fertilizer is produced primarily from the nitrogen in the air, requiring large amounts of energy in its manufacture. Although the largest producers are China, the USA, and the USSR (together accounting for half of global production), many other countries produce it as well (UN, 1982, table 136). Phosphorus fertilizer is largely mined. Suitable deposits are uncommon, with the USA accounting for almost one-third of world production, and four countries (the USA, followed by the USSR, Morocco, and China) for fully three-quarters (UN, 1982, table 110). Jordan, Tunisia, and South Africa are other phosphorus producers of note, together accounting for another 10 per cent of the world total. Potassium fertilizer is also largely mined and again extraction is quite concentrated: the USSR accounts for one-third of world production and Canada one-quarter (UN, 1982, table 138). Other important producers are the two Germanies, France, and the USA, together accounting for all but one-tenth or less of the remaining world production.

It can be concluded that the degree of concentration in the global production of the three major fertilizers is not such that would suggest more than isolated possibilities of international political coercion based on denying fertilizers to a potential consumer.

Finally it must be pointed out that a considerable number of countries grow insufficient food to prevent chronic malnutrition among many of their inhabitants, and even to prevent hunger and starvation on a recurring basis. A high proportion of these countries are located in Africa (Brown, 1985; Sai, 1984). Such conditions of food deficit can lead to political unrest, rioting, and even civil war (Timberlake & Tinker, 1984, pages 38–53; see also chapter 7, section II). The analysis by Wallensteen emphasizes the central position of food adequacy in national security and thus the crucial need in many Third-World nations (*a*) for agricultural development and (*b*) for a change in the internal distribution of political power (see chapter 7).

Ocean fisheries

The world ocean has been yielding about 67 million tonnes (fresh weight) per year of finfish (true fish) plus shellfish (crustaceans and molluscs) in recent years (FAO, 1983, table A-4, 1980–83). This corresponds to a dry weight of just over 22 million tonnes and to a usable protein content of about 10 million tonnes. Thus, the marine fishery currently provides the world's human population with about 9 per cent of its total protein intake (calculated from FAO, 1983, table A-4 plus UN, 1982, table 96). In Japan, fish protein represents about 39 per cent of the total, in the USSR about 13 per cent, and in the USA about 6 per cent. Most ocean fish inhabit the waters over the continental shelves, perhaps 90 per cent of them—and thus most fishing occurs there as well. The continental shelves of the world vary enormously in width, the average distance being about 80 kilometres.

The two major ocean fishing nations are Japan (with 16 per cent of the world catch) and the USSR (with 13 per cent) (see chapter 6, table 6.1). Next in line come the USA, Chile, China, and Norway (together accounting for another 21 per cent of the world catch).

Scores of other nations catch the remaining 50 per cent. Ocean fishing is especially important to the economy of Iceland.

Some 80 per cent of the nations of the world have access to the ocean and the great majority of them claim jurisdiction over the fish resources out to some greater or lesser distance from their coastlines. The distance varies widely from country to country (from 11 to 370 kilometres), and countries have changed their proclaimed widths from time to time. More than half of the coastal countries have over the past decade or so laid claim to a fishery zone or an exclusive economic zone out to a distance of 370 kilometres (Borgese & Ginsburg, 1982, pages 564–68). The USA did so in 1976 (with slight modifications in 1983), thereby establishing for itself an area of ocean jurisdiction of 7.6 million square kilometres; the USSR did so in 1984, creating an area of 4.5 million square kilometres. Virtually all ocean fishing now occurs within 370 kilometres of shore (Copes, 1981), although some species of fish regularly cross this boundary (Colson, 1984–1985). No relevant treaty is in force that supports the legality of such exclusive economic zones (see appendix 6), but nevertheless the concept appears now to be generally recognized (see chapter 6, section IV).

Numerous international disputes have arisen in recent years over fishing in exclusive economic zones, some of which have escalated to armed clashes (see chapter 6, section V). Perhaps the most prominent of these was the Anglo-Icelandic Clash of 1972–73 (see appendix 2, war 9). Moreover, the Falkland–Malvinas Conflict of 1982 was waged in part over control of the offshore fishery resources (see appendix 2, war 12). A number of additional ocean fishery disputes have been alluded to elsewhere (Timberlake & Tinker, 1984, pages 67–76). Peterson & Teal reach the conclusion that future disputes can be expected (although not necessarily armed conflicts) as ocean fishing becomes more intense, as discharges of pollutants into the ocean increase, and as more nations exercise (i.e., police) their proclaimed jurisdictions, especially so in the absence of appropriate international agreements (see chapter 6; see also Morris, 1982).

V. Conclusion

The global land area has long been divided among the nations of the world. Ever greater demands for natural resources have required ever more intense (and more efficient and imaginative) exploitation of national territories as well as ever greater competition for the natural resources of the extra-national territories. Antarctica, the final such terrestrial 'international commons', has been largely claimed by a variety of nations, although these claims are not universally recognized and the interested parties have agreed to defer the question for a time (see appendix 4). A substantial fraction of the oceanic international commons (the high seas) has also been claimed in recent years, at least in terms of its natural resources. If all coastal nations claim an exclusive economic zone (as a majority already have), this would come to about one-quarter of the overall ocean area and to almost all of the area readily exploitable for fish, oil, and other minerals. The natural resources of the moon are still beyond our reach.

In a world that already has too many people for all to be able to enjoy a standard of living approximating that of the developed nations, a heightened level of competition and dispute over natural resources can be expected in the years to come, especially so if consideration is given to the needs of the remaining wild creatures on earth (Westing, 1981e). Some of these disputes could well become overtly hostile and thus lead to armed conflict. Indeed, given that war has been one of the routine means of achieving national aims, it will be difficult to avoid the outbreak of some wars over natural resources. Approaches to avoiding such events are included in the subsequent chapters (chapter 2–8) and are the main theme of the final one (chapter 9).

References

Ager, D. 1985. Ore that launched a thousand ships. *New Scientist*, London, 106(1461):28–29.

Arad, R. W. & Arad, U. B. 1979. Scarce natural resources and potential conflict. In: Arad, R. W. *et al. Sharing global resources.* New York: McGraw-Hill, 220 pp.: pp. 23–104.

Beaumont, P. 1978. Euphrates River: an international problem of water resources development. *Environmental Conservation*, Geneva, 5:35–43.

Bokhari, I. H. 1985. Soviet military challenge to the Gulf. *Military Review*, Ft Leavenworth, Kansas, 65(8):50–62.

Borgese, E. M. & Ginsburg, N. (eds). 1982. *Ocean yearbook. III.* Chicago: University of Chicago Press, 581 pp.

Brigg, P. (ed.). 1985. *BP statistical review of world energy*. London: British Petroleum Company, 32 pp.

Brown, L. R. 1985. Reducing hunger. In: Brown, L. R. *et al*. *State of the world 1985*. New York: W. W. Norton, 301 pp.: pp. 23–41.

Bullis, L. H. (ed.). 1981. *Congressional handbook on U.S. materials import dependency/vulnerability*. Washington: US House of Representatives, Committee on Banking, Finance & Urban Affairs Print No. 97–6, 405 pp.

Carneiro, R. L. 1970. Theory of the origin of the state. *Science*, Washington, 169: 733–738.

Choucri, N. 1983. *Population and conflict: new dimensions of population dynamics*. New York: UN Fund for Population Activities, Policy Development Study No. 8, 47 pp.

Christman, D. W. & Clark, W. K. 1978. Foreign energy sources and military power. *Military Review*, Ft Leavenworth, Kansas, 58(2):3–14.

Colinvaux, P. 1980. *Fates of nations: a biological theory of history*. New York: Simon & Schuster, 384 pp.

Colson, D. A. 1984–1985. Transboundary fishery stocks in the EEZ. *Oceanus*, Woods Hole, Mass., 27(4):48–51.

Copes, P. 1981. Impact of UNCLOS III on management of the world's fisheries. *Marine Policy*, Guildford, UK, 5:217–228.

Eckhardt, W. 1985. Deaths in twentieth century wars. In: Sivard, R. L. *World military and social expenditures 1985*. Washington: World Priorities, 52 pp. + 1 fig.: pp. 9–11, 44.

FAO, 1983. *Yearbook of fishery statistics. LVI*. Rome: Food & Agriculture Organization of the United Nations, 393 pp.

Ferrill, A. 1985. *Origins of war: from the Stone Age to Alexander the Great*. New York: Thames & Hudson, 240 pp.

Galdi, T., Baker, J. & Mayer, L. 1977. *Use of U.S. food resources for diplomatic purposes: an examination of the issues*. Washington: US House of Representatives, Committee on International Relations, 85 pp.

Glassner, M. I. 1970. Río Lauca: dispute over an international river. *Geographical Review*, New York, 60:192–207.

Goose, S. D. 1983. World at war: 1983. *Defense Monitor*, Washington, 12(1):1–24.

Hathaway, R. M. 1983. Food power. *Foreign Service Journal*, Washington, 60(11):24–29.

Heinebäck, B. 1974. *Oil and security*. Stockholm: Almqvist & Wiksell, 197 pp. [a SIPRI book].

Hodson, H. V. *et al*. 1978. Ethiopia; Somalia. *Annual Register*, London, 220:207–210.

Kemp, G. 1977–1978. Scarcity and strategy. *Foreign Affairs*, New York, 56:396–414.

LeCuyer, J. A. 1977. Food as a component of national defense strategy. *Parameters*, Carlisle Barracks, Pennsylvania, 7(4):56–70.

Legvold, R. 1981. Strategic implications of the Soviet Union's nonfuel mineral resources policy. In: Wolpe, H. (ed.). *Possibility of a resource war in southern Africa [Hearing, 8 July 1981]*. Washington: US House of Representatives Committee on Foreign Affairs, 120 pp.: pp. 57–85.

Maull, H. W. 1984. *Raw materials, energy and Western security*. London: Macmillan, 413 pp.

McCartan, B. 1985. Resource wars: the myth of American mineral vulnerability. *Defense Monitor*, Washington, 14(9):1–18.

McNaugher, T. L. 1985. *Arms and oil: U.S. military strategy and the Persian Gulf*. Washington: Brookings Institution, 226 pp.

Meyerhoff, A. A. 1976. Economic impact and geopolitical implications of giant petroleum fields. *American Scientist*, New Haven, 64:536–541.

Morning, J. L., Matthews, N. A. & Peterson, E. C. 1980. Chromium. In: Knoerr, A. W. (ed.). *Mineral facts and problems*. Washington: US Bureau of Mines, Bulletin No. 671, 1060 pp.: pp. 167–182.

Morris, M. A. 1982. Military aspects of the exclusive economic zone. *Ocean Yearbook*, Chicago, 3:320–348.

Myers, N. 1985. Critical link between the environment, natural resources, and war. In: Kelly, A. S. (ed.). *Second biennial conference on the fate of the earth*. San Francisco: Earth Island Institute, 628 pp.: pp. 47–53.

Nincic, M. 1985. *How war might spread to Europe*. London: Taylor & Francis, 109 pp. [a SIPRI book].

North, R. C. 1984. Integrating the perspectives: from population to conflict and war. In: Choucri, N. (ed.). *Multidisciplinary perspectives on population and conflict*. Syracuse, NY: Syracuse University Press, 220 pp.: pp. 195–215.

Papp, J. F. 1983. Chromium. *Minerals Yearbook*, Washington, 1983(I): 203–220.

Rabchevsky, G. A. 1983. Mineral industry of the Federal Republic of Germany. *Minerals Yearbook*, Washington, 1983(III):289–309.

Roper, M. K. 1975. Evidence of warfare in the Near East from 10,000–4,300 B.C. In: Nettleship, M. A. *et al.* (eds). *War, its causes and correlates*. Hague: Mouton, 813 pp.: pp. 299–343.

Russett, B. 1981–1982. Security and the resources scramble: will 1984 be like 1914? *International Affairs*, London, 58:42–58.

Sai, F. T. 1984. Population factor in Africa's development dilemma. *Science*, Washington, 226:801–805.

Shafer, M. 1982. Mineral myths. *Foreign Policy*, Washington, 1982 (47): 154–171.

Sondermayer, R. V. 1983. Mineral industry of France. *Minerals Yearbook*, Washington, 1983(III):257–272.

Tilton, J. E. & Landsberg, H. H. 1983. Nonfuel minerals: the fear of shortages and the search for policies. In: Castle, E. N. & Price, K. A. (eds). *U.S. interests and global natural resources: energy, minerals, food.* Washington: Resources for the Future, 147 pp.: pp. 48–80.

Timberlake, L. & Tinker, J. 1984. *Environment and conflict.* London: International Institute for Environment and Development, Earthscan Briefing Document No. 40, 88 pp. + 6 pl.

UN (United Nations). 1982. *Statistical yearbook. XXXIII.* New York: United Nations, 1088 pp.

UN (United Nations). 1985. *World population prospects: estimates and projections as assessed in 1982.* New York: UN Department of International Economic & Social Affairs Population Study No. 86 (ST/ESA/SER.A/86), 521 pp.

Wallerstein, M. B. 1980. *Food for war—food for peace: United States food aid in a global context.* Cambridge, Mass.: MIT Press, 312 pp.

Weinberger, C. W. 1985. *Annual report to the Congress: fiscal year 1986.* Washington: US Department of Defense, 315 pp.

Westing, A. H. 1980. *Warfare in a fragile world: military impact on the human environment.* London: Taylor & Francis, 249 pp. [a SIPRI book].

Westing, A. H. 1981a. Crop destruction as a means of war. *Bulletin of the Atomic Scientists*, Chicago, 37(2):38–42.

Westing, A. H. 1981b. Environmental impact of conventional warfare. In: Barnaby, W. (ed.). *War and environment.* Stockholm: Royal Ministry of Agriculture Environmental Advisory Council, 154 pp.: pp. 58–72.

Westing, A. H. 1981c. How much of this land is our land? *Environment*, Washington, 23(6): 5,44–45.

Westing, A. H. 1981d. Note on how many humans that have ever lived. *BioScience*, Washington, 31:523–524; 32:6.

Westing, A. H. 1981e. World in balance. *Environmental Conservation*, Geneva, 8:177–183.

Westing, A. H. 1982. War as a human endeavor: the high-fatality wars of the twentieth century. *Journal of Peace Research*, Oslo, 19:261–270.

Westing, A. H. 1984. How much damage can modern war create? In: Barnaby, F. (ed.). *Future war.* London: Michael Joseph, 192 pp.: pp. 114–124.

Wu, J. C. 1983. Mineral industry of Japan. *Minerals Yearbook*, Washington, 1983(III):417–445.

2. Oil as a factor in strategic policy and action: past and present

Alexander A. Arbatov
Institute for Systems Studies, Moscow

I. Introduction

The role of oil as a factor in strategic policy and action has varied with time. Such change has been the result of many factors, including: changes in the importance of oil and in its scale of consumption; changes in the global distribution of known oil deposits; changes in oil utilization; and changes in the economic development of countries.

This chapter traces through time the dynamics of oil-related factors in strategic policy and action as a prelude to an analysis of the present situation. The contrasting roles are emphasized in this contradiction between producer and consumer nations, between developing and developed countries, and between capitalist and socialist states. Some typical oil-related conflicts are illustrated by presenting those in the Middle East, the Aegean region, and Nigeria. It is concluded that oil has been, and remains, an important factor in strategic policy decisions and in some armed conflicts. However, the role of oil is substantially different today than it was prior to the 1980s. The present chapter expands upon prior work by the author (Arbatov & Amirov, 1984).

The chapter is complemented by a somewhat contrasting inter-pretation of past and present events in the one that follows it (chapter 3).

II. Historical background

Prior to the 1930s

Oil has been used in various ways since ancient times. However, it has become a widely used raw material only since the mid-1870s. It was then that an accelerating development of oil and natural gas deposits began in various regions of the world, spurred by the invention of fuel-requiring engines. Oil as a source of motor fuel for vehicles, ships, and aircraft determined the main directions of technical development in both the civil and military spheres; such development was further influenced by the use of oil as a raw material in the chemical industry. During the first 37 years of the twentieth century—while world-wide industrial production increased by a factor of perhaps 2.5—extraction of oil increased by more than 10 times this factor.

The vigorous growth of the US automobile industry early in the twentieth century became possible in large part because of that country's rich domestic oil resources. On the other hand, in order for European industrial countries to develop they were forced to exploit the oil resources of their colonies and dependent countries. Moreover, the availability of oil as a source of energy favoured the rapid development of many industries. This in turn increased the demand for a variety of other raw materials, which for many countries could be met only in part at the expense of extracting domestic deposits of natural resources.

The establishment of the boundaries of most countries predates an interest in oil and many other raw materials or was otherwise independent of their presence. Thus the uneven global distribution of oil has resulted in the existence of some countries with large quantities and others with only negligible quantities of oil and various other crucial natural resources.

As noted above, some industrializing oil-poor states were able to compensate for such a deficit by exploiting their oil-rich colonies. Others—a prime example being Germany—possessed no such source. Indeed, one of the reasons for Germany's entry into World War I (see appendix 2, war 1) was its aspiration to seize the sources of oil and other raw materials available to its competitors in order to satisfy its rapidly growing civil and military needs.

The struggle for oil among the capitalist countries continued after World War I, although mainly by means other than armed conflict. Rather, the struggle expressed itself primarily as a competition between British and US oil companies, supported by their respective governments. The early advantage went to the United Kingdom because its oil companies (including the British-Dutch Royal Dutch Shell Company) had enjoyed exclusive rights to the oil deposits throughout the limits of the then enormous British Empire. These companies were also able to exercise control over the Iranian oil deposits. US oil companies, on the other hand, at that time had access only to domestic sources. Just prior to World War I, the United Kingdom was estimated to have control over about 9 per cent of global oil resources, a proportion which had been enlarged to no less than 75 per cent by 1920 (Santalov, 1954, page 189).

Despite the strong lead by the United Kingdom following World War I in the control over global oil resources, both the USA and France were able in the succeeding years to improve their positions in this regard. The USA, with a much more robust overall post-war economy than the United Kingdom, was able to make these inroads employing economic and political pressures, the latter sometimes including the threat of war. The five largest US oil companies were thus able to attain major oil rights in Iraq, Bahrain, Saudi Arabia, and Kuwait. France was able to make similar though smaller gains.

World War II and its antecedents

On the eve of World War II, five US companies controlled in the Middle East more than 50 per cent of the concessionary areas given out for oil and natural gas exploration, 12 per cent of known oil deposits, and 13 per cent of ongoing extraction (Santalov, 1954, page 193). Similarly, France controlled 6 per cent of the concessionary areas, 9 per cent of the known deposits, and 6 per cent of the extraction. The remainder in the Middle East was still controlled by either Royal Dutch Shell or the Anglo-Iranian Oil Company. Elsewhere at this time, US companies had come to control more than 30 per cent of known oil deposits and of ongoing extraction in South-East Asia; 60 per cent of known deposits and 63 per cent of ongoing extraction in Venezuela; and 33 per cent of ongoing extraction in Canada.

The struggle during the 1930s for control of the oil deposits in Mexico was connected with a number of governmental upheavals, variously supported by the United Kingdom and the USA and occasionally involving attacks on oilfields and pipelines by mercenary troops (Santalov, 1954, page 195). In 1938, Mexico nationalized its oil industry and in response the United Kingdom broke off diplomatic relations with that country.

During the two decades prior to World War II, the USSR was forced to rebuild an economy which had been almost totally destroyed by a combination of World War I and the Russian Civil War. The rapidly growing demand for oil within the USSR during this period of industrialization was able to be satisfied through the discovery and development of domestic resources. Its huge indigenous oil reserves permitted the USSR to remain aloof from the sharpening international struggle for this commodity. On the other hand, these reserves became an important motivation for German aggression against the USSR in World War II, (see appendix 2, war 3).

At the beginning of World War II, Germany, Italy, Japan, and the other Axis powers controlled 3 per cent of the world's land area, 10 per cent of its population, and 5 per cent of its mineral resources (Eckes, 1979, page 84). By 1942, however, the Axis had been able to gain control over 13 per cent of the world's land area, 35 per cent of its population, and about 33 per cent of its mineral resources. When the German thrust against the USSR faltered, Hitler attempted to reverse the situation by extolling to his high command the potential natural resource gains, suggesting to them that after victory they would be able to bathe in oil.

World War II quickly made it clear to all parties that the waging of war required assured access to huge volumes of oil, not only as the fuel for mechanized combat and transport services, but also for the manufacture of synthetic rubber, explosives, plastics, and other vital military products.

In their desire to become powers of the first rank, Germany, Italy, and Japan were each convinced prior to World War II that in order to do so they had to achieve actual possession of oil and other natural resources. While Italy and Japan attempted this via colonial expansion, Germany tried to acquire the territory of the USSR. The promptness and unexpectedness of the German assault on the USSR could be explained in part by Germany's lack of access at the time to Middle Eastern oil supplies.

III. Developments since World War II

The immediate post-war period

The demand for various mineral resources increased greatly follow-ing World War II as a result of rapid technological progress and industrial development. Thus, roughly five times as much oil was extracted world-wide during the 25 years following that war than during the entire 75 years preceding it. The extraction of coal, iron, and other minerals exhibited similar, although not quite such dramatic, growth trends.

World-wide extraction of oil continued to increase during each post-war year, as did rivalry over the control of the sources. From the very beginning of the post-war period the situation was favour-able for the USA, and continued to become increasingly so. In the Pacific theatre, British and Dutch oil interests had suffered more seriously than those of the USA owing to the wartime seizure by Japan of Royal Dutch Shell holdings in South-East Asia. In the Middle East theatre—the most important *vis-à-vis* oil—US com-panies had unilaterally annulled the so-called 'red line' agreement which regulated the sharing of oil concessions among US, French, British, and Dutch interests. The US companies ultimately com-pensated Royal Dutch Shell and the Anglo-Iranian Oil Company, but not the Compagnie Française de Pétroles on the basis that the last had traded with the enemy (Santalov, 1954, page 220).

British oil interests suffered greatly when Iran nationalized its oil industry in 1951. The USA did not at the time intercede on behalf of the United Kingdom, probably in order to permit the position of a serious competitor to weaken. However, shortly thereafter the USA did act as an intermediary in regulating the conflict between the Anglo-Iranian Oil Company and the Government of Iran. When the Iranian Government was overthrown in 1953 with the support of both the USA and the United Kingdom, Iran again denationalized its oil industry. In the newly established Iranian oil production consortium, US companies received a 40 per cent share, the Anglo-Iranian Oil company another 40 per cent, Royal Dutch Shell 14 per cent, and Compagnie Française de Pétroles the remain-ing 6 per cent.

In summary, control over the oil resources available to the capitalist world shifted away from the United Kingdom and the

Netherlands and towards the USA during and after World War II. Thus, in the late 1930s the United Kingdom plus the Netherlands had control over 36 per cent of such deposits, but only 30 per cent in the mid 1940s. By contrast, comparable values for the USA were 57 per cent and 65 per cent, respectively; or, perhaps more interesting, 24 per cent and 48 per cent, respectively, with its domestic resources excluded from the calculation (Santalov, 1954, page 213).

When the decolonization process began, it was thought that the former metropolis states would lose their former sources of raw materials. But, in fact, this did not occur. Delivery of raw materials from the newly independent developing countries to the industrialized countries hardly changed during the 1950s. Even during the Algerian War of Independence of 1954–62 (see appendix 2, war 4)—a severe struggle, indeed—there was little if any inter-ruption in the flow of oil, natural gas, or phosphates between Algeria and metropolitan France. As late as the 1970s, the develop-ing countries together supplied the world market with 84 per cent of its oil, together with disproportionately high levels of many other mineral resources (Arbatov, 1983). Conversely, their domestic consumption of these resources was remarkably low.

The unchanging flow of raw materials between newly independent countries and their former metropolitan states occurs for a number of reasons. Such inertia in economic relations is based on a high degree of dependence on outside capital, technology, and managerial and commercial experience. It is further based on an absence of supportive national industries, a low level of general education, and a lack of co-ordination between economic and political actions.

OPEC

The Organization of Petroleum Exporting Nations (OPEC) was founded in 1960 by a group of five developing countries, since augmented by eight more (see glossary for current membership). In 1983 the OPEC countries together accounted for one-third of world oil production and two-thirds of known oil reserves.

OPEC has been quite successful in determining world oil prices and in otherwise advancing the economic interests of its members. The oil crisis of 1973–74 was especially important in uniting this group and consolidating its strength. Within a single year OPEC was able to quadruple the price of oil and to open the way for further increases. At least five reasons can be offered to explain the unique success of OPEC among the several major extant raw-material cartels.

First, oil is the most valuable of all raw materials and its substitution without huge cost is practically impossible. No nation would be able to change its industrial structure within a period of even several years in a way that would substantially decrease its dependence upon huge volumes of liquid fuel received on a continuous basis. Oil is a unique raw material which makes possible the effective functioning of the energy, transportation, and chemical industries and which is essential to the maintenance of a military establishment. The developed countries consume oil in such gigantic volumes that the creation of adequate strategic stockpiles is not feasible. Moreover, being combustible, large stockpiles of oil are dangerous and vulnerable to attack.

Second, unlike other mineral resources, oil, once it has been used as a fuel, cannot be recycled. Publicized past predictions of a future oil crisis cannot be explained away entirely as attempted market manipulations by speculators. The present state of geological knowledge permits one to suggest with considerable assurance that it is highly unlikely that new oil deposits are yet to be discovered which are comparable in size and accessibility to those of the Middle East, western Siberia, or the Gulf of Mexico.

Third, oil is one of the few mineral resources located in regions controlled mainly by developing countries. None of the developed countries except for the USSR can be considered as significant oil exporters. Canada, a substantial exporter through the mid-1970s, can no longer be counted in that category. Nor can North Sea oil be exported to any major extent. Moreover, it is known that oil extraction in the Middle East could reach 2600 million cubic metres (16 400 million barrels) per year, thereby compensating for the growing shortages of this raw material in the developed countries.

Fourth, the Arab oil-producing countries—the core of OPEC, having the largest proved oil reserves—are bound together by ethnic, territorial, religious, and political ties (see 'OAPEC' in the glossary). Such a common bond—not present in other raw-material cartels—facilitates a tightly knit united strategy despite some contradictions among these countries.

Fifth, the international oil companies, which constitute one of the most highly monopolized spheres in the economy of the capitalist world, have profited much from the successes of OPEC. It is thus in the interest of the international oil industry to support the organization upon which it depends for its raw material.

The situation today

Most of the negative consequences of the oil crisis of 1973–74 have by now been overcome by the capitalist countries, at least for the moment. During the past decade, they have managed to reduce their dependence upon imported oil. At the same time, the OPEC and other oil-exporting countries increased extraction to the point of creating a glut and having to lower prices. Global oil production reached a peak in 1979, dropped annually until 1983, and then rose slightly in 1984, to the level of a decade earlier (Brigg, 1985, page 4). Thus, at present the oil market is clearly a buyer's market.

It is by no means certain how long the present situation of global oil adequacy will hold. This is the case for at least three reasons. First, comparatively little in the way of further gains can be expected from oil-conservation measures. Second, economic activity is beginning to rise, and this will certainly be accompanied by an increase in oil consumption. Third, the industrialization of many developing countries is expected to occur, again inevitably accompanied by an increase in oil consumption.

IV. Oil-related conflicts

The oil crisis of 1973–74 drew world-wide attention to the possibility of international conflict over very important and unevenly distributed mineral resources such as oil. In fact, the role of oil in such events differs from country to country and region to region. Three areas where oil-related conflict is of some importance are presented in detail below—the Middle East, the Aegean region, and Biafra (Nigeria)—several others more briefly. These will serve to illustrate the different types of oil-related conflict.

Oil producers and consumers

The Western world was shocked by the 1967 embargo by the Arab oil-producing countries and by the following oil crisis of 1973–74.

These events demonstrated the possibility for oil-producing countries to exert an influence on the world oil supply and to use their oil resources for political goals. Indeed, many Western scholars and politicians at the time expressed a fear over the threat of oil blackmail. However, further developments showed that OPEC had only limited possibilities to disrupt oil supplies and that such fears had been exaggerated. Nevertheless, the Middle East remains the best known centre of conflict having a considerable raw-material component. To what extent is the threat of oil blackmail real and to what extent myth?

The situation in the Middle East—a region that accounts for 20 per cent of current world oil production (*circa* 35 per cent throughout the 1970s), about two-thirds of it exported to the developed countries (Brigg, 1985, pages 4, 16)—is grave and complex for at least three reasons. First, there is the opposition between the Arab countries plus Palestine and Israel. Second, there are the difficult relations among a number of the Arab countries themselves: between Egypt and Libya; between Syria and Iraq; between the People's Democratic Republic of Yemen (South Yemen) and Saudi Arabia; and, of course, between Iran and Iraq. Third, there are the hostilities within some of the countries based on religious and political differences. The current war between Iran and Iraq has for the moment at least served to remove these two countries from the list of major oil exporters.

The numerous and varied levels of conflict within the Middle East are viewed with favour by at least some of the oil-importing countries for they are thought to maintain the region in a 'dynamic balance'. Indeed, it appears that the foreign policy of the USA and a number of other states is designed to keep these conflicts alive. Thus, the USA at first actively provided Israel and Iran with military and other assistance inasmuch as these two countries were considered to be stabilizing forces within the region. The USA concomitantly provided similar assistance to Saudi Arabia and other conservative Arab regimes as well as to the nearby states of Somalia and Sudan. One of the justifications put forth by the USA for its military aid to Middle Eastern and nearby countries was the prevention of Soviet expansion into the region. The USA let it be known that it did not even exclude the possibility of an armed seizure of the Middle Eastern oil deposits if it looked as if the region would fall into the hands of the USSR.

The downfall in 1979 of the pro-US regime in Iran appeared to be an irrevocable loss to the US position there. Following this event, the USA took compensatory steps to prepare for an alternative presence in the Middle East region. At the time of the so-called Camp David accords in 1978 among Egypt, Israel, and the USA provision had been made for the USA to be able to construct two military air bases for Israel in the Negev desert (Rubner, 1979, page 5). The presence of the USA on the Sinai peninsula also permitted a continuation of the installation, improvement, and operation of an early warning system (Sinai Support Mission, 1980, page 39). In 1980, partly in response to the change of government in Iran, the USA began to develop a rapid deployment force capable of striking the Middle East. Additionally, a number of NATO countries (see glossary for current membership), as part of a multilateral United Nations force, quartered military units on the Sinai peninsula (which Israel had previously wrested from Egypt). This enabled these forces to have control over the Suez Canal and the Red Sea region. Such action strengthened the Israeli position *vis-à-vis* its neighbours.

The volatile Middle Eastern conflict situation of today should be examined from the standpoint of the region's oil deposits. In 1977, the USA met 34 per cent of its oil requirements from the Middle East; 'Western Europe', presumably the then nine members of the European Economic Community (Belgium, Denmark [including Greenland], France, FR Germany, Ireland, Italy, Luxembourg, the Netherlands, and the United Kingdom; see 'EEC' in glossary for current membership), together 61 per cent; and Japan 72 per cent (Hackett, 1981, page 41). In 1984, only 4 per cent of the oil used by the USA came from the Middle East (Brigg, 1985, pages 7, 16). These figures invite the paradoxical conclusion that the degree of involvement by a nation in the Middle East conflict has been inversely proportional to its dependence on Middle Eastern oil.

The USA seeks to create the impression that it is acting on behalf of the whole Western world in striving to guarantee oil supplies for its NATO allies. But this is belied by the US proclamation that 'An attempt by any outside force to gain control of the Persian Gulf region will be regarded as an assault on the vital interests of the United States of America, and such an assault will be repelled by any means necessary, including military force' (Carter, 1980, page 38B). Moreover, the allies of the USA have suffered tangible economic losses as a result of the US and Israeli foreign policies in the Middle East. For example, Arab countries have been provoked into placing embargoes against the Netherlands and the United Kingdom. It is no coincidence that a number of West European nations have made independent, albeit unsuccessful, initiatives to settle the Arab-Israel conflict.

Does the Western economy gain or lose as a result of the attempts by some capitalist countries to increase their military and other influence in the Middle East? Presented here are various reasons to suggest that the effect has, in fact, been detrimental.

Thus, the Arab-Israeli conflict, in which Israel has been from the start actively assisted by the USA, was one of the factors that served to consolidate the OPEC countries. Although it has been suggested that the OPEC-generated increases in the price of oil have been an Arab response to Israeli aggression, this is too simplistic an explanation. On the other hand, the possibility exists that without this conflict oil prices would have climbed at a slower pace, thus enabling the Western economy to adjust to the situation in a less painful way. The confrontation between the Western and Arab nations has, through the explosive growth of oil prices, led to a higher rate of inflation. In some instances this confrontation has also led to the disruption of stable oil supplies. The slow-down in economic growth among the Western nations, largely owing to a decline in oil consumption brought about by the price increases, is thus also to be attributed in part to the Middle Eastern conflicts.

In recognition of the insecurity of oil supplies and the possibility of further oil price increases resulting from the Arab-Israeli conflict, the Western nations are now trying to achieve at least a position of neutrality *vis-à-vis* the Middle Eastern states. In other words, the involvement of the USA and some other Western nations in this conflict is antithetical to overall Western interests. In view of this conclusion one is bound to question whether the conflicts in the Middle East are caused by oil at all. This doubt arises especially because (*a*) the USA is not itself heavily dependent upon oil from the region, and (*b*) the West has as a result suffered economically. In order to analyse this matter, one must distinguish between short-term and long-term considerations.

In the short term, it is important to the USA that it strengthen the position of Israel, its main ally in the Middle East. It thereby ensures its own military presence in the Middle East, a strategic region which is close to the borders of the USSR and which also serves as the crossroads of crucial international communications. But in consideration of the likely response of both world and domestic public opinion to an open pursuit of such a policy, the USA finds it more convenient to claim that it is ensuring regular oil supplies and otherwise defending its vital economic interests. Difficulties connected with more expensive and scarcer oil are easier to present than White House ambitions to dominate the region. As to the US-suggested threat of seizure of Middle Eastern oil by the USSR, even ignoring moral considerations, it has become clear to the majority of Western scholars that it is much simpler and cheaper and free of political risk for the USSR to satisfy its energy needs using domestic energy resources.

In the long term, it would be an obvious oversimplification to think that oil is no more than a smokescreen meant to hide the true expansionist plans of Western states for gaining control over the strategic Middle East. Far-reaching considerations regarding that region's future role in the world energy picture undoubtedly play an essential role as well. This is, of course, the case because the oil deposits of the Middle East far surpass, and are sure to long outlast, all other oil-producing regions outside of the socialist countries.

It is unlikely that the Middle Eastern countries will try to diversify their economies so as to make them less dependent upon oil exports. In recognition of the serious financial troubles being experienced by Mexico, Venezuela, and Nigeria deriving from a one-sided oil orientation, the Arab oil-producing countries are, in fact, already considering definite steps to restructure their economies.

As the development of the Middle Eastern countries proceeds towards diversification, their dependence upon imports of goods, services, and technology is bound to decline. Once they are themselves able to solve many of their socio-economic problems, these countries might well find it advantageous to minimize their oil exports. This will leave their oil deposits as a major natural reserve whose financial value as a raw material for fuel and other uses will continue to increase. In the not too distant future, therefore, oil production in the Middle East might well decline even though its deposits are still considerable.

In conclusion, it is obvious that the USA and other capitalist countries seek to retain control over the course of events in the

Middle East. Their actions serve to channel the regional course of events along definite lines that impose development models upon the Arab countries which suit Western economic interests. Thus, the short-term interest and long-term goal of the USA and other capitalist countries to ensure a continuing abundant and reliable source of oil from the Middle East are closely intertwined.

Regions with contested jurisdiction over oil

With the present world surfeit of oil, the likelihood of conflicts arising between producer and consumer nations is low. This situation does not, however, prevent conflicts regarding the jurisdiction over oil deposits between oil-poor nations.

Discovery of oil deposits in the Aegean Sea in 1973 off the Greek island of Thásos exacerbated rival claims by Greece and Turkey to the mineral rights elsewhere in the Aegean sea-bed. After Greece refused to enter into bilateral negotiations, Turkey in May 1974 began oil exploration operations west of the Greek island of Lesbos. The following month Turkey granted the Turkish Petroleum Company further exploration rights to the Aegean continental shelf. Greece protested these actions and this was followed by a mutual exchange of military threats.

Following some unproductive interactions during the next few years with NATO, with the United Nations Security Council, and with the International Court of Justice, and after coming rather close to open hostilities in 1976, Greece and Turkey finally initiated bilateral negotiations over their Aegean dispute towards the end of that year. The legalities of the claims and counter-claims are complex and to date no resolution of the issue is in sight. However, the problem would never have become acute were it not for the discovery of oil deposits.

In the South China Sea, both China and Viet Nam claim title to the Paracel (Hsi-sha) Islands which are believed to be underlain by rich oil deposits. A Vietnamese garrison stationed there in 1974 was attacked and driven off by Chinese armed forces (see appendix 2, war 10). The dispute has yet to be resolved.

The territorial status of Antarctica remains unsolved (see appendix 4, article IV). Thus, in the event that this region becomes an object of oil or other mineral exploitation, it could become the scene of conflict among some 20 nations.

The separatist movements and oil

Some conflicts arise from separatist movements of ethnic or religious groups within a country, often one with a colonial past. If such a group seeks independence for territory that is rich in mineral resources, the movement is often supported by outside states or transnational corporations. They provide such support in order to change existing international economic or political relations in their favour or to gain control over the mineral resources. The Nigerian Civil War of 1967–70 provides a vivid illustration of this phenomenon (see appendix 2, war 7).

The then so-called Eastern Region of Nigeria—representing 8 per cent of its territory and 22 per cent of its population—seceded in 1967, declaring itself the Republic of Biafra. This region, primarily populated by Ibos, is the industrially most developed one of Nigeria; it is also rich in various mineral resources, especially so in oil, which accounts for two-thirds of the nation's production.

Many Ibos also lived outside of the Eastern Region, often rather well educated and qualified to play a significant role in the social and economic life of the country. In 1966, owing to inter-tribal enmity, a butchery of Ibos took place in the Northern Region which led to a mass escape or migration by Ibos from throughout the country to the Eastern Region. Despite administrative efforts by the central government to alleviate the situation, in May 1967 the Ibos declared the independence of Biafra which soon led to a bloody and disastrous two-and-a-half-year war by Nigeria to regain control over its Eastern Region.

It seems hardly possible that the Ibos decided to fight this war merely in response to the butchery to which they had been subjected in the Northern Region in 1966, especially in view of their obviously slim chance for success. It is here suggested that the real reason for resisting the central government was to gain control over the huge regional oil deposits.

First, Nigeria did not begin its armed attack on Biafra until July 1967, more than a month after the declaration of independence, but only days after Shell (which was extracting oil in the contested region) agreed to pay its royalties to Biafra rather than to Nigeria. Second, Nigeria's attack followed the boycott by Arab oil-producing countries against those states which were supporting Israel, a boycott which had been provoked by the third Arab-Israeli War of

June 1967 (see appendix 2, war 6). This Arab embargo increased the interest shown by the oil-importing states in the non-Arab oil-exporting states. Nigeria was of particular interest to the United Kingdom because Shell and the British Petroleum Company together produced almost 85 per cent of the oil exported from Nigeria, accounting for 10 per cent of total oil imports to the United Kingdom.

A naval blockage and general embargo by Nigeria against Biafra prevented the export of oil. This led the United Kingdom to withhold its support from Biafra. Then, when it appeared that Nigeria was winning, the United Kingdom began supporting Nigeria, by providing military supplies and in other ways.

It was widely assumed that the sympathy of France towards Biafra, as expressed in public declarations and military supplies, was motivated by its interest in the mineral resources of the region. Such an assumption is supported in at least two ways. First, a French-owned oil company was operating in Biafra which is said to have obtained oil rights capable of producing about 2.3 million cubic metres per year of oil. At the same time, the French branch of the House of Rothschild Bank is said to have obtained the exclusive extraction rights in Biafra for a period of 10 years to all of its deposits of niobium (columbium), uranium, coal, tin, oil, and gold (Cervenka, 1971, pages 113–14). Moreover, the pro-Biafra lobby that existed in the USA must be seen in the light of the substantial investments in the region by the Mobil Oil and several other US companies (Cervenka, 1971, pages 123–24).

Irrespective of any governmental positions pro or con, all of the oil companies with interests in Biafra favoured its independence and provided significant support to the secessionists. It has been suggested that Nigeria did not suit the oil companies because for them 'The *ideal* oil state, of course, would be one with just enough land on which to place oil rigs and just enough people to guard the pipelines—a combination which is closely approximated by the sheikdoms of South Arabia' (Fitch & Oppenheimer, 1968, page 35). In the last analysis, it must be concluded that oil was one of the important triggering and sustaining factors in the Nigerian Civil War.

Oil as a lever rather than a goal

Besides being a source of conflict, oil often appears to serve as a lever of foreign policy. For instance, in the Persian Gulf region, a war has been in progress between Iran and Iraq since 1980. Each side is bent upon destroying the oil resources of the other. Both countries have been among the major oil exporters and diminution in oil revenues makes it difficult for them to pursue their war.

In southern Africa, the insurgent forces in South Africa (the African National Congress) periodically assault South African synthetic liquid-fuel production facilities in recognition that such action is a major blow to the regime in power. For their part, the attacks that guerrillas supported by South Africa make on Angola (which supports the South African insurgency) are often aimed at Angola's oil enterprises. The importance of these targets is suggested by the claim that oil supplies up to 80 per cent of Angola's foreign reserve earnings and over 60 per cent of total government revenues (Price, 1981, page 93).

V. Conclusion

The present desire of the major oil-importing nations to maintain the stability of oil production mitigates against their armed intervention in oil-exporting nations to achieve control of their oil resources. Nor is it at present likely that oil-importing nations will fight among themselves over oil owing to the current oil glut. It is at present also unlikely that the oil-exporting nations will go to war with each other because the currently favourable oil prices can remain so only if the main oil exporters remain united in their marketing efforts. Nevertheless, small-scale oil-related conflicts are possible at the interstate or inter-regional level, especially in areas of contested jurisdiction or with ethnic problems.

If the role of oil as a cause of armed conflict has diminished, its role as a lever of foreign policy remains intact. An obvious use of oil as an instrument of foreign policy is the imposition of an oil embargo. However, such action can achieve success only in the short term. On the one hand, a consumer state thus deprived can utilize domestic stockpiles and can reinforce domestic conservation measures; and in time it is able to mobilize its own resources or to find new suppliers. On the other hand, a supplier state that is withholding oil from the market can do so for only a limited period of time because of its dependence on the thus suspended oil revenues. Put simply, it is in the best long-term interests of both consumers and producers to maintain their relationship, whether it deals with oil, wheat, or other large-volume commodity.

References

Arbatov, A. A. 1983. [Peculiarities of mineral-raw material sector functioning in different economy types] (in Russian). *Ekonomika i Matematicheskie Metody,* Moscow, 19(2):197–205.

Arbatov, A. & Amirov, I. 1984. Raw material problems in interstate conflicts. *International Affairs,* Moscow, 1984(8):65–73,103.

Brigg, P. (ed.). 1985. *BP statistical review of world energy.* London: British Petroleum Company, 32 pp.

Carter, J. 1980. State of the Union address. *Department of State Bulletin,* Washington, 80(2035):38A–38D.

Cervenka, Z. 1971. *Nigerian war 1967–1970: history of the war, selected bibliography and documents.* Frankfurt a.M.: Bernard & Graefe Verlag für Wehrwesen, 459 pp.

Eckes, A. E., Jr. 1979. *United States and the global struggle for minerals.* Austin: University of Texas Press, 353 pp.

Fitch, R. & Oppenheimer, M. 1968. Biafra: let them eat oil. *Ramparts,* San Francisco, 7(4):34–35,38.

Hackett, J. 1981. Protecting oil supplies: the military requirements. In: Bertram, C. (ed.). *Third-world conflict and international security. I.* London: International Institute for Strategic Studies, Adelphi Paper No. 166, 58 pp.: pp. 41–51.

Price, R. M. 1981. Prepared statement. In: Wolpe, H. (ed.). *Possibility of a resource war in southern Africa [Hearing, 8 July 1981].* Washington: US House of Representatives Committee on Foreign Affairs, 120 pp.: pp. 91–98.

Rubner, M. 1979. *Camp David and after: the military implications.* Los Angeles: California State University Center for the Study of Armament & Disarmament, Occasional Paper No. 5, 17 pp.

Santalov, A. A. 1954. *[Imperialist struggle for sources of raw materials]* (in Russian). Moscow: USSR Academy of Sciences Publishing House, 586 pp.

Sinai Support Mission, US. 1980. *Watch in the Sinai.* Washington: US Department of State, Publication No. 9131, 39 pp.

3. Oil and natural gas as factors in strategic policy and action: a long-term view

Erik Solem and Antony F. G. Scanlan
Canadian Department of External Affairs and British Institute of Energy Economics

I. Introduction

It was argued a decade ago that global stability, that is, international security and the absence of war, was related to stability in *both* the developing and developed worlds (Solem, 1976). One of the major problem areas and sources of potentially serious conflict pointed to at that time lay in the field of energy resources, involving their availability, development, and distribution. A proper energy strategy for the world presupposed sane national energy policies plus appropriate long-term planning. It was further argued that an ideal global strategy had to include a number of collective restraints on action, an approach not generally accepted at the international level except in the face of severe imminent danger.

The necessity for the approach suggested earlier remains and it is argued here that the necessary international co-operation and restraints are possible. It is further argued that a truly global energy strategy is the *sine qua non* of international security and global survival. This chapter is thus an elaboration of previous work by the authors (Scanlan, 1985; Solem, 1976; 1981; 1982; 1983).

The chapter is complemented by a somewhat contrasting interpretation of past and present events in the one that precedes it (chapter 2).

II. Historical overview

Today, oil plus natural gas globally account for more than twice the amount of energy obtained from coal (table 3.1). In the nineteenth

Table 3.1. Oil, natural gas, and coal production by the major powers (energy equivalents), 1982[a]

Country[b]	Oil[c] (10^{18} J)	Natural gas[c] (10^{18} J)	Coal[c] (10^{18} J)	Lignite (brown coal)[c] (10^{18} J)	Total (10^{18} J)	Proportion of global total (per cent)
China	4.4	0.5	13.3	0.3	18.4	7
France	0.1	0.3	0.5	0.1	1.0	0.4
United Kingdom	4.4	1.4	3.0	0	8.8	4
USA	18.1	17.6	17.6	0.7	54.1	22
USSR	26.1	17.4	12.0	2.3	57.8	23
All others	59.7	17.1	20.9	8.5	106.2	43
Global total	**112.8**	**54.3**	**67.4**	**11.8**	**246.3**	*100*

Sources and notes:
[a] Table prepared by A. H. Westing.
[b] The countries are the five permanent members of the United Nations Security Council.
[c] The values are for 1982 and are derived from *UN Statistical Yearbook*, New York, 33, table 158 plus annex III (1982). Approximate energy contents: for oil, 36.5×10^9 joules per cubic metre (or 42.6×10^9 joules per tonne); for natural gas, 38.3×10^6 joules per cubic metre; for coal, 29.3×10^9 joules per tonne; and for lignite (brown coal), 11.3×10^9 joules per tonne.

century, by contrast, industry depended upon coal for its source of energy; and, owing to the great bulk involved, drew largely on indigenous production. Oil began to gain in importance only after the turn of the century, with the development of the internal combustion engine for land, sea and air transport.

The Middle East became identified as a major source of oil in 1909 with discoveries by the United Kingdom in Persia (now Iran). Within three years the United Kingdom converted its navy from coal to oil and established partial control over the extracting company (later to become the British Petroleum Company) in order to secure its naval supplies. Previously, the production and use of oil had been almost entirely indigenous, with the USA and Russia then accounting for 90 per cent of it.

World War I (see appendix 2, war 1) made clear the strategic importance of oil. The production of oil increased rapidly in the USA after that war, expanding from 70 million cubic metres (440 million barrels) in 1920 to 210 million cubic metres in 1940.

Although domestic use increased as well during that inter-war period, the USA remained an exporter. The production of oil in the USSR also expanded after World War I, but it ceased to export oil for many years. US oil companies had strong interests in acquiring access to oil in the eastern hemisphere, but it was the European states, with essentially no indigenous oil, that were most concerned with securing access to external supplies, especially following further major Middle Eastern discoveries, for example, in 1928 in what is now Iraq. The countries most involved in gaining access to Middle Eastern oil were France, the Netherlands, the United Kingdom, and, to a lesser extent, the USA.

Italy invaded Ethiopia in 1935 and in response Romania and the USSR proposed an oil embargo against Italy, but it was never put into effect (Roberts, 1970, pages 485–87). Japan, too, was threatened by an oil embargo, by the USA in 1941, because of its aggression in East Asia, and this may have been the trigger which caused Japan to initiate World War II in the Pacific theatre (Turner, 1983, page 38).

During World War II (see appendix 2, war 3), Germany had no access to oil except for modest amounts in Romania (Turner, 1983). This led Germany to manufacture oil products from coal, of which it had ample indigenous supplies, despite the costs of such conversion. Today, South Africa is potentially independent of outside oil because of its similar ability to convert domestic coal. It is clear that, given sufficient warning, an oil embargo would have economic but little strategic impact on most of the major powers of the world because of their indigenous coal deposits (table 3.1).

Following World War II, the global oil industry changed remarkably. Not only did global production rise rapidly, but new uses were found for oil. Whereas oil had previously been used almost exclusively for transportation, its use was now diversified to meet various energy needs. Oil replaced coal as the main global source of primary energy in most of the non-socialist countries by 1958 and throughout most of the world by 1966.[1] The USA, which had

---

[1] In the Western oil industry, the nations of the world are often divided for purposes of market analysis into two groups: (*a*) the 'communist world', which consists of the members of the Council for Mutual Economic Assistance (for current membership, see 'CMEA' in glossary) plus China; and (*b*) the 'non-communist world', which consists of all other nations. In this book, the comparable terms are: (*a*) the 'socialist countries'; and (*b*) the 'non-socialist countries'.

dominated the oil industry prior to World War II (accounting for 60 per cent of global production in 1938), ceased to be self-sufficient after 1945. Its interest in Middle Eastern oil increased accordingly. By 1954, the USA had acquired a 40 per cent share of Iranian oil (previously entirely in the hands of the United Kingdom), and soon afterwards a 100 per cent share of Saudi Arabian oil. In addition, development rights to Kuwaiti oil, with known reserves second only to those of Saudi Arabia, were then shared equally by the United Kingdom and the USA. The oil deposits of Saudi Arabia, discovered by US companies before World War II, were in time found to comprise one-fourth of the then known global reserves, putting the USA ahead of any other nation in terms of Middle Eastern oil concessions (Turner, 1983, pages 41–49).

Realization that Kuwait, Iran, Iraq, Saudi Arabia, and the United Arab Emirates together accounted for about 70 per cent of known global oil reserves in just a few giant reservoirs led to the development of supertankers (some now with capacities in excess of 500 000 cubic metres), permitting this relatively cheap and abundant source of energy to penetrate all world markets.

The industrialized countries were for the first time placing their energy lifelines outside their own territories. The USA became apprehensive that free competition in the international oil market might drive prices down to the point where the relatively small oilfields typical of the USA (e.g., those in Texas) could not survive because of their inability to match the economies of oil delivered by supertanker from the giant Middle Eastern fields. The oil-poor nations of Europe began in the 1950s to seek safety by diversifying their sources of supply, turning beyond the Middle East to Latin America, Canada, the USA (Alaska), and Africa. (North Sea oil was not to become important for another decade.)

The need for secure sea lanes for the tankers bringing oil from the Middle East increased the importance of the Suez Canal to a level never imagined by its builders. The Second Arab-Israeli War of 1956, which led to the blockage of the Suez Canal for some six months, was at the time perceived as a major threat to world oil supplies, not because it disrupted production, but because it led to the need for more tankers to carry enough oil via the Cape of Good Hope. In the event, this obstruction turned out to be far less important than had been feared. By the time the Suez Canal was closed again, by the Third Arab-Israeli War of 1967 (see appendix

2, war 6), this time for seven years, supertankers were leading to such economies of scale that their long alternate route around the Cape of Good Hope had transformed the Canal to a mere secondary or regional route.

US moves in 1958 to protect its domestic oil production industry by imposing import restrictions did stimulate domestic production until about 1970. However, the main exporter nations responded to this denial of free access to their largest market, and to the concomitant decline in the value of their oil, by creating in 1960 the Organization of Petroleum Exporting Countries (OPEC; for current membership, see glossary). A combination of the collective strength of OPEC and growing demands for oil in Europe and Japan were among the factors that drove up oil prices after 1970, but the key reason was the rapid increase in demand for oil imports by the USA after 1970, at the time its indigenous production peaked. Before the Fourth Arab-Israeli War of 1973, the delivered price of crude oil in the USA (and elsewhere) more than doubled in one year (Champness & Jenkins, 1985; Steel, 1983). Subsequent imposition of an oil embargo by OPEC against countries considered by the Organization to be sympathetic towards Israel plus a major increase in the price of Iranian oil resulted in a fourfold increase in the price of oil during 1973.

In 1974, a group of 16 oil-importing nations established an International Energy Agency (in Paris) under the auspices of the Organisation for Economic Co-operation and Development, a number which has now grown to 21 (all Western). The Agency works towards curbing excess demands for oil, encouraging alternative sources of energy, and seeking conservation measures. Member states are committed to share oil in certain emergencies, and the Agency is also supposed to develop a co-operative relationship between consumers and producers.

The oil shortages and dramatic price increases that had existed in the major oil-importing countries in 1973–74 can now be seen not to have been the result of an actual shortage of oil in the world, but rather to have stemmed from distortions in the international balance of trade. After 1979, when market prices of oil doubled in the wake of the Iranian revolution and the cessation of Iranian oil supplies for several months, a debt crisis of global proportions had developed, and the ensuing recession damaged the OPEC, OECD, and oil-importing developing nations alike.

III. The world energy situation today

The inequalities, imbalances, and disparities in levels of energy production and consumption, both present and future, among the many nations of the world—as well as those in levels of present and potential affluence—can be resolved only if an expanded concept of security is developed. For this to be achieved, certain economic and political realities must be recognized.

A view of the world energy situation as it stands today reveals serious inequalities among countries in energy consumption, imbalances in many countries between energy supply and demand, and a highly skewed distribution among countries of known energy reserves (Rao, 1980). Therefore, coming to terms with the long-term energy problem on a global basis requires an accommodation to the global system of sovereign states.

A major feature of the global energy regime is the element of uncertainty with regard to economic growth, to energy demand, and to energy supply. The uncertainty associated with future sources of energy and with changes in the use patterns adds to the problem. Another feature of the global energy regime is the variety of national perceptions of what constitutes energy security. These perceptions differ from one socio-political system to the next and from one sector of society to the next. Remarkable differences exist in the level of the energy problem from oil-exporting to oil-importing states; and, among the oil-importing states, from developed to developing nations (Rao, 1980).

Resolution of the global energy problem will require a recognition of the considerations enumerated above. No single approach based upon some static or unidimensional interpretation of the situation will suffice. The approach must be a dynamic and pluralistic one, a prerequisite that is apparently beginning to be more widely understood and accepted. This is not to say that important international problems will not remain. However, it appears that these will be of a more political than economic nature and will therefore be more readily soluble as public awareness and understanding grow.

It is essential to understand that no adequate substitute for oil is likely to be available in the coming few years or decades in quantities sufficient to replace it as the primary commercial fuel for most countries, be they developed or developing. It is probably also true that most of the developed nations will continue to remain dependent upon large amounts of imported oil—Canada, Norway, the USSR, and possibly the United Kingdom being exceptions. Moreover, there is little prospect of the Middle East being displaced as the major supplier of oil, even if the potential sources in the Arctic, far northern North Sea, or offshore China are developed or if the USA and USSR exploit their domestic energy deposits more fully (Solem, 1981; 1981–1982). The uncertainties of oil supply during the 1970s have been largely replaced in the 1980s by the uncertainties of oil demand. Nevertheless, it seems likely that demand for oil by the OECD countries will experience very little growth in the future (Belgrave, 1985).

In considering the global oil regime it must be remembered that the USA and USSR together account for a huge share (about 45 per cent) of all production (table 3.1) and essentially the same proportion of all consumption (Brigg, 1985, page 7). Moreover, the USA is the world's largest net importer of oil (about 20 per cent of the total traded), whereas the USSR is the world's largest exporter (about 10 per cent of the total traded) (Brigg, 1985, page 16). Thus relatively small changes—whether in production, in consumption, or in trade—by either of the two superpowers can have a large impact on the rest of the world (Scanlan, 1985). In fact, it would seem to be advantageous to both of these nations to maintain stability in the global oil market by preventing abrupt distortions in either supply or demand. International energy security is in the interests of both the supplier and the consumer nations. It hinges upon détente between the USA and USSR, stability in the Middle East, co-operation among the oil-importing developed nations, stable monetary exchange rates, and co-operation and trust between the exporters and the importers. In such a setting, the risks of oil disruption would be low, the possibility of collective remedial action high, and the likelihood of armed conflict over oil minimal (Bohi & Quandt, 1984).

It is unrealistic to expect that a benign global energy environment of the sort just alluded to will develop naturally during the 1980s. Indeed, energy security is likely to remain problematic in the 1980s and 1990s. This will not be the result of oil shortages, but rather of political instability in the Middle East, rivalry between the superpowers, and competition among the developed consumer nations.

Approaches to achieving global energy security are addressed below (section V).

The waxing and waning of OPEC

By 1970, the productive output of the OPEC countries had expanded to meet nearly 70 per cent of the demand for oil imports by the non-socialist countries. Furthermore, OPEC controlled more than 75 per cent of proven oil reserves existing in the non-socialist countries (Brigg, 1985, page 2). During the 1970s, OPEC determined the world market price of oil, which increased dramatically in this period. The more or less immediate result of this increase was a drastic reduction in the value of the world's capital.

The huge increase in the cost of oil during the 1970s led to an unprecedented shift in the distribution of world income. In 1980 the oil-importing developing nations imported 13 per cent less oil than in 1973, doing so at four times the cost in real terms (Solem, 1983). Much of the increased purchasing power of the OPEC nations has been used for the acquisition of sophisticated military equipment and large investments in military infrastructure (Ohlson, 1981; Solem, 1983). The increased cost of oil has in many parts of the world contributed to monetary inflation, to unemployment, and to economic recession in general. The world has become poorer as a result.

The international financial system has become unbalanced as a result of huge accumulations of financial surpluses in many of the OPEC nations. The concomitant trade deficits in the oil-importing nations have led to restrictions on total (oil and non-oil) imports by the OECD and other nations. This has hurt the developing countries. The subsequent decline in oil purchases, in turn, has had an adverse effect on the OPEC countries.

Although it is unjust to blame OPEC for all, or even most, of the economic problems now facing the world, it is clear that oil supplies and prices are crucial to the economic life of the entire world. By raising the price of oil so remarkably during the 1970s and early 1980s, OPEC has discouraged oil-importing countries from maintaining fiscal policies conducive to economic growth and full employment. For many oil-importing countries and much of the oil industry the early 1980s have been a period of frustrated expectations and crushed hopes (Petroleum Economist, 1982). The period has been one of unprofitable trading, under-utilized capacity, and plant closures. Oil-exporting countries have not been exempt. They have experienced cuts in production, falling revenues, unbalanced budgets, domestic unrest, and other problems.

Among the factors contributing to the world-wide decreases in oil consumption during 1980–83 (Brigg, 1985, page 7) and the recent uncertainties in the global oil market have been greater emphasis on efficient use of energy and on alternative sources of energy. The situation has also encouraged oil exploration in areas outside of the OPEC countries. For example, in 1981 the five major US oil companies, as well as Shell and British Petroleum, all raised their expenditures on exploration by one-third or more (Petroleum Economist, 1982). By the early 1980s, OPEC appeared to be heading for trouble and various members were obliged to begin cutting production or reducing prices, or both. Of course, the situation differed in various respects from one OPEC country to another. Saudi Arabia, with an annual oil output of up to 500 million cubic metres, has acted as the 'swing producer', attempting to protect price by cutting back on production. Other nations, with less flexibility and larger needs (from, e.g., pressures of population growth or costs of ongoing wars), have tended to cut price and to maximize their share of the market. However, very recent market conditions have caused Saudi Arabia to also change its export policy to a more aggressive one.

Despite its current problems, OPEC cannot be dismissed as a price-setting force. Oil remains a commodity of central importance and the OPEC countries account for a large proportion of known reserves. The price of oil, despite recent declines, remains substantially higher than it might be in a free market, in part owing to high taxes. In the long term, the future of OPEC is tied to the world economy itself, which, it must be noted, shows few signs of rebounding in the immediate future.

IV. The future world energy situation

Any forecast regarding economic growth is subject to major uncertainty and the following predictions must be seen in that light.

In the non-socialist countries, it is likely that overall energy consumption will grow by perhaps 2.2 per cent per year during the next 15 years, that is, at approximately three-fourths the rate of the expected growth in combined gross national products (Chevron, 1985, page 8). Oil consumption, however, is predicted to grow by about 1.1 per cent per year during this period (Chevron, 1985, page 9). Its displacement in the total energy package of the non-socialist countries during these 15 years will presumably be in large part accounted for by coal (the use of which is expected to grow by 3.2 per cent per year) and in small parts by natural gas (expected growth, 2.4 per cent per year) and nuclear energy (expected growth, 5.5 per cent per year).

In the USA, total energy consumption is expected to grow by 1.3 per cent per year over the next 15 years, that is, at approximately half the rate of the predicted growth in its gross national product (Chevron, 1985, pages 5–7). Oil consumption, by contrast, is during this period expected to grow at the rate of only 0.7 per cent per year. The share of oil in the total energy package will thus decline. Oil imports are expected to increase during this period inasmuch as domestic production is forecast to decline by 1.4 per cent per year.

As for the socialist countries, oil exports by the USSR are expected to decline somewhat during the next 15 years, and natural gas exports to increase somewhat (Chevron, 1985, page 11). Overall energy consumption by the USSR is predicted to increase by about 2.6 per cent per year during this period, that is, at roughly the same rate as its expected growth in gross domestic product. The share of oil in the total energy package of the USSR is expected to decline somewhat, to be replaced in large part by natural gas.

In Eastern Europe, total energy consumption is expected to increase by about 2.3 per cent per year during the next 15 years (Chevron, 1985, page 11). Oil consumption by these countries is expected to be constrained since indigenous production accounts for only about one-fifth of consumption and since importation is costly. Domestic supplies of natural gas are inadequate to meet the growing energy demands of the region and the coal, except in Poland, is mainly low-grade lignite.

In China, overall energy consumption over the next 15 years is forecast to increase by a remarkable 4.0 per cent per year, in line with the country's predicted very rapid overall economic growth (Chevron, 1985, page 12). At present, coal accounts for about three-fourths of China's energy consumption, and development of this resource remains a top priority. The already modest share of oil in China's total energy package is expected to decline even further during this period. Domestic oil consumption is tightly controlled in order to permit increasing exports for the acquisition of hard currency.

The total volume of oil that has been extracted to date throughout the world (i.e., since about 1860) is at least 84×10^9 cubic metres (Chevron, 1985, page 2; Scanlan, 1983, page 3). Proved reserves as of the end of 1984 come to about 112×10^9 cubic metres (Brigg, 1985, page 2; Chevron, 1985, page 2). At a global rate of consumption of 3.4×10^9 cubic metres per year (the 1980–84 average; Brigg, 1985, page 7), proved reserves would last for 33 years. It is, of course, unsound to anticipate the rate of success in finding any remaining undiscovered deposits, but it can be expected that they will extend that period by some years.

Projections of the above sort are subject to enormous uncertainties, both technical and political, but the point to be made is that oil production can be expected to peak within a very few decades and that thereafter this resource is likely to become increasingly scarce and expensive. It is therefore essential that today's planning take such an eventuality into serious account. Among other avenues, steps must now be taken towards a renewed reliance on coal and natural gas and on renewable sources of energy.

V. A long-term energy strategy

A long-term energy strategy must recognize the central importance of oil, its vulnerability to disruption, and its finite nature. The supply of oil is vulnerable to accidents, extortion, terrorism, insurgencies, and warfare. Natural gas supplies are equally vulnerable. About 90 per cent of commercial energy comes from oil, gas, and coal, all of which require huge effort and take about a decade to develop. Nuclear and water energies are also difficult and slow to develop. Solar energy is likely to become more important in the future; some so-called passive or background solar heating is already being utilized (e.g., in Greece), but the production of electricity from solar energy is far from commercial realization.

It has become clear that security of oil supply cannot be neglected in favour of keeping oil prices down. Indeed, higher oil prices may simply have to be accepted for reasons of security. Thus it has been a mistake for the USA to encourage the Middle Eastern oil-producing states to increase their production and to keep their prices down (Solem, 1983). Such action has served to increase the dependence of the oil-importing OECD nations on Middle Eastern oil.

A successful oil strategy must strive towards efficiency of use and other aspects of conservation and for a greater reliance on substitutes. There must also be an emphasis on preventing supply disruptions and on avoiding wild fluctuations in price. For example, the decontrol by the USA in 1981 of domestic crude oil prices was a step in the right direction, both with regard to preventing supply interruptions internationally and to keeping world prices more stable (Solem, 1983). A better integration must be achieved of political and economic policies, both nationally and internationally (one of the aims of which must be to avoid protective and tariffs).

During the oil crisis of the 1970s a number of options for action were discussed in the West. Among these were some wildly improbable 'quick-fix' solutions involving drastic political or even military coercion. Such approaches would have been counter-productive; and it is, for example, extremely unlikely that either the USA or USSR harboured contingency plans for taking over the Middle Eastern oilfields. A military take-over would have destroyed the oil infrastructure of the region, would have had profound international economic repercussions, and would have caused almost irreparable political damage to either superpower.

The USSR, only 800 kilometres away from the Middle Eastern oilfields, could be considered as a threat to the continuity of oil supplies from that region (Solem, 1983). In fact, it is in the best interests of the USSR—as it is of the USA—to maintain stability in the Middle East. Much more serious threats to continued regional oil production are sabotage and terrorism, insurgencies, and regional wars. It would perhaps be attractive to the oil-importing developed nations if the Middle East could somehow be neutralized or otherwise internationalized. However, this is at best a case of wishful thinking.

It would be ill-advised for the oil-importing developed countries to attempt to 'break' OPEC at all costs (Solem, 1983). A food embargo on OPEC for the purpose of destroying the price structure imposed upon the world oil market by that organization would be untenable because it could be circumvented and for other reasons (see also chapter 7).

An attempt to destroy OPEC is foolish for a variety of reasons, among them: (*a*) that the feared power of OPEC has been to some extent already undermined by the development of a number of sources of oil—and of other forms of energy—independent of that organization; (*b*) that the existence of OPEC is in the best interests of both producers and consumers; (*c*) that OPEC has never been able to control production rates among its members; and (*d*) that if OPEC were to disappear it would soon be replaced by a comparable organization. In other words, the rest of the world must learn to live with OPEC and to assist it in becoming fully integrated into the world economy. It is important for the world community to avoid the possibility of chaos in the increasingly fragmented oil market of today.

Despite the short-term abundance of oil, what is needed for long-term energy security is formal co-operation among the main oil-importing nations in order to develop a unified long-term strategy (Solem, 1976). The International Energy Agency mentioned above was established with this goal in mind, but only represents one group of nations.

It is useful to observe that conflict in regions rich in oil or natural gas has rarely been caused in the first instance by the presence of that commodity. For example, the Nigerian Civil War of 1967–70 (see appendix 2, war 7) had its antecedents in regional tribal animosities that long predate the discovery of oil in the Biafra region. As for the Middle East, this is a chronically unstable region. Deep-seated mistrust of long standing among the nations of the Middle East makes the prospect for regional stability dim. Those who feel, for example, that resolution of the Palestinian problem will bring stability to the region seriously underestimate the dimensions of the situation.

Although a direct link between oil and war cannot be readily established, there clearly does exist a link between oil and development. The developing nations of the world require sources of energy for their development. It thus becomes crucial to seek additional sources of oil and new sources of energy that would be accessible to the developing world. Serious thought must be given by developing nations to water, solar, geothermal, and tidal energy.

Natural gas

Whereas concerns over the global oil regime centre on the Middle East with its huge proven reserves, those over natural gas centre for similar reasons on the USSR. Indeed, of the known reserves of natural gas as of the end of 1984—96 × 10^{12} cubic metres—fully 43 per cent are located within that country (Brigg, 1985, page 20). Iran, a distant second, has 14 per cent of the known reserves (the Middle East altogether having 25 per cent); and the USA, in third place, accounts for another 6 per cent.

Current global production of natural gas is about 1.6 × 10^{12} cubic metres per year (Brigg, 1985, page 21). Production is dominated about equally by the USSR (accounting for 36 per cent of the total) and USA (accounting for 30 per cent of the total).

Today the USSR is the world's leading producer and exporter of both oil and natural gas, these being its major sources of foreign exchange. About half of the exports are to other members of the Council for Mutual Economic Assistance (for current membership, see 'CMEA' in the glossary) and most of the remainder goes to Western Europe. Soviet production, consumption and export policies regarding oil and natural gas are thus, as noted earlier, of widespread concern.

Of the several major consumption areas in the world outside of the USSR, current interest in natural gas as an export commodity centres on Western Europe because it can be piped there from Algeria, the North Sea and the USSR, sea transport still being too expensive (with the exception of shipment to Japan, which has no alternative). North American demands are being met by domestic sources. Natural gas reserves may soon surpass those of oil, and the likelihood for future discoveries of natural gas deposits is greater than for oil deposits. The reason that the current production of natural gas is only half that of oil (see table 3.1) is in part the prohibitive cost of ocean freight, but is primarily the long lead times necessary for the development of its production, distribution, and consumption infrastructures. Western Europe should develop and begin executing a long-term plan to augment its existing pipeline connections with Norway, Algeria, and the USSR with a major pipeline grid that extends from northern Norway to Algeria, including the United Kingdom, and in time also linking up with pipelines to the Middle East and Nigeria. A willingness by the Western

European nations—a willingness not now apparent—is necessary to provide the right financial and industrial basis for such a long-term energy strategy.

VI. Conclusion

If a global strategy for energy is to be relevant, it must avoid the mistake of dealing with the last crisis. Rather, it must be able to address those factors that, uncorrected, will cause the next crisis. A long-term strategy must be able to look beyond transitory gluts and shortages of oil and beyond the vagaries of the oil price levels of the day. Energy projects require dedicated investment of a decade or more, but it must be recognized that market forces cannot be predicted with any certainty so far ahead. Greater reliance must be placed on the predictions of remaining oil and natural gas resources and long-term plans laid accordingly.

It is important to maintain stable oil prices in order to encourage rational long-term planning and investment. Oil-exporting countries should resist the temptation to use oil revenues as a cure for their short-term financial problems, for this also discourages the necessary investment in the future. Overall policy should emanate, not from individual oil companies, whether private or public, but rather from the industry as a whole. And the proper blend must be discovered of corporate initiative, the role of industry, and governmental legislation.

The world has barely a decade to discover and develop adequate supplies of energy or else face increasing dependence on oil from the most troubled region on earth, the Middle East. It also has to lift itself out of a recession, and at the same time address the dangerous imbalances of development among nations and, in some cases, even within nations. Any national system of economics which fails to recognize these unavoidable problems on the track ahead, whatever label or flag it wears, will shortly derail the train. Energy investments, to maintain the system, must continue to be made despite a lack of appropriate price signals from the market.

Perhaps as evidence that monetarist myopia is more widely understood than many feel it politic to reveal, energy exploration is now at an all-time high on frontiers all over the world, at unprecedentedly high levels of cost. However, in many offshore and polar regions the desire to search for oil and natural gas is moving faster than the necessary agreements can be reached among nations over sovereign rights in these areas, most of which were laid down in an era before the nature of their geology was recognized. Recent examples of the sites of dispute include the North Sea (between the United Kingdom and Norway), the Barents Sea (between Norway and the USSR), the Navarin Basin south of the Bering Strait (between the USSR and USA), the Persian Gulf (between Iran and Saudi Arabia), the Falkland/Malvinas Shelf (between the United Kingdom and Argentina), and many regions in the Indonesian archipelago area, for example, Timor and the Paracel (Hsi-sha) Islands, and in the narrow seas around Europe, for example, in the English Channel, the Baltic Sea, and the Aegean Sea. Other sensitive offshore areas involve the major East Asian powers and also the USA and Canada over their northern waters. Energy agreements must be established in these areas either to recognize individual sovereignty or to allow for co-operative development.

Failure to address the problems of the global energy regime is certain to lead to future tension and perhaps conflict.

References

Belgrave, R. 1985. Uncertainty of energy supplies in a geopolitical perspective. *International Affairs,* London, 61:255–261.

Bohi, D. R. & Quandt, W. B. 1984. *Energy security in the 1980s: economic and political perspectives.* Washington: Brookings Institution, 52 pp.

Brigg, P. (ed.). 1985. *BP statistical review of world energy.* London: British Petroleum Company, 32 pp.

Champness, M. V. & Jenkins, G. I. 1985. *Oil tanker data book.* Amsterdam: Elsevier, 347 pp.

Chevron. 1985. *World energy outlook: forecast through the year 2000.* San Francisco: Chevron Corporation, 21 pp.

Ohlson, T. 1981. World trade in major conventional weapons in the 1970s. *SIPRI Yearbook,* London, 1981:105–120.

Petroleum Economist. 1982. Year of frustrated expectations. *Petroleum Economist,* London, 44:482–483.

Rao, G. V. S. 1980. World energy problematique: an agenda for international co-operation. In: El Mallakh, R. & El Mallakh, D. (eds). *New policy imperatives for energy producers.* Boulder, Colorado: International Research Center for Energy & Economic Development, 257 pp.: pp. 55–68.

Roberts, J. M. 1970. *Europe 1880–1945.* 2nd ed. Harlow, UK: Longman, 575 pp.

Scanlan, A. F. G. (ed.). [1983]. *BP statistical review of world energy 1982*. London: British Petroleum Company, 33 pp.

Scanlan, T. [A.F.G.] 1985. Impact of the superpowers' energy balances on world oil. *Energy Policy*, Guildford, UK, 13(1):5–12.

Solem, K. E. 1976. Energy resources and global strategic planning. *Impact of Science on Society*, Paris, 26:77–90.

Solem, [K.]E. 1981. Strategic implications of resource policy. In: Engelmann, F. & Gillsdorff, J. (eds). *Energy resources and centre-periphery relations*. Edmonton: University of Alberta Press, 509 pp.: pp. 387–394.

Solem, [K.]E. 1981–1982. Energy and changing strategic aspects of Canada's arctic regions. *Canadian Defence Quarterly*, Toronto, 11(3):18–25.

Solem, [K.]E. 1982. *Strategic implications of recent oil and gas developments in the North Sea*. Ottawa: Canadian Department of National Defence, Operational Research & Analysis Establishment Project Report No. 208, 52 pp.

Solem, [K.]E. 1983. *Strategic implications of the world oil glut*. Ottawa: Canadian Department of National Defence, Operational Research & Analysis Establishment Project Report No. 209, 29 pp.

Steel, D. 1983. Oil. In: Ezra, D. (ed.). *Energy debate*. London: Ernest Benn, 252 pp.: pp. 18–21.

Turner, L. 1983. *Oil companies in the international system*. 3rd ed. London: George Allen & Unwin, 279 pp.

4. Minerals as a factor in strategic policy and action

Helge Hveem
University of Oslo

I. Introduction

International conflict over natural resources is basically caused by the concern of governments and private firms over long-term predictability and reliability of resource supplies. Such concern is particularly strongly felt with respect to those natural resources which are perceived as vitally needed for military-political or economic reasons, or both. The present study has selected some such resources for special scrutiny: chromium, cobalt, and uranium. These are among the so-called strategic minerals.

Strategic minerals are not considered strategic solely for military reasons. The overall economic position and the industrial strength of nations are intimately linked to military planning and to programmes for national defence. Many in fact would conceive of the former as pre-conditions for the latter.

The supply of strategic minerals is influenced by several factors: (*a*) political bargaining or intervention; (*b*) the structure of world industry; and (*c*) physical, ecological, economic, and technological constraints. Conversely, demand for such minerals is influenced by such factors as: (*a*) the degree of national self-sufficiency of the main users; (*b*) global availability; (*c*) technological change; (*d*) changes in social structure; (*e*) changes in consumption patterns; and (*f*) the ability to adjust to perceived shortages of or barriers to supply by domestic re-adjustment policies. Several of the enumerated factors are among the chief determinants of conflict among nations and thus represent a considerable potential for such conflict.

The present chapter builds upon previous work by the author (Hveem, 1978; Hveem & Malnes, 1980). It does not cover oil or natural gas (for which see chapters 2 and 3).

II. Conflict over natural resources

For analytical purposes, the potential for conflict can be distinguished from the cause of conflict. Strategic minerals represent more of a potential for conflict than minerals in general. Six aspects appear to be important clues in determining whether or not a potential for conflict over natural resources exists:

1. The extent to which the military sector and industrial system in the short to medium term are dependent on the natural resource, that is, cannot do without it under prevailing technology and applications;

2. The extent to which the industry concerned with the natural resource is subject to monopoly, oligopoly, or other form of dominance or selective control;

3. The extent to which imbalance in the supply position of countries and firms prevails regarding the natural resource, such imbalance being greater the more one country or firm is self-sufficient in supply relative to a competitor;

4. The extent to which there are natural limits to the supply of the natural resource, for example, imminent depletion or lengthy transportation routes;

5. The extent to which locations and routes of supply of the natural resource cross the political-ideological divisions of the international system; and

6. The extent to which a struggle for independence or a struggle over disputed territory involves the natural resource.

Economic factors, such as pricing behaviour on the side of suppliers, may also represent a potential for conflict. Reactions of some major Western powers to the oil-price shock in 1973 indicate this. None of the other minerals which would fall under the term strategic comes close to oil in terms of its importance in the import budgets and the strategic planning of most developed nations (see chapters 2 and 3). It can therefore be assumed that the price of strategic minerals other than oil is a less important factor to consider than those mentioned above. Within wide margins, the demand for the strategic minerals is, in economic terminology, price-inelastic. If supply could be assured, the buyer might be willing to pay a high price in those cases where a total dependence exists on the mineral concerned for some vital application. The threat of an embargo is far more important than that of a price increase.

Policy planners in government and industry turn to the above aspects of the supply situation when they consider their own position. If they are not in a position in which the threat of supply distortion appears to be imminent, their planning strategy would nevertheless probably be attentive to the possibility. As shown below, such a position is normally that of a country or firm not particularly dependent on foreign supplies. Interest in this case lies in the possibility that dependence might come in the future, or in that the country or firm concerned is interested in influencing the supply position of competitors.

If dependence on foreign supplies exists, then the country or firm will be either 'sensitive' or 'vulnerable' to interference with the dependency relationship (Keohane & Nye, 1977). It will be sensitive to the extent that it is liable to suffer costly effects from such interference before policies can be introduced that would change the situation. It will be vulnerable to the extent that it is liable to suffer costs from outside interference even after policies to change the situation have been introduced.

The vulnerability of a nation is a major cause of conflict over natural resources, one of three to be stressed here. The threat or actual imposition of an embargo on supplies of some strategic mineral is normally seen as an act of unfriendly behaviour or aggression by those who are the object of the embargo. But even the fear, realistic or not, of being subjected to such act may cause the affected party to take measures in order to pre-empt interference.

A second major resource-related cause of conflict is linked to the issue of global distribution. If industrialized and non-industrialized countries are compared, the consumption of natural resources is seen to be highly uneven. Moreover, the consumption gap has tended to widen in recent years. The explanation for this, especially in most of the more industrially advanced countries, is that the demand for new products increases faster than their natural resource base can provide the necessary inputs. If depletion of natural resources is anticipated, extra weight is added to the domestic pressure. The outlet for such pressure is to seek increased supplies from abroad (Choucri & North, 1975), thus colliding with the aspirations of other countries to increase their consumption. As may happen in the case of vulnerability, distributive conflict may lead the country to intervene politically or militarily in the supply area.

A third major resource-related cause of conflict is the play of politics or the process of tough bargaining, the latter including threats and counter-threats. These threats may be made in order to interfere in the internal affairs of other nations or firms or otherwise to change the rules of international relations. The demands of developing countries for a so-called new international economic order have meant that prices on primary commodities should be regulated by global multilateral bodies, subject to increased national control by the developing countries themselves; they have further meant that primary commodities be increasingly processed in the producing countries before export takes place. These demands, among others, have led to open conflict with many developed countries and with transnational corporations. If the demands were implemented, the transnational corporations would lose much of their control over the flow of global resources.

When a relatively self-sufficient country seeks to control the sources of supply in another country, the motive may be to hurt some third country which is supplied from these sources. More precisely, the motive here would be to take advantage of the vulnerability of the more dependent country. Such a motive could explain past and present actions of the major powers in the Persian Gulf and it may offer clues to their thinking about change in southern Africa. The dependence of the Western great powers on supplies from southern Africa is a source of considerable concern to those and other countries. This dependence is also a possible source of temptation for the USSR to intervene there, at least in the perception of Western military planners and analysts (Hackett, 1981).

III. Historical experience

Throughout history, conflicts over natural resources have often been associated with competition over concessions or colonies. In many cases, the interests of private firms have been the source of expansionist policies. In many others, national interests have prevailed over private ones. Whereas national and private interests have often coincided, they have in a number of cases clashed.

Publications of scholarly research into past cases of resource conflict are rather scattered and of highly uneven quality. Only very circumscribed conclusions can therefore be drawn from such research. One safe observation would be that conflicts have been located mostly in what is now commonly referred to as the Third World. Disregarding the rather obvious cases of imperialist expansion and the 'colonial scramble' in the past century, past cases of resource conflict appear to have fallen into one or another of three distinct categories:

1. Competition among major powers which led them to intrude upon each others' 'spheres of influence' for some of the reasons already suggested;

2. Conflict between investing or ownership interests (notably in Western capitalist countries) and national or local interests in countries where the resources were located (notably in the Third World); and

3. Conflict owing to strong ideological-political differences, in particular as these resulted from a sudden change in government in one of the countries concerned.

Most observers would agree that conflicts of the first type enumerated above are no longer common occurrences, whereas those of the second two types are. An example of violent conflict that involves a commodity of strategic importance—phosphates—and that was caused by a mixture of ideological dispute, territorial dispute, and external involvement, is the Western Sahara Revolt of 1976– (Kilgore, 1981; see also appendix 2, war 11). In fact, if the above analysis is not restricted to war, then all three types remain common occurrences. Such an extended interpretation of conflict is necessary in order to include, on the one hand, post-war tensions among the major powers and, on the other, so-called trade wars among major capitalist countries. Examples of the latter have become quite common during the 1970s and early 1980s.

Non-violent conflicts in the past which were caused by attempts to control natural resources, or which in some other way involved natural resources, dealt with control over: (*a*) production sites; (*b*) transportation routes; or (*c*) some other key element of control, for example, the local government concerned or the marketing and distribution system.

IV. National vulnerability and international market structures

During periods of crisis and war, governmental control in capitalist countries has assumed a particularly important role in controlling access to natural resources. The declared policy of Germany during World War II was to take control of or else interdict the supply routes of the Allied powers. This strategy led the Allies to organize their supplies from both national and foreign sources into a joint allocation scheme (Leith *et al.*, 1943).

The emergency measures of World War II dealing with natural resources were dissolved after the war as part of the general liberalization of trade that took place in the late 1940s. However, even though governmental control over the supply of raw materials ended in the USA and United Kingdom, this did not re-introduce a fully competitive market. In a great number of primary commodity industries, the degree of concentration of production and exports has remained high. National vulnerabilities therefore not only affect the international industrial structure; they are also influenced by it.

Looking at the problem from the national point of view, high import dependence is a condition of sensitivity only if measures can be taken with great speed and at minimum cost for the purpose of adapting to changes in supply. If measures can be taken only in the long term or at great cost, then the country concerned is in a situation of vulnerability. There is a considerable imbalance in the apparent import dependence position of the major powers regarding minerals of particular importance in military and civilian industrial applications (Hveem & Malnes, 1980, pages 67–75). Whereas Japan is close to completely dependent on imports for these minerals, Western European powers are somewhat less so and the USA is again a little less so. The USSR is substantially less dependent upon mineral imports than the USA; and the USA, in turn, less so than the United Kingdom (table 4.1).

Although data on trends in import dependence are incomplete, the general tendency appears to be in the direction of greater rather than lesser import dependence for the USSR and China. The imbalance in the supply situation of the major powers is, however, still quite considerable and will most probably remain so for the next two decades or so. This imbalance represents an important part of the potential for international conflict.

The high degree of concentration in the global supply of minerals is evident at the level of reserves, at that of production, and at that of exports (Hveem & Malnes, 1980, pages 59–64). As to reserves, only three countries account for 100 per cent of known global

Table 4.1.   Imports of selected minerals by the United Kingdom, USA, and USSR[a]

Mineral[b]	Proportion of domestic consumption imported (per cent)		
	UK[c]	USA[d]	USSR[e]
Aluminium	100	94	50
Antimony	100	53	6
Barium	58	38	49
Chromium	100	91	0
Cobalt	100	93	47
Columbium	100	100	0
Copper	82	14	0
Gold	100	28	0
Iron	89	22	0
Manganese	100	97	0
Mercury	100	49	0
Nickel	100	73	0
Platinum	100	87	0
Silver	100	79	10
Tantalum	100	97	0
Tin	65	84	19
Titanium	100	47	0
Tungsten	99	54	43
Uranium	100	7	0?
Zinc	100	58	0

Sources and notes:

[a]Table prepared by A. H. Westing.

[b]The minerals listed are among those (other than oil and natural gas) of major strategic importance.

[c]The values for the United Kingdom are for 1974–76 and are from Crowson (1979, page 160), except for barium, columbium, and uranium, which are for 1982 and from Karpinsky (1983).

[d]The values for the USA are for 1980 and are from Bullis (1981, page 22), except for silver, which is for 1980 from Bullis (1981, page 79), and uranium, which is for 1983 and from Neff (1984, page 278).

[e]The values for the USSR are for 1983 and are from Levine (1983, pages 783–84), except for columbium, which is for 1980 and from Bullis (1981, page 172), and uranium, which is for 1983 from Levine (1983, pages 802–803).

platinum reserves, three countries for almost 100 per cent of known chromium reserves (table 4.2), and three countries for about 90 per cent of known manganese reserves. As to production, only three countries account for close to 100 per cent of current platinum

Table 4.2. Concentration in the global chromium, cobalt, and uranium regimes[a]

Mineral	Proportion of global total in top three countries (per cent)			
	Known reserves[b]	Production[c]	Exports[d]	Imports[e]
Chromium	South Africa[f] (68) Zimbabwe (30) Finland (1) *Top three (99)*	USSR (30) South Africa[f] (28) Albania (11) *Top three (69)*	South Africa[f] (28) Albania (26) USSR (18) *Top three (72)*	Japan (22) Sweden (12) China (10) *Top three (44)*
Cobalt	Zaire (49) Zambia (15) USSR (9) *Top three (73)*	Zaire (47) Zambia (13) USSR (10) *Top three (70)*	Zaire (55) Zambia (18) Finland (6) *Top three (79)*	USA (44) Japan (13) FR Germany (12) *Top three (69)*
Uranium	Australia (22?) South Africa[f] (21?) Canada (12?) *Top three (55?)*	USA (21) South Africa[f] (20) Canada (17) *Top three (58)*	South Africa[f] (34) Canada (29) Australia (14) *Top three (77)*	Japan (30) France (19) FR Germany (14) *Top three (63)*

Sources and notes:

[a] Table prepared by A. H. Westing.

[b] Known-reserve values: (i) chromium for *ca* 1979 from Morning *et al.* (1980, page 171); (ii) cobalt for *ca* 1979 from Sibley (1980, page 204); and (iii) uranium for 1982 from *UN Statistical Yearbook*, New York, 33, table 104 (1982); the compilation for uranium, however, does not take account of reserves in China, Czechoslovakia, Israel, the USSR, and perhaps elsewhere, for which the data are not made public.

[c] Production values: (i) chromium for 1983 from Papp (1983, page 217); (ii) cobalt for 1983 from Kirk (1983, page 261); and (iii) uranium for 1982 from *UN Statistical Yearbook*, New York, 33, table 104 (1982), adjusted for the missing value for the USSR, assumed here to be two-thirds that of the USA; however, the missing uranium values for China, Czechoslovakia and Israel, assumed to be substantially smaller, are not taken into account.

[d] Export values: (i) chromium for 1983 from Lofty *et al.* (1985, page 43); (ii) cobalt for 1979 from Sibley (1980, page 208); and (iii) uranium for 1983 derived from Neff (1984, pages 215, 217).

[e] Import values: (i) chromium for 1983 from Lofty *et al.* (1985, pages 44–45); (ii) cobalt for 1983 from Lofty *et al.* (1985, pages 57–58); and (iii) uranium for 1983 derived from Nef (1984, pages 227, 235, 241, 247).

[f] The values for South Africa include those for Namibia, a *de facto* possession of South Africa.

production and three countries account for about 90 per cent of current molybdenum production. As to exports, only three countries account for some 85 per cent of current molybdenum exports; and three countries account for about 80 per cent of current cobalt exports (table 4.2).

These high concentrations of mineral supply indicate a potential for monopolistic behaviour and producer or exporter co-ordination in the form of cartels, market sharing deals, and the like. The probability that such co-ordination in fact occurs is a function of several factors, among them political-ideological, economic, cultural, and geographical ones (Hveem, 1978).

A distinction should be made between critical and non-critical supplies. Potentially critical import dependence occurs when supplies come from one or a few suppliers, over long distances, or from a country of different ideology. If all of these factors are present, the situation must be characterized as a highly vulnerable one, indeed.

Diversification of mineral supply has been an important goal for several great powers over the past decade. It is less of a possibility if concentration is high. The significance of high geographical or structural concentration on the supply side is reinforced when it is coupled with a pattern of consumption that is highly concentrated as well. The industrialized capitalist countries consume a very high proportion (more than two-thirds) of the global production of the most important minerals; by contrast, the industrialized socialist countries consume a low proportion (less than one-third); and the developing countries, including China, consume the very small remaining proportion (perhaps one-tenth).

Until the present recession started in the mid-1970s industrialization meant a steady decrease in the self-sufficiency of the industrialized and the newly industrializing countries. For example, whereas the USA in 1950 relied on imports for more than 50 per cent of its requirements for only four important minerals, by 1976 this list had grown to 23 minerals (Hankee & King, 1978). For at least 12 of these minerals, import dependence was more than 80 per cent. A considerable part of this growth has resulted from changes in both intermediate (industrial) and final (consumer) demands. Even though the overall demand for minerals grew over the period, within that aggregation are hidden some important declines as well as some phenomenal increases. Iron consumption, still of huge proportions, declined in relative terms; on the other hand, the demand for certain so-called minor minerals grew rapidly until the beginning of the 1980s. This latter growth was the result of qualitative improvements in products, both in the civilian and military sectors.

All of the five major capitalist countries—France, FR Germany, Japan, the United Kingdom, and the USA—appear to be critically dependent upon foreign supplies for a number of strategic minerals, especially chromium and cobalt (table 4.1; Hveem & Malnes, 1980, pages 67–75). Chromium, the most highly critical mineral from the point of view of these five countries, is supplied largely by South Africa, Albania, and the USSR (table 4.2). The United Kingdom is in a relatively favourable import-dependence position regarding molybdenum, cobalt, and some other minerals because it receives these mainly from Canada, with which it has a close relationship. Here vulnerable transportation routes appear to be the major potential problem. Imports by the USA from Canada and Mexico are even more secure when judged by political, economic, and transportation factors.

For the USSR and China, the two major socialist countries, the picture is quite different. The USSR appears to be dependent—but apparently not critically so—on supplies of aluminium, barium, cobalt, tungsten, and perhaps a few additional minerals (table 4.1). The Soviet imports of cobalt from Cuba could also be vulnerable in the case of major crisis. China appears to be dependent on foreign supplies for at least some of its aluminium, copper, and iron (Chin, 1983, page 184). The current large Chinese industrial expansion programmes could reduce import dependence for some minerals, but possibly increase it for others.

The second main class of concentration factors lies partly in the domain of national politics and partly in that of the transnational corporate dominance of world industries. Governments have made long-term bilateral agreements for a large number of supply lines and for a number of minerals. Of the order of one-third of world trade in minerals takes place under some sort of counter-trade agreement, such as barter, counter-purchase ('offset'), or a compensation ('buyback') arrangement (BusinessWeek, 1982; Maher, 1984). Military items are often tied to such deals (Neuman, 1985).

In addition, transnational corporations conduct intra-firm trade. Perhaps one-third of world trade in minerals might be covered by such organized exchange. Historically, transnational corporations have been dominant in many if not most of the mineral industries in the world. They have integrated the product line vertically. Nationalizations have changed the bargaining situation in many instances, but in far from the majority of cases. If in addition practices of oligopolistic rule continue, with corporations operating cartels or something similar, the corporations could potentially control access to vital supplies. Even if the considerable overlap between negotiated bilateral trade and intra-firm trade is accounted for, the conclusion must still be that world industries are highly organized and highly politicized.

Although there are several possible motives behind the trends that are suggested above, two implications become quite clear: (*a*) access to supplies can be secured only following the completion of bargaining over non-economic factors; and (*b*) corporate dominance constitutes a gateway to supplies that has to be negotiated as well. To the extent that such factors operate, countries with greater bargaining power and transnational corporations having a special relationship with their home governments will enjoy privileged positions.

Demands by developing countries for a new international economic order have led to negotiations at the United Nations Conference on Trade and Development (first held at Geneva in 1964 and subsequently in various cities at three- or four-year intervals) over proposals to regulate trade in a number of minerals and other primary commodities. Various industrialized nations have opposed the idea of regulating raw-material industries in an efficient manner and this has led to considerable North–South conflict. Attempts to put the developing countries into a stronger bargaining position have foundered for several reasons, among them the high indebtedness of the developing countries and resulting lack of economic resilience, and their political disunity. This failure has been a major cause of the worsening economic and social problems being experienced today by many of the developing countries.

Raw-material prices went up in 1974–75 owing to a number of factors, among them (Hveem, 1978): (*a*) inflationary pressures which began in 1971; (*b*) a spurt of industrial growth that led to an increased demand for raw materials; and (*c*) anxiety over access to minerals triggered by the OPEC actions in 1973 (see chapters 2 and 3). Producer-country collaboration was the result rather than the cause of these price increases for a number of raw materials (aluminium, phosphates, and sisal having been notable exceptions). However, the perception of a substantial threat of cartel dominance in the mineral industries (see, e.g., Bergsten, 1973) proved to be largely ill-founded long before the recession in the main industrial countries started (Hveem, 1978; Maull, 1984). Since the late 1970s, raw-material prices have stagnated or declined, causing the terms of trade of most developing countries to deteriorate seriously (World Bank, 1985, pages 59, 153).

V. The strategic imperative and the potential for adaptation

In trying to cope with a situation of potential or actual vulnerability, several possible options could be considered by a country which is powerful enough to influence its environment. Short of war or threat of other violent form of action aimed at influencing the source of trade disruption, the burden of adjustment may be passed on to others, whether the disruption had been intended or not. During the Second Indochina War, the USA successfully pressured its suppliers of nickel into allocating a larger share of available supplies to US defence industries, forcing European and Japanese purchasers to turn to the USSR and suffer a fivefold price increase (Interfutures, 1979, page 53).

A country that produces and exports minerals can be considered vulnerable when it cannot cope with a loss of income from exports without having to undergo major economic and social adaptations. This is the situation which characterizes a great number of Third-World countries. The economic resilience of these countries to falling demand or to political pressures from importing countries is very modest, a condition that was reinforced by the stagnant world economy at the end of the 1970s which had led to high interest rates, balance-of-payment problems, huge foreign debts, and so forth.

Most importing countries have been able to continue to maintain secure sources for their desired raw-material imports. They have accomplished this through their foreign policies or by means of their transnational corporations. If options of this sort are either barred to a country or insufficient for the purpose, then domestic readjustment becomes necessary. Such adjustment involves a consideration of economic, social, and political costs. It is possible to assess where a country is positioned on the sensitivity-vulnerability continuum with respect to minerals. For example, it has been shown that a modest (5–10 per cent) disruption of energy supply would have substantial effects on the US economy, as reflected in a 3–5 per cent drop in gross national product (Levine & Yabroff, 1975). Energy is the most critical resource category in this respect, oil and coal more so than uranium. The impact in terms of gross national product of material shortages in the non-energy categories appears in general to be less dramatic than for the energy raw materials. A 15–30 per cent shortage of supply for only about a dozen minerals could have serious effects on the economy. Some of these are, in decreasing order of impact: titanium, platinum, cobalt, tin, chromium, aluminium, copper, silver, nickel, and tungsten (Levine & Yabroff, 1975). By way of example, for the USA a 20 per cent cut in aluminium supply would mean about a 3 per cent reduction in its gross national product. For FR Germany, a 30 per cent cut in the supply of several minerals could have a profound effect on the economy even though they account for only a small proportion of the monetary value of the nation's total trade (Economist, 1979). Manganese is estimated to be of equal importance to the economy of FR Germany as copper even though the monetary import value of the latter is perhaps 30 times that of the former.

The scope for adjustments to overcome supply disruptions is large. Even if military requirements for a number of strategic minerals are estimated to treble in the case of war or other major crisis, policies of diverting consumption from civilian to military use are believed to be able to keep the economy as a whole of a developed nation running for at least a year (Little, 1974, page 60). Lateral pressure for civilian consumption would ease under such circumstances. If such circumstances did not apply, then the social costs could be considerable in terms of an increased burden on consumers or in employed people being laid off.

In order to protect themselves against having to face the option of costly adjustment, governments (as well as firms) have adopted a series of measures of national preparedness against supply disruptions. The best known is stockpiling. Stockpiling used to be practised chiefly by the USA, but during the late 1970s and early 1980s several other countries also initiated such programmes (Hargreaves & Fromson, 1983; Warnecke, 1980). These programmes have made countries practically invulnerable in some of the most critical minerals, especially in the short term. Governments and firms are able to defuse a threat of price increase or embargo by resorting to their stockpiles.

Conservation is another measure which can strengthen the position of heavily import-dependent consumers. If the efficiency of recovering used material (scrap) is increased and the level of consumption reduced, the life of the resource base (the reserve and the stockpile) could be radically extended. More efficient processing techniques or material-saving designs are among the options. Up to one-third or so of total domestic consumption of some important industrial minerals was derived from recycling in the major industrialized countries in the early 1970s. However, an expansion of recycling is limited by technical and economic factors. The degree of governmental intervention may be a decisive factor in this respect. Thus recycling is more effective in FR Germany and Japan than in the USA, the main reason for the difference appearing to be that the former have instituted tax incentives and other regulatory measures.

A third option is substitution. The range of possibilities for substitution is very great for non-fuel minerals. However, substitution is not easily attained for political, economic, and technical reasons. Long lead times or high investment requirements may reduce the feasibility of substitution. The use of composite materials (i.e., synthetic materials reinforced with embedded fibres or particles) and plastics as substitutes for metals is on the increase. In the long run, these materials could reduce a nation's dependence on mineral imports for a wide range of civilian and military products.

Increased production from domestic deposits and exploitation of the extra-territorial ocean floor and Antarctica are possibilities for developed countries in the medium- to long-term perspective, although increased domestic extraction is not so much of an option for Western Europe or Japan as it is for the USA or Canada. Most major powers did stress this latter option during the raw-material crisis of the 1970s, but reductions in demand, increasing costs, and environmental considerations have thus far precluded such action to a great extent.

The technical feasibility of extracting minerals from the sea-bed has been essentially proved, but when large-scale exploitation will begin is largely an economic question. The nebulous future for the

1982 Law of the Sea Convention (see appendix 6)—not yet in force primarily because of the unresolved issue of control over high-seas mining—leaves a potential for future conflict. Third-World countries have expressed great concern that such mining could weaken their position as mineral producers and suppliers. They have striven for international control of sea-bed mining under the auspices of the United Nations that would serve the interests of all countries. To this must be added the potential for international conflict that arises from the growing interest in mineral exploitation in the two polar regions. The Falkland/Malvinas Conflict of 1982 can be attributed in part to an interest in the natural resources of Antarctica (see appendix 2, war 12).

VI. Southern Africa

The southern African region—primarily the area south of the Equator—occupies a prominent position in the strategic thinking of several, if not all, of the major powers. One reason is the importance of the region for sea transportation routes vital to international trade. Another is the role of the region as a supplier of several strategic minerals. The increased political tension and the possibility of large-scale violent interracial conflict within South Africa have made the region the potentially most volatile one in the coming years.

Various parts of the region were the scene of violent conflict during the 1960s and 1970s, and the cause is believed to have been in part the interaction between political and racial tensions on the one hand and natural resources on the other. For example, the present Zaire was dragged into a resource-related conflict on a number of notable occasions: the abortive Congo Civil War of 1960–64 and its two follow-up actions, in 1977 and 1978 (see appendix 2, war 5).

Apart from the political, economic, and logistical importance of southern Africa in global strategic thinking, there are three aspects of the regional situation that must be pointed out: (*a*) that a major political and racial conflict in South Africa could poison North-South relations and influence the relative positions of the major powers in Africa and elsewhere in the Third World; (*b*) that the region supplies Western powers and Japan with several of the most critical minerals; (*c*) that the largest alternative present and future supplier of some of these minerals is the USSR.

Above it is pointed out that chromium and cobalt are at the top of the list of strategic minerals which are particularly critical to the vulnerability of the USA, Japan, and Western Europe. Manganese should be classed with these also, because of its importance in the ferro-alloy industry, as should platinum and vanadium. Southern Africa is the largest source of supply for these minerals. If to this brief list are added gold (for its special role in financial reserve systems) and uranium (for its role in nuclear energy and in the manufacture of nuclear weapons) then the strategic importance of southern Africa becomes even more evident.

It has been suggested that the worst-case scenario from the point of view of strategic planners in the Western military alliance would be one in which South Africa changed to black rule with a Marxist philosophy that would make it a logical ally for the USSR (Duchêne, 1979). In that scenario, an embargo on supplies of minerals to the Western countries has been suggested to be a possible event. In a variant of this scenario, some kind of cartel behaviour would occur whereby the governments of southern Africa colluded with Moscow in order to dictate the conditions for supplying Western countries.

Less dramatic scenarios would probably be more realistic. Reports of Soviet involvement in the 1978 Shaba revolt (see appendix 2, war 5) have not been substantiated, neither have prophecies that Angola or Zimbabwe would turn against Western interests after decolonization or after changing to leftist governments. Indeed, employment and national economic reasons as well as normal political and diplomatic considerations seem to favour a continuation of existing supply arrangements even if domestic political systems change fundamentally. Moreover, there appear already to exist secret collaborations between the USSR and South Africa on the marketing of gold and of platinum that came to pass irrespective of differences in political philosophy (Hargreaves & Fromson, 1983, pages 12–13). Lastly, if an embargo is to be considered as a serious possibility, then it could be put into effect by the present Government of South Africa as well as by a new government. Indeed, South Africa recently announced the possibility of a cut-off of chromium to the USA and Western Europe (AP, 1985).

Continued violent conflict within South Africa and between it and some of its neighbouring countries, mounting pressure from Western powers, and a growing socio-economic crisis in large parts of southern Africa all emphasize the volatile character of the regional situation. This, coupled with the fact that most of the major powers are particularly vulnerable with regard to some of the minerals for which the region is a prime supplier, warrants special attention to these minerals. An additional reason is what appears to be a growing need by the USSR to import some of these minerals, notably chromium and cobalt (Little, 1977). Such need could lead even the USSR to turn to southern Africa for imports. If this is indeed the case, a potential for East–West conflict over natural resources in the region could, of course, develop.

Uranium is extracted domestically by several of the nuclear powers, but is still the object of considerable international trade. The very special role of uranium as both a source of energy and a base for nuclear weapons also makes it a potential source of international conflict. This further enhances the importance of southern Africa, for the region is also a substantial source of that mineral.

Three of the strategically most crucial minerals associated with southern Africa—chromium, cobalt, and uranium—are singled out below for more detailed examination.

Chromium

By far the largest use of chromium—perhaps three-quarters of it— is for metallurgical purposes. The bulk of the metallurgical applications is in the steel industry, where chromium is added to steel in order to make it harder, less subject to corrosion, and more heat-resistant. It appears to be an indispensible additive, at least in the medium-term perspective.

Reserves, production, and exports are all highly concentrated at the country level (table 4.2). South Africa and, to a lesser extent, Zimbabwe together account for most known global reserves. The USSR and South Africa are the current main producers, whereas South Africa, Albania, and the USSR are the current main exporters. Japan has been the main importer for a number of years.

Countries currently producing moderate amounts of chromium are: Turkey and the Philippines, both allied to the West and both experiencing declining shares of world production; Finland and Zimbabwe, both non-aligned and both with stable shares of world production; and Albania, non-aligned and experiencing a rapidly increasing share of world production. The rapid expansion of production in Albania during the past decade has made it one of the largest exporters. A decrease in Soviet exports of chromium appears to reflect both a real decline in self-sufficiency and a policy of protecting its own reserves from being depleted too rapidly. It is even possible that the USSR will become an important importer before the end of the decade. A similar, if not quite as explicit, tendency to reduce exports can also be discerned in several other producing countries. Such a trend can only lead to an even more concentrated international supply situation.

Another general tendency is for producing and exporting countries to turn into processors (mainly of ferro-chromium) in order to reap a higher share of value-added profit, or for reasons of economic nationalism. This logically challenges the market shares of established metallurgical, refractory, or chemical producers and the mineral policies of major powers that wish to preserve a strategically important processing industry. This represents yet another potential source of conflict.

If the chromium industry is highly concentrated at the country level, then the degree of concentration at the corporate level is even more pronounced. Chromium in the capitalist world is involved in a complex and apparently stable cobweb of conglomerate corporations with ownership, partnership, or other linkages among themselves. The Anglo American Corporation of South Africa is apparently the centrepiece of this oligopolistic system through its dominant position as a controlling agent in GENCOR and some of the other principal South African and Zimbabwean producing companies. Through joint ventures with other corporations such as the Rio Tinto Zinc Corporation in the United Kingdom, and by integrating 'downstream' into the processing and refining of chromium and steel, the Anglo American Corporation of South Africa appears to have secured for itself a key decision-making position in the global chromium industry.

There is relatively little apparent 'upstream' integration by the big steel and ferro-alloy producers in the USA, Canada, or Western Europe. There may, however, be an element of control by such agents in the form of long-term contracts and special relations of a more informal character. Prices are not determined in a free market, but in negotiations by the corporations. There is also an important element of price differentiation in specific market segments, assisted also by tariff and other barriers. Such features could, in a tight supply situation, lead to the less privileged buyers being left out of normal supply.

These structural and political factors create a level of uncertainty that has led to considerable efforts to diversify supplies and to intensify measures of domestic adjustment. Diversification into new territories or old mining sites with lower grade ores is, however, always under the threat of South African producers who are in a position to cut prices and flood the market with cheap chromium, ferro-chromium, and even stainless steel. Domestic adjustment therefore appears to be a more feasible choice. There are stockpiling programmes in all of the major industrialized countries, both in the governmental and private sectors. Recycling is now providing of the order of one-quarter of all chromium needs. Perhaps one-third of the chromium used today could theoretically be substituted for; but for a range of important applications, as in stainless steel, there is simply no substitute. Chromium could be replaced for some purposes by materials such as titanium, nickel, or composite materials based on boron or silicon. However, these substitute materials suffer from either deficient performance or higher cost, or both. Technical innovations have so far not come far in overcoming these problems. Therefore, it appears as if chromium is one mineral that will continue to occupy a highly strategic position in the world arena. The limits of domestic adjustment measures and the uncertainty facing diversification strategies add to the extreme concentration of control over the first links in the production chain, to the unbalanced vulnerability of the major powers, and to the location of reserves, production, and corporate decision-making in an increasingly unstable area. These factors clearly combine to make control over chromium a potential for international conflict.

Cobalt

Cobalt, like chromium, is a strategic mineral that is likely to become involved in conflict. In 1976, transportation of cobalt from two of the three main exporting countries—Zaire and Zambia (table 4.2)—was interrupted for some time by the civil war that had just then started in Angola. In 1978, military forces opposed to the Government of Zaire attacked mining installations in Shaba Province (see appendix 2, war 5), leading to an interruption of production (Commerce, 1981). Belgium responded, backed by some other NATO governments, by deploying a military force in Shaba. The resulting supply disruptions caused the USA to declare cobalt a so-called priority metal in its national stockpile (bringing the list of those to 11) (Guttman *et al.*, 1983).

Cobalt is a vital alloying element in metals for the aerospace industry. In fact, an estimated 17 per cent of US consumption goes into the manufacture of jet aircraft (Maull, 1984, page 215). The crucial property of cobalt alloys is their resistance to high temperatures. The second main application for cobalt is in permanent magnets and thus in electric motors; and the third is for a variety of uses in the chemical industry.

The availability of cobalt is highly dependent on the production of copper and nickel as some 95 per cent of all cobalt is mined in association with these two metals. As cobalt is also usually less than 3 per cent of the metal content of the ores mined, the linkage of cobalt to copper and nickel is an important structural determinant for the world cobalt regime. Only exceptional circumstances could lead to a decision to mine cobalt without first considering the copper or nickel situation. Since the mid-1970s, cobalt production has stagnated owing to reduced demands for copper and, to a lesser extent, nickel.

World resources of cobalt are abundant, especially so if the cobalt content of sea-bed nodules is considered; the quantity of these sea-bed deposits is estimated to be huge (Guttman *et al.*, 1983; Wald-heim, 1975). However, in the short- to medium-term perspective the reserve situation is centered around access to deposits in Zaire, in Zambia, and in the USSR (table 4.2). If low-grade currently non-commercial deposits of cobalt are considered, then Cuba, New Caledonia (an overseas territory of France), the Philippines, and the USA become potentially important producers and, to a lesser extent, also Finland and Morocco. However, the USA at present remains the major importer (table 4.2).

In the short- to medium-term perspective, the two main African producers—Zaire and Zambia (table 4.2)—occupy a strategic position, whereas in the longer term, the Pacific producers may become more important. Reactions to the 1976 and 1978 Shaba events (see appendix 2, war 5) suggest that the short-term perspective cannot be overlooked. For example, the USA started buying cobalt in 1976 in order to double the size of its strategic stockpile (Guttman *et al.*,

1983). This action and subsequent destruction of production facilities in Shaba led to soaring prices. The effect was all the more dramatic as the Shaba incidents coincided with an increasing demand for cobalt during a period of depressed demand for copper and nickel. The price increases led to a sudden increase in purchases from Zambia and a renewed interest in producing cobalt domestically in the USA, where production had ceased in 1971. The response of Zaire was to reduce its selling price to well below the cost of production and to far below what was considered a break-even price for resumed production in the USA or elsewhere. Thus, instead of some form of collusion between Zaire and Zambia, there developed intense competition.

A knowledge of the corporate structure in cobalt is—as is also the case with chromium—crucial to an understanding of the world cobalt regime. The market is highly organized. The Belgian financial-industrial conglomerate, Société Générale, has a part in the management of GECAMINES in Zaire and its trading arm SOZACOM and, through its processing arm in Belgium, is one of the main buyers of cobalt from Zaire, in association with copper. INCO of Canada and Falconbridge Nickel Mines of Canada are important producers of cobalt. Another is the Anglo American Corporation of South Africa, which holds an important share in the Zambian producer, Zambia Consolidated Copper Mines. As dominant producers and as vertically integrated entities, these corporations logically have a common interest in preventing diversification away from areas which they control and in keeping prices low on the raw materials which they process. At the same time, they may feel inclined to compete for market shares when the market is unstable and when demand is down.

As with chromium, there is no world price for cobalt. Prices are set by producers or negotiated in contractual arrangements, or are simply a matter of intra-firm trading and hence a corporate decision. If the Belgian-Zairian sub-system may be considered a price leader in the capitalist world, there are several 'special relationships' where factors other than price count. Additionally, there exist Cuban-Soviet and Japanese-Australian sub-systems. Imports to the USA are also highly concentrated (Kirk, 1983).

If diversification has been inhibited so far by volatile prices, adjustment measures seem to have had some success. Total consumption is being reduced by cutting down on the amount of cobalt being used in specific applications. Cobalt can be applied in smaller quantities and still offer its unique heat resistance, but it cannot be completely substituted for. Besides, some of the substitutes, such as molybdenum, are also critical materials. New techniques to apply a changed material composition already exist; the lead time is therefore not as long as is usually the case when substitution is considered. Recycling, on the other hand, seems to offer few adjustment opportunities because scrap is mostly spread in a large variety and number of products, often in very small quantities.

The medium-term availability of cobalt will be influenced largely by developments in southern Africa. Political instability and fragility of transportation networks are factors that must be taken into account. Again, the highly unbalanced supply situation between the major powers of East and West could provide a potential for conflict. This is partly why the major Western powers, probably even Japan, maintain stockpiles of cobalt. US stockpiles appear to be sufficient for about six years of domestic consumption (Sibley, 1980, pages 206, 209–10).

Uranium

Uranium is used in the manufacture of nuclear weapons and this aspect alone makes it a strategic mineral. Practically all non-military uses are for the production of energy. In the immediate aftermath of the 1973 oil crisis, access to uranium was considered by many countries to be important because of its use in producing energy. For countries with nuclear-energy programmes, it became a special matter of national security in the 1970s to obtain satisfactory control over all relevant links in the extraction and manufacture of uranium.

Although the perceived urgency of ensuring access to uranium has eased somewhat owing to a radical downward revision of many nuclear-energy programmes, this is still considered highly important. The military aspect of access to uranium has become ever more important owing to continued proliferation of the capacity to produce nuclear weapons. In addition, environmental concerns have become far more important to populations all over the world.

The expanded programmes of uranium production in the 1970s led to a perception of impending depletion. A rush developed on those uranium deposits that could still be considered not closely controlled by the nuclear powers, such as those in Australia. Although this rush has now slackened, there remains considerable uncertainty as to the future development of the uranium industry. Inasmuch as fuel being used to make nuclear explosives accounts for only a marginal share of total uranium demand, neither escalation of the nuclear arms race nor nuclear disarmament would exert a big effect on total demand.

A very considerable level of secrecy pervades the uranium industry. The only national system which is relatively transparent is the US one; the Soviet system is especially opaque, as is also that of China. Major reserves are known to exist in Australia, South Africa, and Canada (table 4.2), although the USSR and China are also thought to have large reserves. As regards current production, the USA heads the list, with South Africa and Canada not far behind (table 4.2). However, US production is at present declining owing to a combination of reduced demand and environmental concerns, so that Canada will probably soon become the largest producing country in the capitalist world. As there is a long lead time from initiating uranium production to achieving an output in the form of fuel, changes do not take place rapidly. It is expected that in the 1990s and 2000s the US nuclear industry will be importing up to 35 per cent of its total uranium consumption, largely from Canada, as compared with an import level of less than 10 per cent in the 1970s and early 1980s (Reagan, 1984). Japan, France, and FR Germany are the current major importers (table 4.2).

Uranium extraction and manufacture are tightly regulated. Some 90 per cent of all sales are covered by long-term (at least 10-year) contracts, often containing restrictive clauses. Only a small proportion of these contracts are made without governmental participation. The structure of the market and the high strategic importance of the products imply that there is no world price. This only goes to emphasize that availability and security of supply are considered by most users as being much more important than price. Price competitiveness may, however, be important for small utilities and for those who compete directly with other energy producers.

A considerable part of uranium production is controlled through vertical integration and by conglomerates. Nuclear energy producers (e.g., the Westinghouse Corporation in the USA and Compagnie Générale d'Electricité in France) and energy diversifiers or conglomerates (e.g., Exxon in the USA) are therefore to some extent involved in uranium production. There are also some so-called uranium independents (e.g., American Nuclear). Finally there are the conglomerate mineral producers, some of which are also vertically integrated. The most important ones are the Anglo American Corporation of South Africa, the Rio Tinto Zinc Corporation in the United Kingdom, and the Newmont Mining Corporation in the USA. The two former control practically all of the combined production in South Africa (including Namibia), Anglo American being the leading partner in NUFCOR, the South African marketing cartel. Cross-ownership or minority ownership link several of the large corporations, facilitating co-ordination and co-operation. An international cartel was organized in 1972 (with headquarters in Paris) among uranium producers in Australia, Canada, France, FR Germany, and the USA which is said to have organized a market-sharing agreement that for several years led to major price increases (Bethel, 1977). Since Rio Tinto Zinc is also strong in Australia (the country which has expanded production the most since the 1970s), the Anglo American–Rio Tinto Zinc link must be considered a vital one in future world trade in uranium.

US uranium producers have formed NUEXCO, whereas most of the other corporate producers are members of the Uranium Institute in London. The role of the Uranium Institute is not well known, but it probably serves as a co-ordinating unit and information pool, perhaps even as a quasi-cartel. It can be assumed to have some influence over three of the main uranium trade routes: from southern Africa to Western Europe and Japan; from Australia to Japan and the United Kingdom; and from Canada to Western Europe. However, some of the producing countries are not regulated by the 1968 Treaty on the Non-Proliferation of Nuclear Weapons (for which see Goldblat, 1982, pages 172–74) and this may have an important effect on the international movement of uranium. Thus the uranium regime appears able to secure long-term supplies of uranium for enrichment facilities throughout the capitalist world. However, it must be considered weak when it comes to providing security against military applications or against leakages that threaten the environment during extraction and manufacture.

The French sub-system could become another dynamic factor in the uranium industry (Rydell & Mullins, 1981). France itself has expanded production. More importantly, French interests are dominant in what is a rapidly growing level of production in three African countries with no domestic demand, but apparently with considerable reserves: Niger, the Central African Republic, and Gabon. Indeed, more than one-third of the national budget of Niger now rests on its income from uranium (Rydell & Mullins, 1981, page 34). Supplies to FR Germany are provided through joint ventures within the French sub-system together with producers in southern Africa and Canada. Japan has organized its imports in closely woven relations with producers in Australia and South Africa.

A fear in the mid-1970s over supply shortages in the capitalist world has led to a situation of world-wide over-supply. In 1983, known stocks represented more than three years of consumption. The great gap between forecasted and actual requirements in the recent past is a warning that future developments, even when restricted to the capitalist world, can only be guessed very roughly.

From a strategic point of view, the dynamic factors of importance in relation to uranium are: (*a*) the evolution of the East-West political climate and the arms race; (*b*) the extent to which the policies of countries with a potential to develop nuclear explosives can be controlled or at least foreseen; and (*c*) the developments in southern Africa. All of these factors can exert pressures on the uranium industry and lead to conflicts over access to supplies or over attempts to deny such access.

VII. Conclusion

This chapter shows the extent and importance of strategic considerations *vis-à-vis* those minerals which are seen as critical to military as well as national economic interests. Although there are few examples of direct violent intervention to control sources of mineral supply, there is a clear potential for such conflict. The volatile situation in southern Africa is pointed to as being especially important in this regard. The military and political-ideological competition between the USA and USSR and the economic competition among the major powers are both additional factors of great importance.

Changes in demand and the potential for adjustment domestically are among those factors which influence the strategic mineral industries. However, all of the three minerals which are given special attention here remain indispensible for military and civilian purposes, at least for the next 10 to 15 years. Technological developments and measures of stockpiling can alleviate, but not entirely eliminate, this dependence. And, as most major powers are dependent upon mineral imports, the crucial dimension in policy-making is, and will continue to be, foreign policy.

For mineral-producing countries in the Third World, it is of particular importance that their exports continue in order to provide them with highly necessary income. For mineral-poor countries, it is of particular importance that their imports continue in order to maintain their industries. Multilateral agreements to meet both of these needs would reduce international tensions and are thus a prerequisite for ultimate world disarmament (Hveem & Malnes, 1980).

If attempts are made to make access to foreign sources of supply more difficult, countermeasures can be expected that could in time lead to open conflict. The possibility that this will happen is a function of: (*a*) the East–West relationship; (*b*) policies of control over natural resources in producing countries; (*c*) the extent and form of corporate control over production, marketing, and distribution; and (*d*) the development of new sources of supply. In the short- to medium-term pespective, even the import-dependent countries appear to be in a good position to secure suppliers because: (*a*) they maintain close diplomatic and economic relations with many of the resource-surplus countries; (*b*) many of the corporations running the mineral industry are home-based in—and to a considerable extent dependent upon the assistance of—the countries which they mainly supply; (*c*) much of the international trade is tightly controlled in the form of long-term contracts or intra-firm trade; and (*d*) the probability is not great that an opponent will intervene in their transportation routes.

In closing, two points stand out: (*a*) that the weak link in the mineral supply chains is southern Africa; and (*b*) that the volatility of mineral supply and demand could add to the competition among the major powers and thus to the potential for international conflict.

References

AP (Associated Press). 1985. Botha says chrome to Europe and U.S. could be cut off. *International Herald Tribune,* Paris, 1985(23 Oct):1.

Bergsten, C. F. 1973. Threat from the Third World. *Foreign Policy,* Washington, 1973(11):102–124. Cf. *ibid.* 1974(14):56–90.

Bethel, A. L. 1977. Testimony. In: Moss, J. E. (ed.). *International uranium supply and demand [Hearing, 4 November 1976].* Washington: US House of Representatives, Committee on Interstate & Foreign Commerce Serial No. 94–150, 374 pp.: pp. 62–89.

Bullis, L. H. (ed.). 1981. *Congressional handbook on U.S. materials import dependency/vulnerability.* Washington: US House of Representatives, Committee on Banking, Finance & Urban Affairs Print No. 97–6, 405 pp.

BusinessWeek. 1982. New restrictions on world trade. *BusinessWeek,* New York, 1982(2748–79):128–132.

Chin, E. 1983. Mineral industry of China. *Minerals Yearbook,* Washington, 1983(III):179–195.

Choucri, N. & North, R. C. 1975. *Nations in conflict: national growth and international violence.* San Fancisco: W. H. Freeman, 356 pp.

Commerce, US Dept of. 1981. *Critical materials requirements of the U.S. aerospace industry.* Washington: US Department of Commerce, Report No. EA/OSR–83/001, 319 pp.

Crowson, P. 1979. Geography and political economy of metal supplies. *Resources Policy,* Guildford, UK, 5:158–169.

Duchêne, L.-F. 1979. Not so hidden hand. In: Martin, L. (ed.). *Strategic thought in the nuclear age.* London: Heinemann, 233 pp.: 31–68,221–222.

Economist. 1979. West German raw materials: stockpile maybe. *Economist,* London, 271(7079): 92.

Goldblat, J. 1982. *Agreements for arms control: a critical survey.* London: Taylor & Francis, 387 pp. [a SIPRI book].

Guttman, J. T., Merrick, J. E., Fenwick, V. J., & Graham, J. F. 1983. *Critical non-fuel minerals in mobilization with case studies on cobalt and titanium.* Washington: US National Defense University, Industrial College of the Armed Forces, Report No. AD-A137 681, 140 pp.

Hackett, J. 1981. Protecting oil supplies: the military requirements. In: Bertram, C. (ed.). *Third-World conflict and international security. I.* London: International Institute for Strategic Studies, Adelphi Paper No. 166, 58 pp.: pp. 41–51.

Hankee, W. B. & King, A. H. 1978. Role of security assistance in maintaining access to strategic resources. *Parameters,* Carlisle Barracks, Penn., 8(3):41–50.

Hargreaves, D. & Fromson, S. 1983. *World index of strategic minerals: production, exploitation and risk.* Aldershot, UK: Gower, 300 pp.

Hveem, H. 1978. *Political economy of Third World producer associations.* Oslo: Universitetsforlaget, 237 pp.

Hveem, H. & Malnes, R. 1980. *Military use of natural resources: the case for conversion and control.* Oslo: International Peace Research Institute, Publication No. S–29/80, 138 pp.

Interfutures. 1979. *Facing the future: mastering the probable and managing the unpredictable.* Paris: Organisation for Economic Co-operation & Development, 425 pp.

Karpinsky, T. 1983. Mineral industry of the United Kingdom. *Minerals Yearbook,* Washington, 1983(III):813–831.

Keohane, R. O. & Nye, J. S. 1977. *Power and interdependence: world politics in transition.* Boston: Little, Brown, 273 pp.

Kilgore, A. 1981. Phosphate links with desert war. *South,* London, 1981(4):72–73.

Kirk, W. S. 1983. Cobalt. *Minerals Yearbook*, Washington, 1983(III): 255–263.

Leith, C. K., Furness, J. W., & Lewis, C. 1943. *World minerals and world peace.* Washington: Brookings Institution, 253 pp.

Levine, M. B. & Yabroff, I. W. 1975. *Department of Defense materials consumption and the impact of material and energy resource shortages.* Menlo Park, Calif.: Stanford Research Institute, Report No. AD-A018 613/OGA, 159 pp.

Levine, R. M. 1983. Mineral industry of the U.S.S.R. *Minerals Yearbook*, Washington, 1983(III):773–805.

Little, A. D. 1974. *Industrial preparedness in an arms control environment: a study of the potential impact of sharp increases in military procurement. II. Complete report.* Cambridge, Mass.: Arthur D. Little, Report No. AD-A007 443/5GA, 77 pp.

Little, A. D. 1977. *Dependence of the Soviet Union and Eastern Europe on essential imported materials year 2000.* Cambridge, Mass.: Arthur D. Little, Report No. ADL-C-79515-79614, 188 pp.

Lofty, G. J., Sharp, N. E., Hillier, J. A., Lowe, M. F., Lehall, M. K., Davis, M. M., & Thomas, D. G. 1985. *World mineral statistics 1979–83: production: exports: imports.* London: British Geological Survey, 275 pp.

Maher, P. 1984. Countertrade boom. *Business Marketing,* Chicago, 69(1):50–56.

Maull, H. W. 1984. *Raw materials, energy and Western security.* London: Macmillan, 413 pp.

Morning, J. L., Matthews, N. A., & Peterson, E. C. 1980. Chromium. In: Knoerr, A. W. (ed.). *Mineral facts and problems.* Washington: US Bureau of Mines, Bulletin No. 671, 1060 pp.: pp. 167–182.

Neff, T. L. 1984. *International uranium market.* Cambridge, Mass.: Ballinger, 335 pp.

Neuman, S. 1985. Offsets in the international arms market. In: ACDA (ed.). *World military expenditures and arms transfers 1985*. Washington: US Arms Control & Disarmament Agency, Publication No. 123, 145 pp.: pp. 35–40.

Papp, J. F. 1983. Chromium. *Minerals Yearbook*, Washington, 1983(I):203–220.

Reagan, R. 1984. *United States uranium mining and milling industry: a comprehensive review*. Washington: US Department of Energy, Report No. DOE/S-0028, 103 pp.

Rydell, R. & Mullins, A. F. 1981. *Nonproliferation and the uranium market: the implications of Third World suppliers*. Livermore, Calif.: University of California, Lawrence Livermore Laboratory Report No. COVD–2104, 55 pp.

Sibley, S. F. 1980. Cobalt. In: Knoerr, A. W. (ed.). *Mineral facts and problems*. Washington: US Bureau of Mines, Bulletin No. 671, 1060 pp.: pp. 199–214.

Waldheim, K. 1975. *Economic implications of sea-bed mining in the international area*. New York: UN General Assembly, Document No. A/CONF.62/37 of 18 February 1975, 17 pp.

Warnecke, S. 1980. *Stockpiling of critical raw materials*. London: Royal Institute of International Affairs, Chatham House Paper No. 5, 52 pp.

World Bank. 1985. *World development report 1985*. Washington: International Bank for Reconstruction & Development, 243 pp.

5. Fresh waters as a factor in strategic policy and action

Malin Falkenmark
Natural Sciences Research Council, Stockholm

I. Introduction

Socio-economic development is closely related to the ability to manage water resources in the natural environment. Not only is water fundamental for human survival as such, but also for both plant and fish production, for urban and industrial activities, for energy production, and for navigation and recreation. Water also causes dramatic human suffering and material damage. Massive health problems are caused by infectious diseases transmitted by water. Too much water can lead to immense problems as a result of flooding. A water shortage puts limitations on human activity, and severe deficiency is a disaster for those subjected to the drought.

Consequently, a secured supply of water and control of river flow must be cornerstones in national planning and development, particularly in regions where water is scarce or where increases in population reduce the degree of freedom by decreasing the amount of water available on a per-capita basis.

The problems related to the allocation of a fixed supply of water to support both the demands of growing populations and for an increased quality of life, and to the crucial role of water in plant production, in soil degradation, and in other environmental effects, are dealt with elsewhere (Falkenmark, 1970; 1979; 1981b; 1984a; 1984b; 1985; 1986). The risk for inappropriate knowledge and technologies being transferred between climatic zones with radically different water problems (the risk for so-called climatic bias) has been addressed elsewhere (Falkenmark, 1981c), as have the implications of internationally shared river basins[1] (Falkenmark,

---

[1] A 'river basin' (also known as a 'drainage basin', 'catchment area' [British usage], or 'watershed' [US usage]) refers to the area within which rainfall drains into a given stream. Rivers of interest in the present context are for the most part first-order streams, i.e., streams whose outlet is an ocean or an inland sea.

1984a; Widstrand, 1980). Whereas in the past water problems have been examined largely from a technical standpoint, the author has proposed a wider, more interdisciplinary and ecologically based approach (Falkenmark, 1984a).

This chapter discusses fresh water as a present and future focus of international disputes and as a factor in conflict formation. Examples are given of typical disputes of various sorts. The potential for international tension resulting from problems of freshwater supply is discussed. Also summarized are efforts in conflict resolution and prevention, with a focus on current progress towards an internationally agreed code of conduct.

II. Water as a natural resource

Availability of water

Water is necessary for domestic use, industrial purposes, and agriculture (irrigation). Bodies of water are available for fishing, navigation, recreation, and other important uses. Water is brought to a country in two ways: (*a*) as precipitation over the national territory; and (*b*) as inflow from upstream countries in the same river basin. In the absence of upstream interference, the amount of water coming into a country is fixed when seen in a long-term perspective, although both seasonal and annual fluctuations can be considerable, particularly in zones with a dry climate.

The inflow from upstream countries depends on the nature of water-consuming activities in the upstream country. Water-consuming activities, such as irrigation or water transfer out of the basin, reduce the inflow to the downstream country and often degrade its quality as well.

The demand for water in a country and the level of competition among different uses depend on the numbers of individuals to be supplied from the amount available and on the nation's degree of development. The larger the population, the less water is available on a per-capita basis, making population increases a real dilemma in countries where the supply of water is scarce.

The natural territorial boundaries applicable to water are defined by the position of the water divides separating neighbouring river basins. When landscape features are large or countries small, several countries might belong to the same river basin and be forced to co-operate in sharing and controlling the joint resource. However, in many river basins, downstream countries are at the mercy of their upstream neighbours. As a result, the location of a country along a river can have a considerable influence on its international relations.

Socio-economic development

Most human activities depend directly or indirectly upon water, the demand for which increases rapidly with an increasing level of socio-economic development (Postel, 1984). The United Nations is pursuing a world-wide campaign for water supply and sanitation that addresses itself to the exceedingly poor health conditions that prevail in developing countries (Valdes-Cogliano, 1985). The goal is to provide an adequate amount of safe water close to every dwelling, each individual being considered to require approximately 100 litres of water per day in order to maintain an adequate quality of life.

Water is the basic 'lubricant' in industry, used *inter alia* for cooling, processing, boiling, and transporting. There are great differences among various branches of industry in terms of the amount of water needed, which depends upon the processes employed and the degree of in-plant circulation (UNWC, 1978, pages 28–30). Thus the amount of water used can be reduced by altering the processes or by increasing the re-use. The industrial development that is occurring in developing countries today involves rapidly increasing water demands.

The human activity which consumes most water is agriculture, currently accounting for some 75 per cent of global water use (L'vovich, 1979). Large increases in irrigation needs are foreseen in those countries striving towards increased self-sufficiency in food production and faced with rapid population increases. At the same time, irrigation efficiencies are generally quite low. It is not uncommon that 70 per cent or more of the water withdrawn from rivers or aquifers for irrigation never reaches the crop (UNWC, 1978).

As water passes through a country it is likely to be used for a variety of complementary purposes: (*a*) for hydropower production; (*b*) for fishing; and (*c*) for navigation. Navigation is particularly important for land-locked countries, especially if they can use the rivers to obtain access to the sea.

Water management

The need for water-resource development and regulation in order to adapt the supply of water to a continuously changing demand is reflected in the management infrastructure and in the successive development of water projects. The tools and practices of water management become more and more complicated as socio-economic development proceeds. It becomes more and more difficult to balance supply and demand.

As water demands increase in size and number, water management proceeds from being supply-oriented to being resource-oriented and then to being demand-oriented (Dávid, 1976). In the early stages, measures are taken to satisfy the demands as they develop. As demands increase, water storage and water redistribution projects are undertaken to regulate the supply. Finally, when the river systems are as developed as is considered acceptable and there is no more water to allocate, further development must be supported by re-allocations and by the control of demand, that is, by accepting water availability as a regional constraint. The control of demand could lead to changes in the crops grown, to increases in the efficiency of irrigation (e.g., by changing from furrow irrigation to drip irrigation), to recirculation and re-use of water, and so on.

In view of the fundamental importance of water for many different sectors of the economy, it is evident that protection from water-related natural hazards (e.g., flood, drought), from health hazards (e.g., water-borne diseases), and from hazards to aquatic ecosystems (e.g., pollutants) must form cornerstones of national policy. It is also clear that measures taken by upstream countries that in some way threaten the water supply of downstream countries, will be sure to create strong feelings of uneasiness among the latter. Diplomatic activities of downstream countries such as Jordan, Bangladesh, and Egypt certainly seem to reflect a fear that their future is being endangered in this way.

III. Water disputes and conflicts: some case histories

Many countries are tied together by joint dependence on the same river system, which can lead to conflict. The nature of such potential conflict varies from river basin to river basin. In humid (non-arid) regions, the typical dispute is related to either water pollution or the environmental impact of dam projects. In arid regions, the typical dispute is generated by increasing water competition combined with problems of water scarcity during the dry season. Downstream countries may depend on upstream countries not only for water, but also for water storage and flow-control facilities (e.g., Bangladesh, Egypt). Land-locked upstream countries may find incentives to adapt to downstream desires if they in turn can benefit from free access to the sea. Quite often semi-arid countries co-operate actively in increasing dry-season flow, which generally is the most critical resource constraint (e.g., Egypt and Sudan based on the Aswan Dam and Lake Nasser and on the Jonglei canal project on the Nile River; and Mali, Mauritania, and Senegal based on dam projects along the Senegal River).

Upstream withdrawal

Three cases are discussed: (*a*) the Jordan River, with an ongoing armed conflict; (*b*) the Ganges River, with a dispute resulting from insufficient dry-season flow; and (*c*) the Nile River, with frustrations owing to increasing water consumption in upstream countries.

Jordan River

The river basin in which competition for water is stronger than anywhere else in the world is that of the Jordan River, which is shared by Lebanon, Syria, Israel, and Jordan (see table 5.1, note *b*). Israel diverts water from the Sea of Galilee (through which the Jordan River passes) to its Kinnert-Negev conduit; and Jordan diverts water from the Yarmuk River (a tributary to the Jordan River and which forms the border between Syria and Jordan) to the East Ghor Canal, its national water artery (Charnock, 1983).

Controversial water issues have helped to block any peace agreement in the area since 1947. According to Cooley (1984, page 3): 'The constant struggle for the waters of the Jordan, Litani, Orontes, Yarmuk, and other life-giving Middle East rivers, little understood outside the region, was a principal cause of the 1967 Arab-Israeli War and could help spark a new all-out conflict. It is also a major aspect of the Palestinian question and of the struggle over the future of the West Bank' (see also appendix 2, war 6). A contributing factor to the 1967 war, into which Israel entered against Syria and Syria's ally, Egypt, was the fact that 'the Arabs

Table 5.1. Selected countries dependent upon the Jordan River or Nile River[a]

Country[b]	Total water availability[c] (10^6 m^3/year)	Water withdrawal in year noted[c] (10^6 m^3)	Year of withdrawal[c]	Cereal production in 1980[d] (kg/capita)	Per-capita water withdrawal circa 1975[e] (m^3)	Population doubling time[f] (years)	Per-capita water availability in 2000[g] (m^3)
A. Jordan River							
Israel	1 650	1 720	1975	78	506	30	307
Jordan	850	380	1975	65	141	30	133
Syria	35 300	7 000	1976	441	959	21	1 950
B. Nile River							
Egypt	56 000	43 000	1972	198	1236	27	859
Sudan	84 000	18 150	1970	157	1156	22	2 550

Sources and notes:

[a] Table prepared by M. Falkenmark and A. H. Westing.

[b] The countries are the major ones in the two river basins. The Jordan River is *circa* 320 kilometres long, flowing from Syria to Israel and Jordan (their border) and into the Dead Sea. Its basin includes: Jordan (54 per cent); Syria (30 per cent); Israel (10 per cent); and Lebanon (6 per cent). The Nile River is *circa* 6700 kilometres long, flowing from Sudan to Egypt and into the Mediterranean Sea. Its basin includes: Sudan (63 per cent); Ethiopia (12 per cent); Egypt (10 per cent); Uganda (8 per cent); Tanzania (4 per cent); and Kenya, Zaire, Rwanda, and Burundi (3 per cent).

[c] The water-availability values and water-withdrawal values plus year of withdrawal are from Forkasiewicz & Margat (1980, tables III, IV, VI, and VIII).

[d] The cereal (grain) production is calculated from the 1980 values for total cereals (wheat, rice, barley, oats, maize [corn], etc.) and population in *UN Statistical Yearbook*, New York, 33, table 76 (1982) and 1980 population values from the UN (1985, table A–2). The 1980 global average was 351 kilograms per capita.

[e] The per-capita water-withdrawal values are from Forkasiewicz & Margat (1980, tables III, IV, and VIII); they are based on total withdrawal in the year noted and population values for 1975. Per-capita water-withdrawal values for the year of withdrawal (using population values for that year, derived from the UN [1985, table A–2]) are, respectively: 498, 146, 910, 1280, and 1323.

[f] The population doubling-time values assume exponential growth and are based on extrapolations using the 1975 and 1980 population values from the UN (1985, table A–2).

[g] The per-capita water-availability values for the year 2000 are based on population values from the UN (1985, table A–2, medium variant).

had unsuccessfully tried to divert into Arab rivers Jordan River head-waters that feed Israel' (Cooley, 1984, page 3). This diversion idea was originally part of a coordinated water development plan for the river basin initiated by the United Nations (Inbar and Maos, 1984). However, diversion of the salt-free headwaters direct to a Syrian tributary to the Yarmuk River turned into an extremely controversial issue, which has been in abeyance as a result of the 1967/73 cease-fire lines which fall outside the hydrological border of the Jordan basin.

Rivers were also involved in the Lebanon conflict (World Water, 1984b). In the Israeli incursion into Lebanon of 1982–85, Israel gained access to the low reaches of the Litani River, which strengthened an Arab conviction that diverting those waters to Israel has been an important long-term Israeli goal (Cooley, 1984). Also involved was the Orontes River, which originates in Lebanon's fertile Bekaa Valley and waters western Syria. To protect this region, its best farmland, Syria has sought guarantees that the headwaters of the Orontes River would never fall into the hands of Israel.

Different socio-economic levels in the countries involved add to the problem: it has been claimed that Israel uses five times the amount of water on a per-capita basis as do the neighbouring Arab countries (Cooley, 1984). However, this must refer to municipal use only, as the total per-capita water consumption by Israel is very modest. Indeed, on a per-capita basis Israel, with its modern agro-industrial society, uses about half as much as either Egypt or Syria, although about three times as much as Jordan (table 5.1).

The future water developments of Jordan could be based either on withdrawals from the Sea of Galilee (depending on Israeli approval), or on the Maqarin project on the Yarmuk River (depending on Syrian approval) (Charnock, 1983). Another possibility for Jordan would be to transfer water from the Euphrates River which, however, would create a dependence on Iraq (World Water, 1984c). The planned Israeli Mediterranean–Dead Sea project to transfer salt water to the Dead Sea in order to produce hydropower and to compensate for Israel's withdrawal from the upper Jordan River, adds to the present frustrations in the area by threatening Jordan's potash industry and its ongoing conservation of agricultural lands (World Water, 1984d).

Ganges River

The Ganges River—the basin of which is shared primarily by India and Bangladesh—passes through one of the poorest regions of the world. Its waters have traditionally been regarded as an inexhaustible gift of nature (Choudhury & Khan, 1983). However, the regional population explosion and the rapid development of agriculture and industry in both India and Bangladesh are increasingly straining this water resource, both through increased consumption and by contributing to a deterioration of the water quality.

A 30-year dispute is still going on regarding the sharing of the waters of the Ganges River, recently focused on the water diversion by India at the Farakka Dam (Barrage) just upstream from the border with Bangladesh. The aim of this project is to flush more water through the Hooghly River and port of Calcutta in order to reduce silting. Bangladesh has felt threatened by the decrease of the dry-season flow that can be caused by this withdrawal (Zaman, 1983a). After about 20 years of fruitless negotiations on the joint use of the river water, a temporary agreement was finally reached in 1975 on a six-week trial withdrawal at the Farakka Dam. However, India prolonged this diversion for more than two years, which created large problems in Bangladesh. The dry season which followed the agreed trial period turned out to be extremely dry and produced a series of adverse effects in Bangladesh. The extent of sea-water intrusion was exacerbated by the extremely low water level in the river, the upstream (inland) penetration extending some 160 kilometres further than usual. Ground-water salinization occurred over vast areas.

Bangladesh brought the issue to the United Nations, and the General Assembly in 1976 urged the parties to meet in order to negotiate a fair and expeditious settlement (UNGA, 1976). In November 1977, a five-year Ganges Water Agreement was reached. This treaty *inter alia* provides for the seeking of a long-term solution for augmentation of the dry-season flow. Unfortunately, Bangladesh and India envisage divergent solutions as to how to increase the dry-season flow of the Ganges River (Zaman, 1983a). India has proposed a transfer of waters from the Brahmaputra River in Assam through a long canal partly passing through Bangladesh. Bangladesh's proposal, on the other hand, rests on storage dams in the upper reaches of the Ganges River in

Nepal and India that would store wet-season flow for release during the low-flow period. Bangladesh rejects the canal scheme as ecologically ruinous and technically and economically infeasible. However, the Bangladesh proposal involves Nepal as well, whereas India's scheme is only bilateral. Nepal has not yet expressed itself on the matter, but must be aware of the potential benefits to it of the canal scheme, including the possibility for generating hydropower and for gaining access to the sea.

Nile River

Successful sharing of the waters of the Nile River—the basin of which spans Sudan, Ethiopia, Egypt, and six other states (see table 5.1, note *b*)—has been the key to regional socio-economic development since ancient times, and past disputes seem to have been settled in a friendly atmosphere. The hydrological unity of the Nile River basin has long been recognized despite its former subdivision among various colonial powers, and now among nine diverse states (Mageed, 1985). A number of agreements during colonial times prohibited any construction, even on the tributaries, which would obstruct the flow to the main river. As early as 1899, basin-wide plans included reservoirs for seasonal storage, water-loss reduction in the flood-prone Sudd region of southern Sudan, flood-control works, and long-term storage at the equatorial lakes in order to reduce drought hazards. The 1929 Nile Water Agreement allocated river flow between Egypt and Sudan, and required East African countries not to construct any works in the equatorial lakes before consultating with the downstream countries.

After independence, Sudan in a 1959 agreement with Egypt allowed Egypt to construct the Aswan Dam as a long-term storage facility. A permanent river commission was established. The upstream countries have not significantly interfered with the natural flow even though vast opportunities for hydropower production have been identified.

A number of obstacles form immense challenges for the future of the Nile River basin, given the aspirations and development needs of the riparian countries, where the majority of the population still lives in absolute poverty, short of food and other basic human needs. Egypt, Ethiopia, and especially Sudan all have rapidly growing populations and must meet their increasing food demands via irrigated agriculture (table 5.1). Egypt, receiving practically all of its water as inflow from Sudan, was extremely worried during the drought of 1984 that Sudan and Ethiopia would be forced to use more water for themselves from the Nile River. Egypt therefore prepared for water rationing (World Water, 1985b). The fact that Sudan has now asked for a revision of the 1959 agreement on water sharing increases the downstream unease (World Water, 1985a). Egypt has instituted long-term water planning that puts stress on water conservation, including increased irrigation efficiency.

The Jonglei Canal project in southern Sudan was started in 1978 and has been funded jointly by Egypt and Sudan. The two countries have agreed to share its benefits. However, the project has met with internal rivalry between Sudan's northern and southern regions. The latter see the project as a means of channelling their water to the north. The construction work had to be stopped as a result of hostilities in the area, including guerrilla attacks and a kidnapping in November 1983, the victims of which were not released until January 1985 (World Water, 1984a; 1985b; 1985c).

Upstream pollution

Upstream waste disposal can degrade the water entering down-stream countries and thereby lead to conflict. For example, the Rhine River basin, with a population of 40 million people, contains one of the largest industrial complexes of the world, causing severe pollution to the river. In spite of friendly relations among riparian countries—FR Germany, Switzerland, France, the Netherlands, and four other states—disputes are still difficult to settle. After 25 years of negotiations, the salt load of the river is higher than ever before (Volker, 1983). A main problem of dispute is caused by the waste salts from potassium mines in the Alsace region of France. Even though downstream Netherlands is prepared to carry part of the cost of reducing the salt input in France, there is opposition in France to the proposal to re-inject the waste salts into the mines, owing to the risk to the aquifers from which the local water supply is drawn.

The Colorado River provides another example of conflicting interests and international dispute. The river is shared between upstream USA and downstream Mexico. Increasing salinity emerging in the wake of large-scale irrigation in the USA started to create problems in the 1960s, including excessive crop losses in Mexicali

Valley, Mexico, where 7 per cent of all irrigated crops in Mexico are grown (Murphy & Sabadell, 1985). Some 10 years of negotiations were needed before the USA agreed to guarantee Mexico a certain maximum level of river salinity. A desalinization plant may have to be constructed just upstream of the international border in order to comply with this agreement.

International borders

Conflict can develop where rivers form international borders. Problems might develop owing to natural processes of erosion and sedimentation, whereby river bends and islands can change their locations.

The border between the USSR and China is, according to an 1860 treaty, drawn along the thalweg of the Ussuri (Wu-Su-Li) River (the line following the lowest part of the valley). Natural processes of fluvial erosion have since that time led to shifts in the thalweg. When Chinese forces crossed the original line in March 1966, this led to a severe clash with Soviet forces (Macadam *et al.*, 1969, pages 199–201).

A portion of the border between Iran and Iraq is formed by the Shatt-al-Arab channel (the confluent downstream portion of the Euphrates and Tigris Rivers), on the basis of a 1937 agreement. Frustration by Iraq over this agreement has been suggested in press reports to be a contributing factor to the present Iran-Iraq War.

In many regions where deep soils or fissured rocks underlie international borders, ground water can move from one country to another. For example, disputes over ground water have occurred between France and FR Germany and also between France and Belgium (Falkenmark, 1981a). In that between France and Belgium, an understanding was reached in 1971 in which both countries agreed to curtail their withdrawals from the shared aquifer (IRAL, 1985b).

Another example of a recent aquifer dispute occurred in the USA between the states of Texas and New Mexico (IRAL, 1983b). At dispute was the right for the city of El Paso, Texas to benefit from the ground-water resources in the Mesilla Bolson aquifer. This aquifer extends over a wide area of Texas and New Mexico within the USA and also reaches southwards into Mexico. El Paso, rapidly exhausting its own supplies of water, wanted to gain access to the New Mexico ground water by tapping the aquifer close to the Texas–New Mexico border. However, New Mexico strongly opposed this and attempted to enforce a total ban on out-of-state transportation of ground water.

IV. The potential for future conflict

Multinational river basins

The problem of upstream/downstream water competition is by no means a small one. About 50 countries have 75 per cent or more of their total area falling within international river basins (UN, 1978, pages 21–47) and a number of these have severe population problems (table 5.2). In 1973, an estimated 35–40 per cent of the global population lived in multinational river basins (Widstrand, 1980, page 124). At least 214 river basins are multinational: 155 of these are shared between two countries; 36 among three countries; and the remaining 23 among four to 12 countries (UN, 1978, pages 5–29). Indeed, in Africa and Europe most river basins are multinational.

The types of conflict between countries in international river basins differ greatly from one river configuration to another, among different climatic zones, and among different socio-economic levels of development. Countries may be sequentially aligned in a river basin, so that the river passes from one country to another, or they may be placed in parallel, sharing the river as an international border. In humid regions flow increases along the river and problems are generally related to water pollution or to water projects with adverse downstream effects. Under arid conditions, by contrast, river flow generally decreases along the river owing to evaporation. The competition for water is at its most intense in arid river basins with rapid population increases.

It is clear that the problem of reaching agreement on sharing the joint water resources in a river basin increases with the number of nations involved. Measures taken upstream that influence river flow or quality will generally influence the water resource available to downstream countries. The interests of basin countries can be either parallel (e.g., regarding navigation, flow control, or perhaps

Table 5.2. Selected countries dominated by international river basins[a]

Country[b]	Number of international river basins[c]	Area in international river basin(s)[c] (per cent)	Population density in 1980[d] (persons/km²)	Cereal production in 1980[e] (kg/capita)	Population doubling time[f] (years)
Bangladesh	3	86	613	246	24
Burundi	2	100	146	73	44
Ghana	3	75	48	54	22
Iraq	2	83	30	168	19
Malawi	2	96	50	222	24
Nepal	2	100	104	259	29
Nigeria	5	87	87	121	20
Paraguay	1	100	8	224	21
Rwanda	2	100	195	51	21
Sudan	5	81	7	157	22
Swaziland	3	100	32	188	24
Uganda	2	100	56	82	21
Venezuela	6	80	17	105	20
Zaire	3	99	12	28	24
Zambia	2	100	8	185	22
Zimbabwe	5	100	19	269	21

Sources and notes:

[a]Table prepared by A. H. Westing.

[b]The countries represent all developing countries the area of which is 75 per cent or more in international river basins and the populations of which will double in 25 years or less or which have a present population density of at least 100 persons per square kilometre.

[c]The number and area of international river basins are from the UN (1978).

[d]The population density is calculated using the 1980 population values from the UN (1985, table A–2) and area values from *UN Statistical Yearbook*, New York, 33, table 19 (1982). The 1980 global average was 33 persons per square kilometre.

[e]The cereal (grain) production is calculated using the 1980 values for total cereals (wheat, rice, barley, oats, maize [corn], etc.) from *UN Statistical Yearbook*, New York, 33, table 76 (1982) and 1980 population values from the UN (1985, table A–2). The 1980 global average was 351 kilograms per capita.

[f]The population doubling time assumes exponential growth and is based on an extrapolation using the 1975 and 1980 population values from the UN (1985, table A–2). The 1975–80 global value was 39 years.

hydropower development) or divergent (e.g., regarding upstream withdrawal or pollution).

Growth in population

Multinational river basins provide a constant reminder that water is distributed with no regard to the world's administrative and political divisions, and that most water-related activities within such shared systems have an impact on the other countries concerned (Caponera, 1983). Functionally speaking, such water resources must be considered to be common resources and not the exclusive property of any one state. If a state ignores this principle and behaves as if it had full sovereign jurisdiction over the water while it was temporarily flowing through its territory, such behaviour will only lead to dispute.

The potential for dispute, and in the long run also for armed conflict, increases as the importance of water for the satisfaction of human economic and social needs grows. Until the 1960s, most water conflicts were related to navigation and small-scale uses, but with the present ability to carry out massive, large-scale projects, upstream water diversions can mean famine and destruction for other nations sharing the resource. There is a constant potential for dispute, and even violent action, in regions with scarce resources and rapidly increasing water demands.

It is clear that many regions depend for their development on the successful sharing of joint water resources. In some regions most of the rivers are, indeed, international. When the same region is additionally characterized by rapid population increase—as, for example, throughout much of Africa—a rapid development of national water resources is called for. The water competition may be particularly aggravated in regions of water shortage where countries are striving towards self-sufficiency in food production and are therefore dependent on irrigation, a measure which will increasingly reduce the water resources of downstream countries. The degradation of water quality from future industrial development will add to the problem.

The regions which seem most exposed to future water competition are Africa, the Middle East, and South Asia. The existence in these regions of multinational river systems brings the following basins into focus in terms of dispute potential: (*a*) Middle Eastern rivers, in particular the Jordan and Euphrates Rivers; (*b*) African rivers, in particular the Nile, Zambezi, Niger, Senegal, and perhaps Medjerda Rivers; and (*c*) South Asian rivers, in particular the Ganges, Brahmaputra, and perhaps Mekong Rivers.

In the case of the Jordan River, it is quite evident that both Israel and Jordan already face serious problems of water shortage, problems that can only worsen in the years ahead. Israel now uses the entire amount available to it under present circumstances (table 5.1). Its level of per-capita use is already somewhat below the minimum of 500 cubic metres that appears to be necessary in the region for sustaining high socio-economic standards even under conditions of sophisticated water management. That Israel has begun to exceed the lower limit is suggested by the trouble it is beginning to encounter with ground-water salinity, the result of too great a reliance on water recycling (Shuval, 1981). Israel's level of staple food production is very low and its population is growing rapidly (table 5.1).

Jordan has not been using all of the water available to it, but its per-capita level of use has been exceedingly low (table 5.1). Only the most modest increases in demand resulting from development could be met under present circumstances. The situation is precarious since Jordan produces an exceedingly low level of staple foods and is at the same time experiencing dramatic increases in its population.

In the case of the Nile River, increased problems for Egypt can be envisaged. Egypt now uses much of the water available to it under present circumstances (table 5.1). Its population is growing rapidly and severe problems appear to be in store for the country within a few decades.

It is clear that serious disputes could soon arise among arid-zone countries over water quantity as well as quality. The problem is exacerbated when industrialization based largely on industrial techniques imported from the developed world is adopted. Having been developed under humid conditions, these techniques often depend upon volumes of water that are lavish by arid-zone standards. Among the consequences of such adoption is that the water coming to a downstream country during the dry season might be highly polluted.

Multinational aquifers

Aquifers are important water resources in arid regions. Problems will arise when several countries plan to develop the same aquifer. Indeed, this appears to be an imminent problem with the Nubian sandstone aquifer (UN, 1983, pages 303–310). This impressive ground-water reservoir, 500–1000 metres deep, is shared by four countries: Egypt, Sudan, Chad, and Libya. The aquifer is seen as an important resource by Egypt for agicultural development in its New Valley project (Charnock, 1985). By Libya it is seen as the corner-stone in providing water for a huge artificial river, planned to be the country's major artery (George, 1985).

Other sources of water-related tension

In the long-term, tensions are expected to develop between neighbouring regions of surplus and deficiency. As mentioned above, Jordan is exploring the possibility of co-operation with Iraq for water transfer. Other types of fundamental dependency are exemplified by the desire of Bangladesh to store water in India or Nepal which would increase dry-season flow of the Ganges River; or by the interest of Egypt in the Jonglei Canal project in Sudan which would provide more water for its bulging population.

Another issue that might lead to disputes is related to inadequate safety conditions in a river basin owing to poor maintenance of upstream dams. Many dams in the Third World are leaking, creating a risk of flood disasters. Some dams that impound large tropical lakes are becoming exposed to unpredicted water levels that threaten their stability, for example, the dam at the outlet of Lake Victoria at Owen Falls (Gunnell, 1985). Conversely, unanti-cipated low water levels might also lead to dispute if irrigation pumps ceased to be supplied with adequate water. The African drought of the 1970s and 1980s led to this problem in the Lake Chad basin (Evans & Gunganesharajah, 1985).

Uncontrolled land erosion is a further problem of international dimensions (Mosely, 1985; Ongwenyi, 1985; Gong & Mou, 1985; Volker, 1983). Silt transported from upstream countries which are experiencing massive soil erosion settles in downstream river beds and reservoirs, thereby reducing hydropower production and increasing the severity of inundations during floods.

V. Conflict prevention and management

International law of water resources

In order to be able to avoid water related conflicts, rules and means must be available for solving the disputes as they emerge. Codification is necessary in the form of international conventions as well as incentives for countries to adhere to the principles involved. Tools are required for successfully sharing the joint water resources, including the appropriate technology, infrastructure, and administrative skills. Moreover, a suitable arena must be available in which the nations can discuss the problems.

What must be reconciled is the desire of upstream states for unlimited territorial sovereignty with the desire of downstream states for what has been referred to as unlimited territorial integrity (Caponera, 1983; Utton, 1977–78).

The strict application of either of these two doctrines would breed permanent conflict. In fact, international practice has tended towards a softening of the principle of absolute territorial sovereignty. In practice, this doctrine has been modified by the ancient Roman principle *sic utere tuo ut alienum non laedas,* that is, the principle of using things belonging to you in such a way that no other person is harmed.

Thus, the water resource must be governed by a doctrine that transcends the exclusively nationalistic approach, doing so on grounds of equity, fairness, and peaceful relations. A juridical base for such a principle has been furnished by a case involving the Oder River in which the International Court of Justice in 1929 ruled that countries have a common legal right to the resources of a shared river, the essential characteristic being the community of interest of all parties in the use of the river (Caponera, 1983). A number of subsequent rulings by the Court, together with the implications of a number of international treaties, have further developed this principle of equitable apportionment of utilization.

A number of basic principles in the law of international rivers have achieved the status of legal norms, even if there does not as yet exist a consolidated international convention (Hayton, 1983a). The Institute of International Law (Geneva) has been working on the issue since the beginning of the century and has produced resolutions on the use of international non-maritime waters and on the pollution of rivers and lakes. The International Law Association (London) has formulated a principle of equitable utilization in its 1966 'Helsinki Rules on the Uses of the Waters of International Rivers' (ILA, 1967). These model rules cover procedures for the prevention and settlement of disputes and for the control of water pollution, navigation, and timber floating. The fundamental principle of the Helsinki Rules is that 'Each basin State is entitled, within its territory, to a reasonable and equitable share in the beneficial uses of the waters of an international drainage basin' (article IV). Thus, they embrace the crucial concept of the river basin being the basic territorial unit of concern.

The International Law Association has also developed model rules dealing with flood control, marine pollution of continental origin, maintenance and improvement of naturally navigable waterways separating or traversing several states, protection of water resources and water installations in times of armed conflict, administration of international water resources, regulation of flow, and the relation between water and other natural resources and with the environment in general (Hayton, 1983a). Work is in progress by the Association on international ground waters.

The United Nations system

In the absence of an internationally agreed upon convention, the use of international fresh waters is still largely based on the general principles and rules of customary international law, including any relevant bilateral or multilateral agreements. In 1959, the United Nations General Assembly recommended preliminary studies on the problems involved (UNGA, 1959). It took 11 years before the Assembly noted that the use of such rivers was ripe for codification, turning the task over to its subsidiary body, the International Law Commission. Although 26 years have now passed since then, the Commission has not even been able to agree on the concept of an international river (Biswas, 1983b). This pace does not invite optimism.

The United Nations Conference on the Human Environment, held in Stockholm in 1972, declared as one of its basic principles (No. 21) that 'States have . . . the responsibility to ensure that activities within their jurisdiction or control do not cause damage to the environment of other States or of areas beyond the limits of national jurisdiction' (UNGA, 1973b, page 5). In 1977, the United Nations Water Conference, held in Mar del Plata, Argentina, urged that national policies take into consideration the right of each state to equitably utilize water resources shared with other countries (UNWC, 1977).

In response to a request from the United Nations General Assembly (UNGA, 1973a), the United Nations Environment Programme in 1978 forwarded to the Assembly 'Draft principles of conduct in the field of the environment for the guidance of States in the conservation and harmonious utilization of natural resources shared by two or more States' (UNEP, 1978a; 1978b). The Assembly has yet to take action on these recommended principles (Biswas, 1983a). It is worth noting that two of the countries voicing the strongest criticisms to them—Brazil and Ethiopia—are upstream countries.

International river commissions

The traditional tool in sharing multinational water resources is a treaty or similar agreement among the countries concerned. The practical application of such instruments requires close co-operation among the states concerned, preferably by establishing a joint river commission. According to the United Nations Charter of Economic Rights and Duties of States (UNGA, 1974, article 3): 'In the exploitation of natural resources shared by two or more countries, each State must co-operate on the basis of a system of information and prior consultations in order to achieve optimum use of such resources without causing damage to the legitimate interest of others'.

The role of international river commissions in preparing joint schemes is often confined to the technical and factual core that provides the basis for subsequent policy-level negotiations. The authority to approve a chosen scheme for equitable utilization of a shared resource seldom, if ever, rests with such a commission. Indeed, few existing commissions have the express authority or the capability to carry out thorough planning. It has even been suggested that this is the case because many governments consider it to be in their interests to prevent balanced development (Hayton, 1983b).

The accomplishments of existing river commissions have varied greatly from river basin to river basin (Fox & Le Marquand, 1979).

In many cases the commissions are advisory bodies only. In other cases, the countries involved have transferred the decision-making capacity to the commission itself. If the nations involved have a common cultural heritage and a history of good working relations with one another, the task is much simpler than where such conditions are absent. River commissions for the Senegal River basin (Guinea, Mali, Mauritania, and Senegal), the Columbia River basin (Canada and the USA), and the Nile River basin (Egypt and Sudan) provide examples of well-functioning commissions (Fox & Le Marquand, 1979; Mageed, 1985). In the Danube River basin, flow forecasting is said to have functioned even during World War II. In Latin America, there seems to be a general reluctance on the part of national governments to delegate power to an international body over which they do not have full control (IRAL, 1985c). In general, the river commissions or similar entities in Latin America are only given authority to decide on strictly technical matters, whereas policy differences are addressed through traditional diplomatic procedures.

Problems of incentive

The doctrine of equitable sharing in principle places the countries on an equal footing, although in practice this will depend upon existing incentives to conform to such a principle. Technical and economic considerations may induce basin states to co-operate, for example, via integrated development projects, and in some cases may even force them to do so. In other situations, the downstream state may suffer from adverse consequences of upstream withdrawals, projects of waste disposal, and so forth. The natural inducement to co-operate is small for the upstream state and large for the downstream state. Economic and political incentives could be helpful (Zaman, 1983b). The desire to develop an international image of being a responsible country might be another powerful factor, as was apparently the case for the USA in its relations with Mexico regarding the Colorado River (Fox & Le Marquand, 1979).

Another effort in creating a stronger incentive has been the general call for an international code of conduct, as was, for example, clearly articulated at the 1977 United Nations Water Conference alluded to earlier. Those international statements that stress the responsibility of states in the protection of shared resources and of their joint use help reduce the issues to be settled in negotiations. They do this by pointing out the responsibilities expected of all countries and by setting out principles for the equitable division of the benefits and costs resulting from the development and use of international water resources.

A private International Water Tribunal, now supported by some 85 European environmental organizations, serves to focus attention on apparent infractions of international water agreements (IRAL, 1983a; 1984b). Evidence has been gathered by the Tribunal and verdicts rendered in some 19 pollution cases in Western Europe (IRAL, 1985a). In many of the cases the attendant publicity has led to corrective action.

Problems of international codification

It is cause for considerable concern that, in spite of its fundamental relevance for socio-economic development in regions where water is scarce, an international code of conduct dealing with international rivers (such as the Helsinki Rules) has not as yet been adopted. Clearly, the issue is undermined by the dichotomy between states with upstream and downstream interests, and consensus seems far off.

In 1970, the United Nations General Assembly gave the task of codifying the non-navigational uses of international watercourses to its subsidiary International Law Commission (UNGA, 1970). Navigational uses had already been codified in 1815 at the Congress of Vienna. However, the Commission has met with extreme difficulties in fulfilling this task. It has not yet been possible to define the basic concept of an international watercourse, in particular whether it should cover only the watercourse as such or also the water in it, and therefore also the origin of that water, including the ground water in the river basin.

The present view of the International Law Commission is that a framework convention should provide general principles governing international watercourses in the absence of agreements among states concerned, and at the same time provide guidelines for the drafting of such regional agreements (IRAL, 1984a). In other words, the Commission recognizes the necessity and validity for having a specific agreement for each watercourse in view of its unique characteristics (IRAL, 1985d). The framework convention would provide for the peaceful solution of disputes via negotiations, consultations, and some form of compulsory settlement. Entitlement to a reasonable or equitable share of the use of the waters of an international watercourse by each state within the river basin is also recognized. The Commission has agreed to the term 'international watercourse' in lieu of such more contentious terms as 'international drainage basin' or 'international watercourse system' (IRAL, 1985d). Although the importance of ground water had earlier been acknowledged by the Commission, that specific resource is now not to be included within the general terms of a framework convention.

The considerable difficulties and delays encountered by the International Law Commission are cause for pessimism. Their task of codification would probably benefit from the development in individual countries of customary law that articulates local doctrines and ways of understanding the mutual rights and duties of countries sharing a joint water system. It would probably also be beneficial to test existing doctrines by bringing selected cases to the International Court of Justice. Particular attention should be paid to those existing conventions in the field of environmental law that provide for protection from negative impacts of measures taken in other countries.

Problems of defining equitable share

The criteria to be employed in objectively determining what constitutes a reasonable or equitable share of an international water resource, defined in such a fashion that disputing nations will accept them, are most difficult to arrive at (Biswas, 1983a; Falkenmark, 1984a). The crucial point is the conflict between national self-interest and international equity or even morality. Among the major problem areas are:

1. Difficulties in anticipating the long-term implications of irreversible water development projects;

2. The multi-dimensional character of the major components related to conflict resolution;

3. A lack of reliable and acceptable methods for allocating the benefits and costs of proposed long-term projects; and

4. The differences among existing national water-law regimes.

These difficulties become especially serious when taking into consideration rapid population increases and their potential for increasing the probability of disputes.

VI. Conclusion

It has been shown that frustrations over scarcity of water and over dependence for water upon upstream countries may develop into disputes. Indeed, water can be a strong contributing factor to armed conflict, even if this is not often recognized.

It has also been demonstrated that competition for water rises in direct response to population growth. At the same time, the amount of water demanded per individual rises with increases in standard of living. The problem is exacerbated not only by rapid population increases, but also by the water needs associated with the long-term goal of many developing countries to become self-sufficient in food staples. The highest levels of frustration that will arise from increasing water scarcities can be expected to develop in Africa (where populations are increasing dramatically and where most of the rivers are international) and in south-western Asia (where populations are also increasing rapidly and where dry-season flow is scarce). Problems will worsen as long as countries with common sources of water cannot reach agreements on equitable management policies for this vital natural resource.

References

Biswas, A. K. 1983a. Shared natural resources: future conflicts or peaceful development? In: Dupuy, R.-J. (ed.). *Settlement of disputes on the new natural resources.* Hague: Martinus Nijhoff, 487 pp.: pp. 197–215.

Biswas, A. K. 1983b. Some major issues in river basin management for developing countries. In: Zaman, M. *et al.* (eds). *River basin development.* Dublin: Tycooly, 239 pp.: pp. 17–27.

Caponera, D. A. 1983. International river law. In: Zaman, M. *et al.* (eds). *River basin development.* Dublin: Tycooly, 239 pp.: pp. 173–184.

Charnock, A. 1983. Maqarin deadlock forces major revision of Jordan's water plans. *World Water,* Liverpool, 6(7):35,37–38.

Charnock, A. 1985. Egypt seeks usage overview. *World Water,* Liverpool, 8(5):29,31.

Choudhury, G. R. & Khan, T. A. 1983. Developing the Ganges basin. In: Zaman, M. *et al.* (eds). *River basin development.* Dublin: Tycooly, 239 pp.: pp. 28–39.

Cooley, J. K. 1984. War over water. *Foreign Policy,* Washington, 1984(54):3–26.

Dávid, L. 1976. River basin development for socio-economic growth: general report. In: UN Development Programme (ed.). *River basin development: policies and planning.* New York: UN Development Programme, 2 vols (250+310 pp.) vol. 1, pp. 25–37.

Evans, T. & Gunganesharajah, K. 1985. Lake Chad at risk if drought goes on. *World Water,* Liverpool, 8(6):34–35.

Falkenmark, M. 1970. [Water in nature: regarding supply and demand] (in Swedish). *Ymer,* Stockholm, 1970:47–69.

Falkenmark, M. 1979. Main problems of water use and transfer of technology. *GeoJournal,* Wiesbaden, FR Germany, 3:435–443.

Falkenmark, M. 1981a. Groundwater is a natural resource too. *Ambio,* Stockholm, 10:49.

Falkenmark, M. 1981b. Integrated view of land and water: the new cornerstone in environmental planning. *Geografiska Annaler,* Stockholm, Ser. A, 63:261–271.

Falkenmark, M. 1981c. Transfer of water know-how from high to low latitudes: some problems and biases. *Geophysica,* Helsinki, 17(1–2):5–20.

Falkenmark, M. 1984a. New ecological approach to the water cycle: ticket to the future. *Ambio,* Stockholm, 13:152–160.

Falkenmark, M. 1984b. Water: the silent messenger between cause and effect in environmental problems. *Water International,* Lausanne, 9(2):62–65.

Falkenmark, M. 1985. Urgent message from hydrologists to planners: water a silent messenger turning land use into river response. In: Plate, E. (ed.). *Scientific procedures applied to planning, design and management of water resources systems.* Wallingford, UK: International Association of Hydrological Sciences, Publication No. 147, 647 pp.: pp. 61–75.

Falkenmark, M. 1986. Macro-scale water supply/demand comparison on the global scene: a hydrological approach. In the press.

Forkasiewicz, J. & Margat, J. 1980. *Tableau mondial de données nationales d'économie de l'eau: ressources et utilisations [World table of national data on water economy: resources and utilization]* (in French). Orléans: Ministère de l'Industrie, Bureau de Recherches ·Géologiques et Minières, Département Hydrogéologie, Publication No. 79 SGN 784 HYD, 37 pp. + 13 tbls + 5 figs.

Fox, I. K. & Le Marquand, D. 1979. International river basin co-operation: the lessons from experience. *Water Supply & Management,* Oxford, 3(1):9–27.

George, A. 1985. Great man-made river debate surfaces. *World Water,* Liverpool, 8(7):33,35.

Gong Shiyang & Mou Jinze. 1985. Methods of land and water conservation in the Wuding river basin. In: Lundqvist, J. *et al.* (eds). *Strategies for river basin management*. Dordrecht, D. Reidel, 346 pp.: pp. 81–89.

Gunnell, B. 1985. Could coup curb Uganda power plan? *World Water,* Liverpool, 8(8):43,45.

Hayton, R. D. 1983a. Law of international water resources systems. In: Zaman, M. *et al.* (eds). *River basin development.* Dublin: Tycooly, 239 pp.: pp. 195–211.

Hayton, R. D. 1983b. Progress in co-operative arrangements. In: United Nations (ed.). *Experiences in the development and management of international river and lake basins.* New York: UN Document No. ST/ESA/120 (Natural Resources/Water Series No. 10), 424 pp.: pp. 65–81.

ILA (International Law Association). 1967. *Helsinki rules on the uses of the waters of international rivers.* London: Intl Law Association, 56 pp.

Inbar, M. and Maos, J. O. 1984. Water resource planning and development in the northern Jordan valley. *Water International,* Urbana, Illinois, 9(1): 18–25.

IRAL. 1983a. International Water Tribunal announced. *International Rivers and Lakes,* United Nations, NY, 1983(3):8.

IRAL. 1983b. United States federal judge rules on the dispute between the city of El Paso (Texas) and the state of New Mexico over the use of ground water. *International Rivers and Lakes,* UN, NY, 1983(3):6.

IRAL. 1984a. International Law Commission: new report on international rivers law. *International Rivers and Lakes,* UN, NY, 1984(4):3–4.

IRAL. 1984b. International Water Tribunal: new cases filed. *International Rivers and Lakes,* United Nations, NY, 1984(4):4.

IRAL. 1985a. Cases decided by the International Water Tribunal. *International Rivers and Lakes,* United Nations, NY, 1985(5):5.

IRAL. 1985b. Ground-water regulation: the international dimension. *International Rivers and Lakes,* United Nations, NY, 1985(5):3–4.

IRAL. 1985c. International river basin co-operation in Latin America: developments since the Mar del Plata conference. *International Rivers and Lakes,* United Nations, NY, 1985(5):9–11.

IRAL. 1985d. Report on the law of non-navigational watercourses. *International Rivers and Lakes,* United Nations, NY, 1985(5):13–15.

L'vovich, M. I. 1979. *World water resources and their future.* Washington: American Geophysical Union, 415 pp.

Macadam, I. *et al.* 1969. USSR. *Annual Register,* London, 211:194–206.

Mageed, Y. A. 1985. Integrated river basin development: the challenges to the Nile basin countries. In: Lundqvist, J. *et al.* (eds). *Strategies for river basin management.* Dordrecht: D. Reidel, 346 pp.: pp. 151–160.

Mosely, P. 1985. Upstream-downstream interactions as natural constraints to basin-wide planning for China's River Huang. In: Lundqvist, J. *et al.* (eds). *Strategies for river basin management.* Dordrecht, Netherlands: D. Reidel, 346 pp.: pp. 131–140.

Murphy, I. L. & Sabadell, J. E. 1985. Impact of water resources public policies on international river basin conflicts. In: Kosinsky, V. de & De Somer, M. (eds). *Water resources for rural areas and their communities.* Ghent: Crystal Drop Publications, 1106 pp.: pp. 883–892.

Ongwenyi, G. S. 1985. Problems of land use and water resources management in the upper Tana catchment in Kenya. In: Lundqvist, J. *et al.* (eds). *Strategies for river basin management.* Dordrecht, Netherlands: D. Reidel, 346 pp.: pp. 123–130.

Postel, S. 1984. *Water: rethinking management in an age of scarcity.* Washington: Worldwatch Institute, Paper No. 62, 66 pp.

Shuval, H. I. 1981. Impending water crisis in Israel. In: Shuval, H. I. (ed.). *Developments in arid zone ecology and environmental quality.* Rehovot, Israel: Balaban International Science Services, 418 pp.: pp. 101–114.

UN (United Nations). 1978. Register of international rivers. *Water Supply & Management,* Oxford, 2(1):1–58 + 5 maps.

UN (United Nations) (ed.). 1983. *Experiences in the development and management of international river and lake basins.* New York: United Nations Document No. ST/ESA/120 (Natural Resources/ Water Series No. 10), 424 pp.

UN (United Nations). 1985. *World population prospects: estimates and projections as assessed in 1982.* New York: UN Department of International Economic & Social Affairs, Population Study No. 86 (ST/ESA/ SER.A/86), 521 pp.

UNEP (United Nations Environment Programme). 1978a. *Co-operation in the field of the environment concerning natural resources shared by two or more states.* Nairobi: UN Environment Programme, Decision No. 6/14 of 24 May 1978, 1 p.

UNEP (United Nations Environment Programme). 1978b. *Draft principles of conduct in the field of the environment for the guidance of states in the conservation and harmonious utilization of natural resources shared by two or more states.* Nairobi: UN Environment Programme, Document No. UNEP/GC.6/17 of 10 March 1978, 3 + 14 pp.

UNGA (United Nations General Assembly). 1959. *Studies of legal problems relating to the use of international waters.* New York: UN General Assembly Resolution No. 1401(XIV) of 21 November 1959, 1 p.

UNGA (United Nations General Assembly). 1970. *Progressive development and codification of the rules of international law relating to international watercourses.* New York: UN General Assembly Resolution No. 2669(XXV) of 8 December 1970, 2 pp.

UNGA (United Nations General Assembly). 1973a. *Co-operation in the field of the environment concerning natural resources shared by two or more States.* New York: UN General Assembly Resolution No. 3129(XXVIII) of 13 December 1973, 1 p.

UNGA (United Nations General Assembly). 1973b. *Report of the United*

Nations Conference on the Human Environment, Stockholm, 5–16 June 1972. New York: UN General Assembly Document No. A/CONF.48/14/ Rev.1, 77 pp.

UNGA (United Nations General Assembly). 1974. *Charter of economic rights and duties of states.* New York: UN General Assembly Resolution No. 3281(XXIX) of 12 December 1974, 10 pp.

UNGA (United Nations General Assembly). 1976. *Situation arising out of unilateral withdrawal of Ganges waters at Farakka.* New York: UN General Assembly Decision No. 31/404 of 26 November 1976, 1 p.

UNWC (United Nations Water Conference). 1977. *Report of the United Nations Water Conference, Mar del Plata, 14–25 March 1977.* New York: United Nations Document No. E/CONF.70/29, 181 pp.

UNWC (United Nations Water Conference). 1978. *Water development and management.* Oxford: Pergamon Press, 2646 pp.

Utton, A. E. 1977–1978. Some suggestions for the management of international river basins. *Water Supply & Management,* Oxford, 1(4):355–364.

Valdes-Cogliano, S. J. 1985. International drinking water decade. *Environment,* Washington, 27(8):41–42.

Volker, A. 1983. Integrated development of the delta and upland portions of a river basin. In: Zaman, M. *et al.* (eds). *River basin development.* Dublin: Tycooly, 239 pp.: pp. 40–61.

Widstrand, C. (ed.). 1980. *Water and society. II. Water conflicts and research priorities.* Oxford: Pergamon Press, 99 pp.

World Water. 1984a. Guerrilla attacks force contractor off Jonglei site. *World Water,* Liverpool, 7(3):8.

World Water. 1984b. Israel accused of stealing water. *World Water,* Liverpool, 7(11):7.

World Water. 1984c. Jordan considering 600 km water pipeline. *World Water,* Liverpool, 7(11):8.

World Water. 1984d. Powerhouse investigations bring Med-Dead scheme one step nearer. *World Water,* Liverpool, 7(4):12.

World Water. 1985a. Airships set to cut hydro costs, but will be too late to relieve African famine. *World Water,* Liverpool, 8(8):7.

World Water. 1985b. Egyptians braced for drought emergency. *World Water,* Liverpool, 8(4):6.

World Water. 1985c. Jonglei hostages released in Sudan. *World Water,* Liverpool, 8(1):10.

Zaman, M. 1983a. Ganges basin development: a long-term problem and some short-term options. In: Zaman, M. *et al.* (eds). *River basin development.* Dublin: Tycooly, 239 pp.: pp. 99–109.

Zaman, M. 1983b. Institutional and legal framework for co-operation between Bangladesh and India on shared water resources. In: Zaman, M. *et al.* (eds). *River basin development.* Dublin: Tycooly, 239 pp.: pp. 185–194.

6. Ocean fisheries as a factor in strategic policy and action

Susan B. Peterson and John M. Teal
Boston University and Woods Hole Oceanographic Institution

I. Introduction

Many conflicts of interest have arisen between coastal states and states with distant-water fleets over the right to harvest given species of fish or given waters for a variety of species. This chapter discusses not only conflicts of interest, but also armed conflicts and those diplomatic skirmishes that lie between a conflict of interest and an armed response to violations of fishing rights.

Discussed first are the distribution of the world's major fisheries, the factors that influence the relative richness or abundance of resources, and the physical and environmental constraints on harvesting those resources. Next described are the current fish harvest, species mix, and trends in demand for fish. Described after that are fishery conservation zones, 370 kilometre (200 nautical mile) limits, and exclusive economic zones, as well as recent changes in territorial and high-seas fishing regimes. This discussion includes the 1982 Law of the Sea Treaty, its system of dispute settlement, and enforcement systems and their costs. This is followed by examination of fishery-related disputes in the Indian Ocean and in the North Atlantic. Considered next are the high-seas and Antarctic fisheries. Comments regarding fishery disputes and likely sources of conflict in the coming decades conclude the chapter.

II. Marine fishery resources

The productivity of marine fisheries, ultimately determined by the overall production of the oceans, is generally controlled by the supply of nutrients to the sunlit surface waters. Production is high in areas where upwelling of nutrient-rich bottom waters occurs or in areas shallow enough for bottom waters to be mixed into the surface waters by winds, waves, or tides. Examples of the former are the west coasts of Africa and the Americas, the Antarctic divergence, and the northern part of the Indian Ocean. Examples of the latter include the rich banks of the north-west Atlantic, the shallow North Sea, and the Alaskan shelf areas. These are the regions that come closest to providing sustained, highly productive fisheries.

There are areas in which fish are plentiful even though productivity is low because slowly growing stocks can accumulate in the absence of fishing. Examples are deep-water and mid-water fishes of the open oceans. But once fishing begins, these areas will certainly exhibit a rapid decline in stocks. Mid-water stocks are dispersed within a large volume of water, and catching them is much more costly than catching the highly productive coastal stocks; this is also true for zooplankton, except for the Antarctic krill.

The simple and attractive notion that fish populations will come into balance with marine productivity on the one hand and fishing pressure on the other is flawed (Hennemuth, 1979). Experience demonstrates that such a balance is rarely achieved. Indeed, the stability of fisheries has decreased markedly as fishing activity has increased. Moreover, the total mortality rate—which is low in the absence of heavy fishing—increases in proportion to fishing effort. There is, therefore, some doubt that humans can be prudent predators, taking only what would otherwise die or what is produced as a result of fishing activities.

How much fish of all kinds can be taken from the world ocean on a sustained basis? Estimates based on reasoning about marine food chains and primary productivity result in values of about 200 million tonnes (fresh weight) per year (Ryther, 1969). But much of this biomass, when considered as individual species, has little or no market value or is very difficult to catch. Thus a more reasonable maximum total catch would be 75–100 million tonnes (Levinton, 1982, page 210; Robinson, 1982, page 3). This is an estimate of total catch, not of total potential harvest. Aquacultural (maricultural) techniques would permit the exploitation of some of the ocean's primary productivity not available to a purely capture-based fishery.

Marine fisheries are vulnerable to pollution, although some species are more readily affected than others. Anadromous species, which come into rivers to spawn and rear their young, estuarine species such as oysters and clams which cannot escape, and those species raised in coastal maricultural systems are the most vulnerable categories. Such pollutants as pesticides, municipal, agricultural or industrial wastes, oil, radioactive wastes, and heated water can be major obstacles to coastal fishing or mariculture. In Singapore, for example, the heavy use of chemical fertilizers in agriculture and the dumping of industrial wastes has had a serious effect on coastal fisheries (Chia, 1979). Pollutants can damage fish via direct toxicity, by killing their food species, by destroying their habitat, or by making them unpalatable (Ruddle, 1982).

III. World catch and consumption

The world catch of marine fishes was 68 million tonnes (fresh weight) in 1968 (table 6.1). This is close to the theoretical limit of the ability to catch the traditional fishery species (including krill) with the methods and expenditures of energy used at present. However, both the mix of species going into the harvest and the countries catching them have been changing dramatically in the past decade.

In considering the state of the fishery and stocks in the different fishing areas, it must be emphasized that many of the numbers reported are unreliable. This is particularly true for estimates of fishery potential. But, given this caveat, data indicate that stocks are being fished to the maximum, that is, with little potential for increase in yield, in the North and South Atlantic, Mediterranean, North Pacific, and Southern Oceans. There is significant overfishing in the western central Atlantic and concern that overfishing may soon occur on the Patagonian shelf of the South Atlantic. Many of the total annual catches recommended for the north-east Atlantic are substantially exceeded by the actual catch, with some herring stocks (*Clupea harengus*) overfished more than threefold (FAO, 1985).

On the brighter side, there is potential for increase in the demersal (bottom-dwelling) fish catch in the western central Atlantic. At present there is considerable waste from the discarding at sea of this resource by shrimp fishermen. There is some room for expansion in the squid catch in the southern parts of the western Pacific and for small pelagic (open-sea) species of finfish in the south-west Pacific. The largest unused potential lies in the western

Indian Ocean where 0.6 million tonnes of demersal fish and 0.7 million tonnes of pelagic fish were taken in 1981, whereas the estimated potentials were, respectively, 1.2 and 2.6 million tonnes, thereby suggesting the possibility of a threefold increase in stable yield. Most of this potential lies off Somalia, an area that has so far been harvested primarily by Romanian vessels (FAO, 1985, page 17). Overall, it is possible that another 20 to 30 million tonnes could be harvested world-wide, provided better management of the stocks were achieved (Robinson, 1982, page 2).

The two major fishing nations are Japan, with 16 per cent of the world catch, and the USSR, with 13 per cent (table 6.1). The two dozen or so developed nations together account for about half of the world catch (Infofish, 1985, page 25), a proportion that has decreased slightly in favour of the developing nations over the past decade. (It should be noted that when ocean fish catch is examined on a per-capita basis, Iceland stands far ahead of the other major fishing nations, as do—to a lesser extent—Norway, Denmark, and Chile.) The value of the world catch has continued to rise by about 3 per cent per year (even over years when the catch was relatively stable); shrimp remains the single most valuable commodity, followed by other crustaceans. The rise in fish caught for food has paralleled the rise in total catch, whereas that for fish-meal or oil has varied considerably, rising to a peak during the 1960s and falling since (Robinson, 1982, page 1).

Fish provides about 20 per cent of the world's total supply of animal protein in direct consumption, and, if the contribution of fish-meal to animal feed is included, then this value would be about 25 per cent (Loftas, 1981). Except for Iceland, Japan, Norway, Portugal, and Spain, fish is far more important in the diet of the developing world than in that of the developed world, although demand for fish is growing in both domains. Population growth is expected to account for more than half of the increase in demand, with the greatest growth, at 5 million tonnes per year, predicted for China, 2 million each for the USSR and Japan, 1 million for India, and several tenths of a million each for Indonesia, the USA, Brazil, and Nigeria (Loftas, 1981).

International trade in fish, now dominated by developed countries, is expected to change in favour of the developing world because those nations have access to and jurisdiction over large supplies of marine fish. The major fish importers at present are

Table 6.1. Ocean fish catches for selected countries, 1953–83[a]

Country[b]	Catch[c] (10^6 tonnes, fresh weight)			
	1953	1963	1973	1983
Canada	0.9	1.2	1.1	1.3
Chile	0.1	0.8	0.7	4.0
China	(1.9)	?	2.8	3.4
Denmark	0.5	1.0	1.7	2.3
Iceland	0.4	0.8	0.9	0.8
India	(0.8)	(1.0)	1.2	1.6
Indonesia	(0.6)	(0.9)	0.9	1.6
Japan	(4.6)	(6.7)	9.9	11.0
Korea, DPR	(0.1)	?	0.9	1.5
Korea, Rep.	(0.3)	(0.5)	1.5	2.4
Mexico	(0.1)	(0.2)	0.4	1.0
Norway	1.6	1.4	2.9	2.8
Peru	0.2	6.9	2.3	1.5
Philippines	(0.3)	(0.6)	1.1	1.3
Spain	0.6	1.1	1.6	1.2
Thailand	(0.2)	(0.4)	1.5	2.1
United Kingdom	1.1	1.0	1.1	0.8
USA	2.7	2.8	2.7	4.1
USSR	(2.0)	(4.0)	7.8	9.0
All others	—	—	12.9	13.9
Global total[d]	**18.9**	**36.3**	**55.9**	**67.6**

Sources and notes:

[a] Table prepared by A. H. Westing.

[b] The countries are all those whose ocean fish catch was one million tonnes (fresh weight) or more in at least one year during 1953–83. The values for Denmark include those for the Faeroe Islands and Greenland.

[c] The catch is the total ocean catch of finfish plus shellfish. However, the values in parentheses include the inland (freshwater) catch. The values for 1953 are from *FAO Yearbook of Fishery Statistics*, Rome, 24, tables A1 and A2–1 (1967); those for 1963 are from *ibid*. 26, tables A1 and A2–1 (1968); those for 1973 are from *ibid*. 54, table A–4 (1982); and those for 1983 are from *ibid*. 56, table A–4 (1983).

[d] The total global ocean catch increased in essentially a straight line during 1953–83, at the rate of 1.657 million tonnes (fresh weight) per year (on the basis of a linear least-squares regression analysis).

Japan, the USA, and the European Economic Community nations (see 'EEC' in the glossary for current membership). The major fish exporting nations number eight from the developed world and five from the developing world (Infofish, 1985, page 26).

Ocean fisheries are a renewable resource the potential of which can only be realized when the resource is properly managed. Examples of overfishing abound. Even when exclusive economic zones have been established, many countries have been unable to control either domestic or foreign fishing in order to maintain the fish stocks at reasonable levels. Thus, while demand for fish will continue to grow in the coming decades, the supply of marine fish from capture fisheries is likely to decline.

IV. The legal regime in ocean fisheries

The international law governing ocean fisheries has evolved over several centuries (Peterson, 1980). During that time, several principles have emerged, two of which have become dominant: (*a*) that there is freedom of the high seas, which carries with it the rights of navigation, overflight, laying of submarine cables, construction of artificial islands, scientific research, and fishing; and (*b*) that the oceans are part of the 'common heritage' of humankind, a concept which dominated the third and most recent United Nations Conference on the Law of the Sea (UNCLOS-III), during 1973–82.

It is the four treaties that emerged from the first United Nations Conference on the Law of the Sea, held in Geneva in 1958, that have provided the modern basis for codifying international ocean law (Oda, 1972, pages 3–26; UNEP, 1985, pages 33–38): (*a*) the Convention on the Territorial Sea and the Contiguous Zone (entry into force, 1964); (*b*) the Convention on the High Seas (entry into force, 1962); (*c*) the Convention on Fishing and Conservation of the Living Resources of the High Seas (entry into force, 1966); and (*d*) the Convention on the Continental Shelf (entry into force, 1964). They established, *inter alia*, that a coastal state has the unquestioned right to control the fish in its territorial sea; and, conversely, that no state is allowed to impose its jurisdiction upon any foreign vessel on the high seas.

The 1982 Law of the Sea Convention, the final product of UNCLOS-III, is to go into effect after 60 nations become parties (for excerpts from the text and potential parties, see appendix 6).

Although not in force, the convention has had the effect of codifying customary international law in relation to ocean fisheries. It has already led to altering the jurisdictions of coastal states by giving them a tacit right to claim exclusive economic zones to 370 kilometres from their coasts (appendix 6, articles 55–75) and has in large measure undermined the traditional dichotomy between the territorial seas and the high seas. In its exclusive economic zone, the coastal state would have 'sovereign rights for the purpose of exploring and exploiting, conserving and managing the natural resources' (article 56.1.a), including fishing, while other states would continue to enjoy such freedoms as navigation and overflight that they enjoy on or above the high seas.

Fishery disputes over access, allocation, management methods, or enforcement can now take place in three arenas—the high seas, the exclusive economic zones, and the territorial seas—each to be discussed in turn.

High-seas fishing

High-seas fishing, considered as one of the basic freedoms for many centuries, would become somewhat restricted by the 1982 Law of the Sea Convention (appendix 6, articles 87,116–20). On the high seas, fishing nations are supposed to co-operate in management, determine allowable catch, not discriminate against fishermen of other states, and conserve and manage marine mammals. Various international fishery commissions—for example, the International Commission for the Conservation of Atlantic Tuna, the International Whaling Commission, and the International Pacific Halibut Commission—were established to conserve and manage specific stocks of fish; commissions such as the Northwest Atlantic Fisheries Organization and the Indo-Pacific Fisheries Commission were designed as research and conservation organizations for living resources within a specific geographical area. Membership in international fishery commissions is voluntary, and management measures promulgated by them would not hold within exclusive economic zones. High-seas fisheries are discussed further below (section VI).

Exclusive economic zone fishing

The 1982 Law of the Sea Convention would have coastal states abide by new rules of fishery management. Each nation that claims an exclusive economic zone should determine the allowable catch in its zone as well as its capacity to harvest those fish; the country is to develop a management programme with the optimal use of fishery resources in mind, and then allow access by other countries to the surplus, including land-locked or otherwise geographically disadvantaged states. This system is based firmly on the principle that the oceans are the common heritage of humankind and that its benefits ought thus to be available to everyone.

Although the general sentiment following the establishment of exclusive economic zones has been to exclude all foreign harvesting from domestic waters, this may not be the most advantageous choice for developing nations in need of foreign exchange. A system of tariffs on foreign fishing might be the best tool to ensure optimal use and income from coastal resources (Chan, 1978; Munro, 1982). Thus the question from the point of view of the coastal state is whether or not such arrangements would be financially advantageous. But any arrangement with a distant-water nation must be tempered with a firm understanding of the condition of the resource; a short-term bilateral arrangement may result in long-term damage to fragile stocks.

To avoid overfishing, bilateral agreements which give foreign vessels access to fish within exclusive economic zones should include measures to ensure implementation and to enable dispute settlement. Under existing arrangements the foreign fleet is required to indicate the total number and names of vessels and their gross tonnage and/or horsepower. The fleet or individual vessels may be required to report catch on a weekly or monthly basis as well as to abide by closed seasons, gear restrictions, and minimum fish-size restrictions.

Coastal states may establish fees based on the amount or the value of fish caught, on the total tonnage of the vessels, or on the number of vessels (Carroz & Savini, 1979). Some fees are for days spent fishing, some vary according to where the catch is landed. There may be obligations to land some fish in the coastal country, to train local fishermen, or to buy fish from local fishermen if the offshore vessel has processing facilities. Under a 1976 agreement between Tunisia and Italy, Italy undertook to contribute a sum of money annually for implementation of fishery development projects in Tunisia. In a 1976 agreement between Senegal and Poland, Poland undertook to cover construction costs for a fishing wharf in Senegal.

A 1977 agreement between the European Economic Community and Sweden provided that if no settlement could be reached following consultations, or if it was claimed that a contracting party had manifestly failed to comply with a specified provision or condition established by the agreement, the dispute would become the subject of arbitration (Carroz & Savini, 1979). In 1976 a joint commission was established by Finland and the USSR to deal with claims for compensation for damage sustained by vessels and equipment while the fishing fleet of the USSR was fishing in Finnish waters. A 1976 agreement between Mexico and the USA provided that a specific number of US vessels, which had habitually fished in a defined area off the Pacific coast of Mexico, were authorized to continue their operations in accordance with past practice, it being understood that these vessels could not be replaced by others and that if they failed to fish during one year they would be disqualified from receiving further permits.

Permits to fish in exclusive economic zones have been used as political tools rather than as methods for allocating excess resources to distant-water fleets. For example, when the USSR entered Afghanistan in 1979, the USA *inter alia* severely curtailed the Soviet fish allocation in the US fishery zone (Cooper, 1980).

The ideal established by the proposed concept of fishery management that 'Thou shalt not waste fish' (Copes, 1981, page 218) is likely to be difficult to carry out. It will not be easy to implement the whole scheme—which requires the coastal state to determine the allowable catch for the purpose of conservation, its capacity to harvest the fishery resource, and its assignment of the surplus to other states—since marine biology is not sufficiently advanced and the 1982 Law of the Sea Convention not sufficiently precise. Thus, however ideal they may appear, the coastal state's obligations in its exclusive economic zone with respect to conservation and optimal use of fishery resources are sure to result in great difficulties when put into practice. Moreover, disputes are bound to occur if other states protest the failure of the coastal state to conserve living resources, its arbitrary refusal to determine the allowable catch, or its refusal to allocate the resources of its exclusive economic zone among interested states.

The 1982 Law of the Sea Convention provides a comprehensive system for dispute settlement (appendix 6, articles 279–99). The dispute settlement procedure could be distorted in ways that might jeopardize the economic or legal security of the coastal state, a coastal state not meeting the established obligations could be harassed by having to appear before international tribunals at considerable loss of time and money, and the machinery for dispute settlement that the Convention suggests may not only come up against practical difficulties, but could even fail to function properly owing to intrinsic flaws (Oda, 1983; Rosenne, 1979).

Enforcement in exclusive economic zones

Although UNCLOS-III debated ocean management problems for a decade to establish workable international arrangements for fishery and other ocean resources, the resulting treaty would provide only a framework for appropriate acts of national enabling legislation. Each country remains responsible for formulating a management and enforcement policy, based upon its legal system and fishing history.

All nations need to be concerned that attempts by a coastal state to enforce fishery regulations within its exclusive economic zone do not affect other freedoms, particularly the freedom of navigation. Enforcement can be a particular problem when a vessel claiming the right to pass through an exclusive zone is a fishing vessel. At the same time that the freedom of navigation is being protected, it is important to recognize that the coastal state must appear to have a strong enforcement capability if its fishery management measures are to work. The countries for whom the fishery resource is vitally important and which lack enforcement capability include most of the developing island states in the central and south-west Pacific and in the Indian Ocean, and also a number of west African coastal states (Burke, 1983). Thus there are trade-offs which must be considered between effective fishery-zone enforcement and freedom of navigation.

A number of measures have been considered for protecting fisheries within exclusive economic zones, among them (Burke, 1983): (*a*) application of territorial-sea restrictions to fishing vessels passing through; (*b*) prohibition of entry by unlicensed fishing vessels; (*c*) restriction of transiting fishing vessels to certain sea-lanes; (*d*) requiring the reporting of entry and exit, together with route used; (*e*) requiring the stowage of fishing gear during passage; (*f*) requiring the use of transponders during passage; and (*g*) requiring observers on board during passage. But most of these proposals would appear to be unworkable because they accommodate the interests of the coastal state at the expense of those of the international community as a whole. It has been suggested that only limited authority to affect navigation should be recognized, and then reserved to developing countries with special dependence on fisheries and little enforcement capability (Burke, 1983).

The impact of fishery enforcement and surveillance on other freedoms which are to exist within an exclusive economic zone have yet to be measured. Coastal states need to be concerned with the effects of pollution on their fisheries, and may try to enforce relevant fishery and other regulations, not only on vessels within the area, but also on vessels in neighbouring areas and on coastal facilities. Fishery enforcement vessels may also interfere with scientific research. Extension of the regime to control pollution or scientific research is likely to prompt protests from some major powers and might even lead to costly enforcement machinery and occasional physical conflict (Mtango & Weiss, 1984).

Although there is concern over the ability of developing nations to enforce fishery regulations associated with exclusive zones, most of the data on cost and use of enforcement come from the developed world. A number of coastal countries—especially the developing ones—have increased their fishery enforcement capability since the establishment of the exclusive economic zone concept. It should be noted that most enforcement effort is directed towards individual fishing vessels whose operators have violated regulations rather than towards a foreign government. Described here are enforcement systems used in Canada, the USA, and the United Kingdom.

Canada patrols some 6.6 million square kilometres of ocean on its east coast, employing both surface vessels and aircraft (Travis, 1978–1979). Eight offshore patrol vessels carry out 68 per cent of the surface work, ships of the armed forces do 20 per cent, and Ministry of Transport ships do the remaining 12 per cent. All airborne observations are made by the armed forces, each of which is linked by computer to a system that provides details about each fishing vessel that should be in the area.

In the USA, fishery enforcement is carried out by the Coast Guard working with enforcement officers from the National Marine Fisheries Service; however, none of the patrols operates solely to enforce fishery laws (Hoagland, 1985). It has been estimated that the cost of fishery enforcement by the USA amounts to somewhat more than 20 per cent of the worth of the nation's fishery (Sutinen & Hennessey, 1984, page 33).

Not all fishery violations are clear-cut, and many jurisdictional issues continue to be worked out. In one recent instance, a Japanese fishing vessel, which had been fishing without permission in the US fishery zone, was pursued by the US Coast Guard onto the high seas and arrested there (Mtango & Weiss, 1984, page 26). A US court supported the Coast Guard action, holding that article 24 of the 1958 Geneva Convention on the Territorial Sea and the Contiguous Zone (Oda, 1972, pages 3–8), to which both the USA and Japan were parties, permitted the USA to establish a contiguous zone for fishery purposes from which hot pursuit could commence.

The United Kingdom has a long history of concern over enforcement of its coastal fishery zone. Enforcement services also play an important role in gathering fishery information, including catch rates, seasonal variations, and concentrations of fishing effort by vessels of different countries. It is the Fishery Protection Squadron of the British Navy that provides the protection for fishery endeavours in the waters of the United Kingdom. The Squadron has 10 to 12 ships on patrol at any one time, of which about half are under separate Scottish control (Munro, 1984, page 49). Aerial surveillance by the government amounts to some 160 hours per month, and additional aerial partrolling of inshore areas is carried out via private contracting. As in the case of the USA, the United Kingdom undertakes hot pursuit onto the high seas of ships violating its exclusive fishery zone, although it does not pursue them into a foreign fishing zone, perhaps because of its reliance on naval rather than civilian vessels for enforcement (Mtango & Weiss, 1984).

Artisanal fisheries pose special enforcement problems for coastal states. In many cases, small fishing boats lack navigational equipment and therefore may not know whether they have entered a neighbouring nation's exclusive economic zone. Perhaps bilateral agreements should be sought among bordering states in which the accidental presence of small fishing vessels of either country is not regarded as constituting a violation of the sea boundary (Mtango & Weiss, 1984). The 1975 agreement between Kenya and Tanzania to recognize a common fishing zone that extends to 22 kilometres on either side of the sea boundary provides an example.

In the Persian Gulf, fishery management and enforcement are relatively unimportant to the coastal nations (Amin, 1983). This is the case owing to: (*a*) an abundance of offshore fishing resources; (*b*) the primitive fishing methods and ships employed, which do not often venture beyond territorial waters; and (*c*) a disinclination or inability to claim authority under international law to regulate or enforce fishing rights beyond the territorial seas.

As the value of coastal fisheries rises, one can expect to see greater interest among all coastal nations in fishery management and enforcement and an even greater diversity in surveillance methods, enforcement procedures, and types of sanction devised for violation of fishery regulations.

Territorial seas

In territorial seas, all of the freedoms attributed to the high seas are denied. Fishery disputes arise in territorial seas, sometimes when boundaries have not yet been negotiated between neighbouring states and at other times when countries claim territorial seas beyond the generally accepted 22 kilometre zone. Many countries do not recognize extended territorial sea claims, but do not choose to challenge them. The USA does not recognize territorial sea claims beyond 22 kilometres (some of which extend out to 370 kilometres), and counters them by traversing the area, claiming freedom of navigation or overflight. Such action has led to military conflict. In 1981, the US Navy shot down two Libyan military aircraft in a skirmish over the Gulf of Sidra, an area over which the USA claims freedom of overflight to exist (Gao, 1984; Weinberger & Gast, 1981).

In 1973, Tanzania extended its territorial waters to 93 kilometres (Iceland in 1972 having claimed a fishery zone of that size) and announced that this was needed to keep foreign fishing vessels away. In retrospect, it appears that Tanzania was concerned more about security than about fishery resources, at a time when its new government was consolidating its power (Mtango & Weiss, 1984).

When the 370 kilometre economic zone of the Democratic People's Republic of Korea (North Korea) came into force in 1977, a 93 kilometre military zone was also proclaimed in order 'to reliably safeguard the economic sea zone and firmly defend the national interests and sovereignty of the country' (Park, 1978, page 866). Japan protested immediately because the action defied recognized international law and also because it was concerned about whether or not Japanese fishermen would be allowed to continue fishing within the military boundary. At the time, Japanese fishermen were catching 80 thousand tonnes per year of fish in the waters around North Korea (Park, 1978). A provisional agreement was reached between Japan and North Korea in 1977 allowing the Japanese to fish inside the 370 kilometre zone, but not inside the 93 kilometre zone. This angered the republic of Korea (South Korea), which felt that the Japanese action had given substance to the North Korean claim to a 93 kilometre military zone.

Thus it appears that accidental intrusion by a fishing vessel into an exclusive economic zone could be viewed not only as a threat to coastal resources, but also as an invasion of territory, to be warded off by a military presence rather than a fishing patrol.

V. Fishery disputes

There exist multilateral and bilateral agreements, international commissions, joint ventures, and licensing arrangements, all of which have evolved to clarify the rules over the catching, processing, transporting, and selling of fish. As fish have grown in economic importance, these accommodations have become more complex, more contentious, and more difficult to reach. In several regions conflict over fishing is endemic; in other areas, one can foresee the potential for conflict as fishing pressure increases. In this section, information is presented on fishery disputes and accommodations in the Indian Ocean and the North Atlantic.

The Indian Ocean fisheries

The Indian Ocean fisheries are now underexploited; indeed, the present fish catch appears to be one-third of the potential catch

(Cheng *et al.*, 1984; Devaraj, 1982). Estimates of potential catch for the Indian Ocean range from 10 to 17 million tonnes (fresh weight) per year, while the actual recent yield has been about 4 million tonnes. India has an exclusive economic zone of 2 million square kilometres having an estimated potential yield of 4.5 million tonnes per year (Sarkar, 1984), yet harvested only 1.6 million tonnes in 1983 (table 6.1). By the end of this century, the population of those 34 nations bordering the Indian Ocean should reach 2000 million, thereby closing the gap between the demand and the potential (Devaraj, 1982).

Some of the 34 countries which border the Indian Ocean, for example, India and Thailand, have substantial commercial fishing industries (see table 6.1), but many of the others today have only artisanal fisheries. Among the non-coastal nations that fish in those waters are Japan, South Korea, the USSR, the German Democratic Republic, and Spain. The growth of the catch in Indian Ocean fisheries varied from nation to nation during the 1970s (Devaraj, 1982). Whereas these non-Indian Ocean countries collectively accounted for 29 per cent of the annual growth, the significant contributors were Iraq (7 per cent), South Africa (6 per cent), Bahrain and Yemen (5 per cent each), and India, Thailand, Qatar, and Tanzania (4 per cent each).

Foreign fishing is possible in the Indian Ocean for several reasons. Some outside countries have bilateral agreements with coastal countries which allow specified levels of fishing in exchange for fees, fish, or technology transfer; many Indian Ocean nations have not yet adopted exclusive economic zones (in 1982, only 14 out of 34 had done so), and thus distant-water fleets may fish without permission within 370 kilometres of the coast; and there is a fishery outside the 370 kilometre zones.

Pressures upon the Indian Ocean fishery increase each year as distant-water fleets, displaced from newly established exclusive economic zones (mostly those of other developed nations) make bargains with coastal nations in underexploited areas. But increased fishing effort comes not only from industrial or mechanized fisheries, but also from the artisanal fishing fleets of the Indian Ocean nations. Small boats, often powered by sail, which fish within 20 or 30 kilometres of the coast are capable of overfishing, and are more difficult to regulate than the large, offshore, easily visible foreign fleets.

One of the underexploited fisheries in the Indian Ocean is the tuna (*Thunnus*) fishery. The potential fishery is for skipjack (*Katsuwonus pelamis*) around the island groups; and for yellowfin (*T. albacares*), bigeye (*T.obesus*), southern bluefin tuna (*T. maccoyii*), and albacore (*T. alalunga*) on the high seas. Most of the existing fishing is carried out by Japan, Taiwan, and South Korea. Management of the tuna stocks would call for active co-operation between the nations whose fleets operate in the Indian Ocean and those Indian-Ocean nations in whose waters the tunas spend part of their lives (Devaraj, 1982). More important among the coastal states are Australia (with the breeding and nursery ground of southern bluefin and yellowfin tunas being located in Australian waters), India (with the fishing grounds for adult yellowfin and bigeye tunas overlapping India's exclusive economic zone), and Mauritius and Tanzania (with adult yellowfin migrating annually to east African waters).

There are two international organizations which could help in managing Indian-Ocean fisheries, both within and outside the exclusive economic zones: the Indian Ocean Fishery Commission and the Indo-Pacific Fisheries Council. Both of these agencies do research, but neither has powers over allocation or enforcement.

Even within their exclusive economic zones, many nations have difficulty in managing the resources. In India, where there is no centrally planned fishery development programme, foreign-owned vessels are inadequately supervised. This has provoked a growing spate of protests, at times violent, by local fishermen. India exports a large amount of fish, mostly prawns and lobster, amounting in 1984 to about 3 per cent of the world value of exported fish products (Infofish, 1985, pages 25–26). But because fish is not an important dietary component in India (annual per capita consumption being 3.7 kilograms [fresh weight] whereas that of the rest of the region ranges from 20 to 40 kilograms), India has not established a detailed fishery policy nor developed a strong enforcement capability.

Illegal fishing by foreign fishing boats is rampant in Indonesia's vast exclusive economic zone (Awanohara, 1984). In recent times, about 50 fishing boats have been caught fishing illegally each year, and this does not include those boats which pay their way to freedom. But the recent completion of a naval base on Aru Island in the Moluccas has reduced infringements.

Eighty per cent of Thailand's fish come from outside its own exclusive economic zone, from the waters of India; Bangladesh, China, Burma, Viet Nam, and Malaysia; many of these fisheries are exploited without formal agreements with the other states (Sheldon, 1984). Thailand is forced to seek non-indigenous fishing grounds for several reasons. First, in the past decade Thailand's coastal waters have been polluted by effluent into the inner gulf. Second, the coastal fishery has been depleted by large numbers of trawlers, built to replace the 'inefficient' artisanal fleet. Third, former traditional fishing areas were lost when the neighbouring countries expanded their fishing zones; the recent new division of the region into various exclusive economic zones has resulted in a loss to Thailand of an estimated 900 thousand square kilometres of fishing ground, equivalent to a catch of perhaps 0.5 million tonnes per year, the total Thai ocean catch for 1983 having been roughly 2.1 million tonnes (table 6.1). The loss of fishing grounds has pushed Thai fishermen to fish in the exclusive economic zones of other nations, resulting in arrests and detainment. In 1983, there were approximately 1000 Thai fishermen held in Vietnamese or Burmese jails for illegal fishing.

In some areas near the Thai border with Malaysia on both the west and east coasts, violence between Thai-crewed trawlers and local Malaysian fishermen has become endemic; trawlers (that one Malaysian fishery adviser described as Thai vacuum cleaners) seldom obey Malaysian laws designed to keep them well offshore (Clad, 1984).

Burma has extensive offshore fisheries within its exclusive economic zone; the attractiveness of these fisheries became clear in the 1960s when a large number of Thai and Taiwanese fishermen started fishing there (Tun, 1984). Now that the fishery resources within its own exclusive economic zone are claimed by Burma, government policy is evolving for management and enforcement. The general feeling in Burma is that a well-developed marine fishing industry is needed in order to keep out foreign poachers and to provide fish for domestic use. Even with rapid growth in the domestic fleet, Burma currently uses only an estimated 10 per cent of the fish resource within its exclusive economic zone. In 1983 Burmese naval patrols captured 59 Thai boats plus 512 Thais.

Seventeen foreign trawlers operated in Pakistani waters in 1983 and a number of them have been charged with violating terms of joint ventures by fishing inside the 65 kilometre wide coastal belt which is reserved exclusively for Pakistani fishermen (Aftab, 1984). It has also been alleged that they were fishing for shrimp rather than the fish for which they had been licensed.

Foreign fishermen in Australian waters have to abide by strict regulations on gear and location (Rees, 1984). Most must report their position every two days and their catch by weight and species; they must keep log books, allow observers on board at any time, and be inspected at the beginning and end of a trip. Even with a fairly rigorous enforcement programme, the Australians have had trouble with unauthorized Taiwanese fishing vessels coming in to harvest giant clams from the Great Barrier Reef.

The North Atlantic fisheries

The fishery resources of the North Atlantic have both economic and strategic significance. The natural resources are not only fish, but also oil and gas, and all of these have grown in value over the past decade. The evolution of exclusive economic zones has taken a considerable proportion of these resources out of the high seas into coastal state control.

At the beginning of the 1970s, fishing disputes in Iceland were the most politically sensitive in the region. For many years, Iceland resisted the intrusion of foreign fishing vessels into coastal waters, claiming ever-larger exclusive fishing zones in order to protect its fragile economy. British fishing vessels, pressured by declining stocks in the north-east Atlantic and accustomed to a traditional fishery near Iceland, continued to fish despite Iceland's claims, first for a 93 kilometre fishery zone (in 1972) and then for one of 370 kilometres (in 1975).

Iceland's responses to fishing by the United Kingdom were several (Mitchell, 1976). It developed a bilateral agreement with the USSR, which was perceived as a threat to NATO. The USA had a military base at Keflavik which Iceland threatened to expel if the United Kingdom continued to fish in Iceland's waters. It also reacted aggressively at sea by cutting the British trawlers' wires, causing them to lose their fishing gear. This last action resulted in the arrival of the British Navy, leading to the so-called Anglo-Icelandic Clash (or 'Cod' War) of 1972–73 (see appendix 2, war 9). Both the United Kingdom Trawlers' Association and Iceland hired public relations firms to help them present their cases to the world press.

Although a diplomatic solution to this argument could eventually be reached, the dispute had far-reaching strategic implications (Archer & Scrivener, 1982–1983). Subsequently Iceland developed bilateral fishing arrangements with the United Kingdom (as well as with Norway and Belgium) to allow limited fishing on a seasonal basis. In its threat to expel the US military base if the United Kingdom would not capitulate in the Cod War, Iceland was prepared to link resource and security issues. The conflict also demonstrated the potential danger from resource wrangles to maintaining good relations among the NATO allies themselves.

Jan Mayen (71°N,09°W) has substantial fisheries in surrounding waters for herring, blue whiting (*Gadus poutassou*), and capelin (*Mallotus villosus*). The island was annexed by Norway in 1929, but had no permanent population (which is needed by an island in order to claim an exclusive economic zone) until 1959, when military navigation facilities were established and people stationed there the year round. In 1980 Norway declared a 370 kilometre exclusive economic zone around Jan Mayen (Archer & Scrivener, 1982–1983). Denmark and Iceland questioned whether the island should have such a zone, or whether it should be defined as a skerry with no such right. However, neither Denmark nor Iceland has pressed the case.

The unresolved political problems in devising a solution to the Jan Mayen dispute have had repercussions within the nations involved. In Norway, fishermen's votes are highly valued, and accommodations satisfactory to the fishing industry influence governmental stability, as is also the case in Iceland, where the government is not able to accept second-best solutions on fishery issues because of the economic importance of the fish harvest and export to the nation.

When Denmark claimed a 370 kilometre fishing zone around its island of Greenland, Iceland contested the delineation between its zone and this one (Archer & Scrivener, 1982–1983). Although Danish patrol vessels were dispatched to the contested zone, no contact occurred between the two parties. A conciliation commission was established in time and the dispute resolved.

In the Barents Sea, most of the problems are between Norway and the USSR, and stem from an as yet unresolved boundary on the shelf (Archer & Scrivener, 1982–1983). Thus far, fishery allocations have been resolved by having two defined exclusive economic zones with a grey zone between them. Whereas total catches and quotas are to be agreed upon by a Norwegian-Soviet fishery commission, each state is to maintain jurisdiction over its own vessels and those of third countries licensed by it.

The Svalbard archipelago lies in a militarily strategic place 'under the flight-paths of US and Soviet ICBMs and long-range bombers' (Archer & Scrivener, 1982–1983, page 73). The 1920 Spitsbergen Treaty gave virtual sovereignty over Svalbard to Norway, but provided all of the parties to the treaty with equal rights to economic activity on the islands and their territorial waters (see appendix 3). The major problem is the scope of Norwegian authority over the Svalbard islands and the jurisdictional delimitation in the waters around them. However, it appears that Norwegian exercise of sovereignty could accommodate Soviet security concerns by effectively controlling the form and intensity of any future offshore activity by other states (Archer & Scrivener, 1982–1983).

Whereas Norway has not renounced the provisions of the 1920 Spitsbergen Treaty that permits parties to mine and fish on the islands and in their territorial waters (at that time a zone out to 7 and now to 22 kilometres), it has recently claimed a 370 kilometre fishing zone that additionally reaches without interruption to the North Pole and *inter alia* includes the Svalbard archipelago. The NATO powers have neither agreed to nor rejected this claim, whereas the USSR has objected to it. In a compromise reached in 1983 between the USSR and Norway, the USSR allows its fishing vessels within the zone to be boarded, but does not report its catches to Norway.

VI. Some areas of potential dispute

Demand for fish is expected to rise to between 113 and 125 million tonnes (fresh weight) per year by 2000, thereby substantially exceeding the sustainable harvest of 75–100 million tonnes (Robinson, 1982). The world catch of marine fishes has increased quite steadily over the past 30 years, at the rate of 1.7 million tonnes (fresh weight) per year (table 6.1), but it is obvious that this rate cannot be sustained.

The fish catches by developing nations are predominantly from within their own or neighbouring exlusive economic zones, whereas those by developed nations often depend upon distant-water fleets fishing in the exclusive economic zones of other states. There has been a downward trend in catches by distant-water fleets in recent years, but the decline has been greater in the exclusive economic zones of the developed countries than in those of the developing world. For example, 52 per cent of the catch in the north-west Atlantic fishery (off the coast of developed nations) in the early 1970s was by distant-water fleets, but only 9 per cent in the early 1980s (FAO, 1985, page 39). By contrast, 63 per cent of the catch in the east-central Atlantic fishery (off the coast of developing nations) was by distant-water fleets in the earlier period as compared with 51 per cent in the latter.

Although the absolute catch of coastal nations in the developing world (as illustrated by those of west Africa) has grown substantially since 1970, that of the distant-water fleets has grown even more (Kaczynski, 1979). The distant-water fleets have moved in large measure from the exclusive economic zones of the developed nations to those of developing nations, which are likely to lack the technical or financial resources for proper management and enforcement within their zones.

The proportion of the world fish catch that comes from the high seas—that is, from outside all of the world's 370 kilometre exclusive economic zones—falls between 1 and 15 per cent (Copes, 1981), but the high-seas stocks are not necessarily separate from those in the exclusive economic zones. Political boundaries rarely conform to ecological divisions, with the result that many fish stocks are at the mercy of several management regimes, that is, those of exclusive economic zones of various individual coastal states as well as those of international fishery commissions. On the high seas, conditions of near-anarchy often prevail.

As developing nations improve their ability to harvest, manage, and enforce the regulations for their exclusive economic zones, it is likely that they will be less willing to accommodate distant-water fishing fleet requests for access to coastal stocks. Whereas multilateral, bilateral, or joint-venture arrangements are certain to continue for many exclusive economic zone fisheries, distant-water fleet managers must consider alternative fishing grounds to exploit—the high seas or Antarctic Ocean—or else discontinue their distant-water efforts.

South Korea's distant-water fleet (developed with substantial help from the USA during the late 1950s and 1960s) at one time contributed substantially to that state's annual harvest (Ensor, 1984). Only 29 per cent of the value of the ocean fish catch now comes from the offshore fleet, while 71 per cent is from the inshore fleet. Heavy fishing has depleted the inshore stocks, so that South Korean boats have been venturing into neighbouring exclusive economic zones. Some of these have been captured by North Korean patrol boats, and minor disputes with Japan are a continuing problem.

Of South Korea's total current fish export, over 60 per cent goes to Japan and another 25 per cent to the USA (Infofish, 1985, page 26). Its distant-water fleet fishes off Alaska (which accounts for 50 per cent of the distant-water catch), off north-western Africa (where the concentration is on octopus and squid), and off Suriname and Brazil (where the concentration is on shrimp). But because South Korea is now restricted from many areas in which it formerly fished, the number of distant-water vessels has dropped from 878 in 1976 to 646 in 1983. Moreover, South Korea must now pay high fees to fish in the exclusive economic zones of other countries and be satisfied with lower quotas than were common in the mid-1970s. This turn of events is driving small South Korean firms out of business and is forcing the government to support some of the large firms with special programmes. France, FR Germany, Japan, Portugal, and Spain have all reduced the number and tonnage of vessels in their distant-water fleets (Kaczynski, 1984, page 27).

But other distant-water fleets have expanded—those of Cuba, the German Democratic Republic, Poland, Romania, and the USSR—and have made a number of accommodations to the new exclusive economic zone regime. These nations have developed bilateral relationships with both developing and developed nations which have fish stocks that are not being exploited, have expanded their high-seas fisheries, and have begun to exploit stocks off Antarctica.

There exists a clear need to expand high-seas fishery management. In the past, the high seas were to some extent monitored by international fishery commissions, but management concerns were largely ignored. This need was recognized during UNCLOS-III, but as yet no effective system of management or enforcement has been established.

For decades the area off the east coasts of Canada and the USA were studied and monitored under the auspices of the International Commission for Northwest Atlantic Fisheries. With the advent of 370 kilometre fishing zones, this Commission lapsed and was replaced by the Northwest Atlantic Fisheries Organization (in Dartmouth, Nova Scotia), with more than 20 member states (but not including the USA). The Organization's fishery management interests lie in those fisheries harvested outside of the exclusive economic zones (Surrette, 1981–1982). The member states allow observers on board one another's fishing boats, but surveillance and enforcement are weak. On the other hand, surveillance by Canada within its 370 kilometre north Atlantic zone makes use of both civil and military patrol boats and aircraft.

One must anticipate that high-seas fisheries will continue to be over-exploited because international commissions lack fishery enforcement capability, because nations in need of fish are unlikely to conserve these common-property resources, and because the competition for the resources is among a very small number of countries (those needing fish protein and possessing the technological and financial resources to fish in very deep water) and thus attracts little international attention.

Antarctic fisheries

The commercial fishery for whales dominated the Antarctic fishery until this decade. It has suffered from serious over-exploitation for almost half a century (McElroy, 1984). Pelagic whaling was the most profitable Antarctic fishery and has the potential to regain this status with prudent management.

It is estimated that Antarctic finfish could sustain a fishery of up to 0.2 million tonnes (fresh weight) per year (McElroy, 1984). In recent years 80 per cent of the finfishing and 90 per cent of the krill fishing has been carried out by vessels from the USSR. Most of the krill is used for high-protein feed supplements for the pig and poultry industries in the USSR. Japan, which catches 9 per cent of the krill harvested, uses it for meal, for bait used in game fishing, and, in small amounts, for feed for cultivated fish. When these fisheries began, the vessels had been displaced from their traditional distant-water fishing grounds by the nearly universal establishment of exclusive economic zones.

Neither the Japanese nor Soviet fishing operations in Antarctic waters appear to be cost-effective when subjected to rigorous economic analysis, even when the capital savings which had been achieved by the use of existing ships is included (McElroy, 1984). In this regard, it is of interest to note that the Soviet krill catch has recently been declining (FAO, 1985).

The 1980 Convention on the Conservation of Antarctic Marine Living Resources has been in force since 1982 (UNEP, 1985, pages 174–75). It provides the forum for discussion of disputes, but the problems of land-based fishing operations override strict fishery management questions and also intrude on territorial claims (Frank, 1983). The Convention, in accommodating to various national political and economic interests, provides several loopholes in the key areas of voting, data collection, and non-party participation. Moreover, in seeking to perpetuate the regime of the 1959 Antarctic Treaty, it maintains the *status quo* regarding Antarctic territorial claims.

It would be most economical to establish fishing bases in Antarctica. There are many problems associated with this, not least the disputed claims over sectors of the continent. Another serious problem is the need to consider trade-offs already being made between whales and krill (Frank, 1983). Today management is on a species-by-species basis without regard for effects on the ecosystem; and with a fishery exploited by a diversity of nations this approach can lead to disaster. Each nation can take its own management approach without regard to a potential response from the total system, for example, the USSR practising heavy whaling while Japan is concentrating on krill.

VII. Conclusion

Solutions to the thorny problems of fishery management and enforcement under the new exclusive economic zone regime can come from several directions. Iceland attempted to protect its fishery through the use of public relations experts, and the diplomatic compromises by Tanzania attempted to protect that nation's fishery by establishing a common fishing zone with a neighbour. And various licensing, monitoring, and enforcement systems can be established based on biologically and economically rational allocations of resources.

Despite all of the difficulties associated with exclusive economic zone fisheries, the negotiated accommodations which have been reached in the heavily exploited North Atlantic provide hope that similar diplomatic efforts could resolve the disputes in an under-exploited fishery such as the Indian Ocean. Indeed, the Regional Seas—recently renamed Oceans and Coastal—Programme of the United Nations Environment Programme has for the past decade been serving to defuse conflicts over ocean resources in a growing number of ocean areas. To date, the programme has led to various regional conferences, action plans, and draft treaties; and to the consummation of three regional treaties that deal with pollution control (UNEP, 1985, pages 133, 157, 182): (*a*) a Mediterranean Sea Convention (signed at Barcelona in 1976; entry into force, 1978); (*b*) a Persian Gulf Convention (signed at Kuwait in 1978; entry into force, 1979); and (*c*) a West-African South-Atlantic Convention (signed at Abidjan in 1981; entry into force, 1984). But successful accommodations for high-seas and Antarctic fisheries are less likely for a number of reasons: (*a*) because these fisheries are less well understood than coastal fisheries; (*b*) because international sanctions against overfishing are rarely enforced; (*c*) because these fisheries are not under the territorial jurisdiction of any nation; and (*d*) because of possible future mutually exclusive claims on the resources.

Conflict can also arise over competing claims on whales versus krill or seals versus capelin. In the Antarctic region, the decrease in whales resulting from intensive harvesting may have led to an increase in krill, as indicated by an increase in populations of other krill predators, especially the crab-eater seal (*Lobodon carcinophagus*). It is possible that the direct harvesting of krill in large amounts could slow or prevent full recovery of whale populations. In the north-west Atlantic, public protest has led to a reduced harvest of harp seal (*Pagophilus groenlandicus*) pups and to reduced killing of grey seals (*Halichoerus grypus*). As a result, Canadian fishermen now claim that seals are severely diminishing their catches. Some may consider that insufficient concern is being given to the need of marine mammals for food to sustain or restore their population levels, whereas others claim that insufficient consideration is being given to the plight of commercial fishermen.

Pollution can certainly lead to conflict, especially in a world in which it is attempted to fully exploit the fishing resource. Most of the ocean pollution problems of today which are severe enough to inhibit fishing are confined to territorial seas or even to estuaries and bays. Coastal pollution represents more of a potential problem to aquacultural production of molluscs which, being filter feeders and fixed in one spot, accumulate pollutants to a greater extent than many finfishes. Instances in which international pollution has or could have effects on fisheries include the spread of anoxic conditions inimical to fish and the fear that some long-lasting halogenated organic compounds or radioactive substances could pollute fishing grounds other than those of the dumping country itself. For example, radioactive wastes discharged by the United Kingdom are detectable in the waters of nations on the eastern side of the North Sea.

Incursions by fishing boats into the fishery zones of other nations will continue to occur, and such trespassers will continue to be pursued and arrested. On the other hand, the customary law that has developed regarding exclusive economic zones makes armed conflict between states over fisheries unlikely in the future. Thus, exploitation of these common-property resources is more likely to lead to a scramble to harvest what remains—and thereby lead to commercial exhaustion of the fish stocks—than to armed conflict.

Technological advances will reduce the incidence of disputes over fishing resources to the extent that they increase the effective harvest through more efficient harvesting, through reductions in post-harvest losses, through more nearly complete utilization, and so forth. Technological advances will also reduce disputes through improved maricultural techniques. Indeed, any major increases in the production of protein marine sources will have to come from mariculture, an endeavour which is, however, particularly vulnerable to damage from pollution. The discharge of pollutants into coastal waters could therefore give rise to disputes in the future, although technological advances will be able to mitigate these sources of dispute as well.

In the last analysis, however, long-term security with respect to ocean resources cannot rely on technological advances. Only an accommodation to the magnitude of the fishery resource, based on sound stock assessments translated into equitable international agreements on allocations, can accomplish this.

References

Aftab, M. 1984. Pakistan: tightening up on poachers. *Far Eastern Economic Review,* Hongkong, 125(31):57–59.

Amin, S. H. 1983. Law of fisheries in the Persian/Arabian Gulf. *Journal of Maritime Law & Commerce,* Washington, 14:581–593.

Archer, C. & Scrivener, D. 1982–1983. Frozen frontiers and resource wrangles: conflict and cooperation in northern waters. *International Affairs,* London, 59:59–76.

Awanohara, S. 1984. Indonesia: there's room enough for trade and modern methods. *Far Eastern Economic Review,* Hongkong, 125(31):43–44,49.

Burke, W. T. 1983. Exclusive fisheries zones and freedom of navigation. *San Diego Law Review,* San Diego, Calif., 20:595–623.

Carroz, J. E. & Savini, M. J. 1979. New international law of fisheries emerging from bilateral agreements. *Marine Policy,* Guildford, UK, 3:79–98.

Chan, K.S.-Y. 1978. Economic consequences of the 200-mile seabed zone: the replenishable resources case. *Canadian Journal of Economics,* Toronto, 11:314–318.

Cheng, E. *et al.* 1984. Fishing in Asia. *Far Eastern Economic Review,* Hongkong, 125(31):35–44,49–60.

Chia, L. S. 1979. Coastal changes, marine pollution and the fishing industry in Singapore. In: Librero, A. R. & Collier, W. L. (eds). *Economics of aquaculture, sea-fishing, and coastal resource use in Asia.* Los Banos: Philippine Council for Agriculture & Resources Research, 384 pp.: pp. 333–344.

Clad, J. 1984. Malaysia: the reality of poverty is grim. *Far Eastern Economic Review,* Hongkong, 125(31):50–53.

Cooper, R. N. 1980. Export restrictions on the U.S.S.R. *Department of State Bulletin,* Washington, 80(2043):45–47.

Copes, P. 1981. Impact of UNCLOS III on management of the world's fisheries. *Marine Policy,* Guildford, UK, 5:217–228.

Devaraj, M. 1982. Critique of Indian Ocean fisheries development. *Ocean Management,* Amsterdam, 8:97–123.

Ensor, P. 1984. South Korea: deep-sea waters are getting murkier. *Far Eastern Economic Review,* Hongkong, 125(31):38–40.

FAO. 1985. *Review of the state of world fishery resources.* 4th rev. Rome: Food & Agriculture Organization of the United Nations, Fisheries Circular No. 710, 61 pp.

Frank, R. F. 1983. Convention on the conservation of Antarctic marine living resources. *Ocean Development & International Law,* New York, 13:291–333.

Gao Changyun, 1984. Territorial dispute handled wrong: United States. *Beijing Review,* Beijing, 27(33):12–13.

Hennemuth, R. C. 1979. Marine fisheries: food for the future? *Oceanus,* Woods Hole, Mass., 22(1):2–12.

Hoagland, P. 1985. Role of the U.S. Coast Guard. *Oceanus,* Woods Hole, Mass., 28(2):67–73.

Infofish. 1985. Marketing digest. *Infofish,* Kuala Lumpur, 1985(3):1–53.

Kaczynski, W. 1979. Problems of long-range fisheries. *Oceanus,* Woods Hole, Mass., 22(1):60–66.

Kaczynski, W. 1984. *Distant water fisheries and the 200 mile economic zone.* Honolulu: Law of the Sea Institute, Occasional Paper No. 34, 50 pp.

Levinton, J. S. 1982. *Marine ecology,* Englewood Cliffs, New Jersey: Prentice-Hall, 526 pp.

Loftas, T. 1981. FAO's EEZ programme. *Marine Policy,* Guildford, UK, 5:229–239.

McElroy, J. K. 1984. Antarctic fisheries: history and prospects. *Marine Policy,* Guildford, UK, 8:239–258.

Mitchell, B. 1976. Politics, fish, and international resource management: the British-Icelandic cod war. *Geographical Review,* New York, 66:127–138.

Mtango, E. E. E. & Weiss, F. 1984. Exclusive economic zone and Tanzania: considerations of a developing country. *Ocean Development & International Law,* New York, 14:1–47.

Munro, G. N. 1984. Fisheries enforcement: the United Kingdom experience. In: OECD (ed.). *Experiences in the management of national fishing zones.* Paris: Organisation for Economic Co-operation and Development, 159 pp.: pp. 39–51.

Munro, G. R. 1982. Fisheries, extended jurisdiction and the economics of common property resources. *Canadian Journal of Economics,* Toronto, 15:405–425.

Oda, S. 1972. *International law of the ocean development: basic documents.* Leiden: Sijthoff, 519 pp.

Oda, S. 1983. Fisheries under the United Nations Convention on the Law of the Sea. *American Journal of International Law,* New York, 77:739–755.

Park, C.-H. 1978. 50-mile military boundary zone of North Korea. *American Journal of International Law,* New York, 72:866–875.

Peterson, S. [B.] 1980. Common heritage of mankind?: regulating the uses of the oceans. *Environment,* Washington, 22(1):6–11.

Rees, J. 1984. Australia: small industry, big contribution. *Far Eastern Economic Review,* Hongkong, 125(31):58–59.

Robinson, M. A. 1982. *Prospects for world fisheries to 2000.* 1st rev. Rome:

Food & Agriculture Organization of the United Nations, Fisheries Circular No. 722, 16 pp.

Rosenne, S. 1979. Settlement of fisheries disputes in the exclusive economic zone. *American Journal of International Law,* New York, 73:89–104.

Ruddle, K. 1982. Environmental pollution and fishery resources in Southeast Asian coastal waters. In: Soysa, C. *et al.* (eds). *Man, land and sea.* Bangkok: Agricultural Development Council, 322 pp.: pp. 15–36.

Ryther, J. H. 1969. Photosynthesis and fish production in the sea. *Science,* Washington, 166:72–76;168:503–505.

Sarkar, J. 1984. India: traditional and disorganised. *Far Eastern Economic Review,* Hongkong, 125(31):56–57.

Sheldon, M. 1984. Thailand: its contraction rather than expansion now. *Far Eastern Economic Review*, Hongkong, 125(31):49–51.

Surette, R. 1981–1982. 200-mile limit brings more offshore problems. *Canadian Geographic,* Ottawa, 101(5):44–51.

Sutinen, J. G. & Hennessey, T. M. 1984. *Enforcement: the neglected element in fishery management.* Kingston, RI: University of Rhode Island, Agricultural Experiment Station Contribution No. 2232, 37 pp.

Travis, R. 1978–1979. Policing our enlarged coastal fishing zones. *Canadian Geographic,* Ottawa, 97(2):46–51.

Tun, M. C. 1984. Burma: trying to balance surplus fish profits with rice earnings. *Far Eastern Economic Review,* Hongkong, 125(31):55.

UNEP (United Nations Environment Programme). 1985. *Register of international treaties and other agreements in the field of the environment.* Nairobi: UN Environment Programme, Document No. UNEP/GC/INFORMATION/11/REV.1, 209 pp.

Weinberger, C. W. & Gast, P. J. 1981. U.S. plans attacked by Libyan aircraft. *Department of State Bulletin,* Washington, 81(2055):57–62.

7. Food crops as a factor in strategic policy and action

Peter Wallensteen
Uppsala University

I. Introduction

To secure a reliable supply of food remains a basic requirement for any society. For many societies, grains such as wheat or rice meet this requirement. Greater or lesser fractions of these staple food products are used by different countries to produce meat, luxury drinks, automotive fuels, and other products that go beyond basic human needs.

A threat to the supply of the basic staple food requirements of a country is likely to lead to conflict. Such threats could arise in many ways, notably through the political manipulation of access to food (e.g., via an embargo), through environmental degradation (e.g., via soil erosion), or through competition among conflicting land-use or consumption interests (e.g., between nomadic and sedentary populations).

This chapter is devoted to conflict over food in recent times and to the possibility of such conflict in the future. The analysis begins by examining the relation between food and political power and then turns to the use of food as a political weapon, with special emphasis on wheat. Next discussed is the role of food in conflict formation, including societal responses to food shortages, and then, in conclusion long-term trends. This chapter builds upon previous work by the author (Wallensteen, 1976).

II. Food and political power

The availability of food for different groups in the global community or in a given society depends on purchasing power, production patterns, and influence over central decisions concerning food. It is a recurrent pattern that, in the midst of starvation, there is food available either in the area hit, in neighbouring territories, or in the global community at large. The simultaneous collapse of food production in all layers of society is a rare event. Only in the gruesome aftermath of a nuclear war with 'nuclear winter' would that be a plausible scenario today, but the phenomenon is known from history, for example, from the period 1846–48 (Hobsbawm, 1962, page 208). A long-term projection suggests that the potential for solving the food problem is available (Higgins *et al.*, 1982). This means that the availability of food will depend either on the economic strength of those hit by a shortage or on their political impact, or on both.

In any society, the power over food production and distribution is of great importance, perhaps exceeded in significance only by access to military power. It is therefore to be expected that the patterns of production are constantly monitored, that the pricing of food products is closely controlled, and that the exports and imports of food are kept under governmental scrutiny.

The importance of food suggests that governments are sensitive to food shortages, to imbalances between wages and food prices, and to food riots. Indeed, the following several recent revolts relating to food illustrate the political significance of food:

1. In Poland in 1980 increases in the price of food led to the formation of the Solidarity trade union, the collapse of the Communist Party, and the creation in 1981 of a military government (Hodson *et al.*, 1980; 1981a).

2. In the Sudan in 1981 demonstrations against price rises took place following the announcement to phase out food subsidies (Hodson *et al.*, 1981b).

3. In Tunisia in 1983–84 riots following marked increases in the price of food resulted in changes in national policy (Hodson *et al.*, 1983, 1984).

4. In Morocco in 1984, as in Tunisia, riots broke out in several towns to protest against a cut in subsidies on food and other basic commodities, followed by a governmental cancellation of the price rises (Fraser, 1984).

5. In the Sudan in 1985, the regime was overthrown following strikes and riots over rising food prices (Fraser, 1985).

Tensions over consumer prices occur frequently in food markets in many parts of the world. Most of these events are not reported. From a political perspective such tensions are normal events, but at some point they become 'abnormal', that is, turn into conflict. The resulting riots are more often reported. Although internal, such events can have international ramifications. For example, the events in Poland in 1980–81 alluded to above served to increase tensions between Poland and the USSR as well as between East and West.

The linkage between food production and politics has rarely been explored in depth. Rather, attention has focused on issues such as the use of food as a political tool (e.g., via grain embargoes or via food aid) or on the impact of such measures on particular policies or on international trade. In industrial economies it has been more interesting to focus on the development of industry, taking agriculture as a given.

Historians focusing on economic development now point out that European industrialization would not have been possible without the successes of agriculture in increasing production and in accumulating capital; and thereby in being able to contribute to the financing of the industrial development. The emergence of capitalist landowners as opposed to feudal ones during the eighteenth century provides an example (Hobsbawm, 1962, chapter 8; 1975, chapter 10), as does the growth of the textile industry in the United Kingdom during the nineteenth century based on rural manufacture and a big domestic market (Landes, 1969, chapter 2). In other words, the agricultural sector has probably been underestimated as an originator of change and as a sector operating on conditions of its own. It is obvious that such neglect could result in the formulation of disastrous agricultural policies.

Fully two-thirds of the global population lives in the developing countries, but its share of world agriculture is less than 40 per cent (FAO, 1981). Therefore, the remaining one-third of the global population, living in the developed countries, accounts for more than 60 per cent of world agriculture. A huge number of people in the Third World—estimated at over 400 million—is seriously undernourished (FAO, 1981). It is also in the Third World that repeated famines have occurred. These statistics suggest that the development of agricultural production is important for societal development as a whole. The disparity between the developed and developing worlds additionally suggests the possibility of future conflict over access to food resources.

In order to tackle the problem of conflicts over natural resources, two primary aspects are concentrated on in this chapter:

1. The use of food as a political weapon. This topic leads into a discussion of the uses of food embargoes. (It could further lead to an analysis of the motives and impact of extending food aid as well as to one of food trade between countries, but these are covered elsewhere [Wallensteen, 1976].)

2. The role of food in conflict formation. This topic relates societal cleavages to cleavages resulting from food production, food distribution, or food trade. It is a most intricate problem because social phenomena are seldom isolated from one another. However, the experiences of food shortage can help illuminate the dynamics involved. To be considered here primarily are intra-state relations inasmuch as most food production in the world (*circa* 90 per cent) is for domestic consumption.

III. Food as a political weapon

World trade in grain has not only increased remarkably over the past four decades, but has also shifted from a situation of consumer domination to one of producer domination. Prior to World War II the only region of the world to be a net importer of grain was Western Europe (Cathie, 1985). Today, Western Europe, Eastern Europe, Africa, and Asia are all substantial net importers of grain, including especially China, Japan, and the USSR (table 7.1). The only truly major grain exporter is the USA; other important exporters are Argentina, Australia, Canada, and France (table 7.1).

Third-World countries in Africa and Asia have become increasingly dependent on external supplies of food (FAO, 1981). Especially in Africa, increases in food production have not been able to keep pace with population growth. The pressures on available land have increased, forcing food production to move into more ecologically fragile or otherwise unsuitable areas. Nomadic societies have been especially seriously affected by these pressures.

The debate on the use of any scarce commodity as a political instrument focuses primarily on the supplier (i.e., on the producer or the seller). In theory, and sometimes in practise, the consumer can also exert influence, as there has to be someone buying the goods. There are four conditions, at least in theory, for any scarce good to become a potential instrument of political influence (Wallensteen, 1976): (*a*) scarcity of the good; (*b*) supply concentration of

Table 7.1. **Major world trade in grain (cereals), 1983–84**[a]

Country[b]	Wheat[c] (10^6 tonnes)	Rice[c] (10^6 tonnes)	Maize[c] (corn) (10^6 tonnes)	Total[d] (10^6 tonnes)
A. Exports				
Argentina	9.6	—	5.9	15.5
Australia	11.6	0.4	—	12.0
Canada	21.8	—	0.4	22.2
France	14.0	—	4.7	18.7
USA	38.9	2.1	47.4	88.4
Others[e]	4.1	8.3	6.4	18.8
Total[e]	**99.9**	**10.8**	**64.8**	**175.5**
B. Imports				
China	9.6	—	0.1	9.7
Japan	5.9	—	14.5	20.3
USSR	20.0	0.5	9.5	30.0
Others[e]	64.4	10.3	40.7	115.5
Total[e]	**99.9**	**10.8**	**64.8**	**175.5**

Sources and notes:

[a]Table prepared by A. H. Westing.

[b]The countries are all those whose trade in grain was 10 million tonnes per year or more.

[c]The data are from the US Department of Agriculture (Lane, 1986, page 157). The data for wheat are for July 1983–June 1984; those for rice, January–December 1984; and those for maize (corn), October 1983–September 1984.

[d]The trade in grains not included here (barley, oats, etc.) would increase the presented world total by about 10 per cent.

[e]The category 'others', and therefore also the 'total' values, do not account for a number of very minor grain exporting and importing nations.

the good; (c) demand dispersion for the good; and (d) independence of the supplier of the good (so-called action independence).

Scarcity is a fundamental condition for a good to be able to become a political tool. If the demand is not greater than the supply within a given geographical entity, then there is no way in which the supplier can exert influence. In a situation of balance or abundance, the potential power of the consumer increases. Normally, scarcity results in increasing prices. The use of a scarce good for political purposes can, consequently, be described as adding a political price to the economic one. However, not all situations of scarcity will have political implications.

Supply concentration is the second condition for a good to be able to become a political tool. If there are many suppliers they will compete, and then the consumer will be in a position to exert leverage by playing one supplier against another. However, if the suppliers are few, or even only one, the market becomes close to, or actually, a monopoly. Not only will this permit the regulation of prices, but political strings can also be added. If there are few alternative suppliers, the buyer will find the situation highly constraining. The cartel of suppliers is a classical example of such a situation.

Demand dispersion is the third condition for a good to be able to become a political tool. This provides a situation in which the supplier can play one buyer against another. Again, not only can this result in a price favourable to the supplier, but also political conditions can be attached such as the threat of reduced quantities if certain conditions are not met. The remedy here is well known: the formation of a consumers' club which aims at improving the strength of the demand side.

Independence of the supplier (action independence) is the fourth condition for a good to be able to become a political tool. The supplier state must be able to control its own assets, both politically and technologically. Since the good in question is attractive, a supplier nation might easily find itself in a politically exposed situation were it to manipulate the supply of the good. The consumers could unite in an attempt to control the good. Indeed, the entire colonial expansion into the Third World during the nineteenth century could be interpreted in that light. In this way, European powers brought under their control highly important resources, thereby simultaneously preventing competitors from doing so and preventing resource-rich nations from embarking on independent courses of action. The possession of an attractive good creates a particularly difficult problem of national security.

It is obvious that the situations with respect to these four conditions will vary with the good concerned, with political conditions, and with time. Thus, sometimes the political use of a good can be attractive while at other times it might be counter-productive. These conditions merely specify the situations; whether they will, in fact, be exploited for political purposes are separate questions.

Grain

In dealing with the international trade in foodstuffs, it is sensible to concentrate on grain as this is the commodity most widely traded and as it is a staple food product for a large number of industrialized countries. There are at least five trends that make grain interesting in the context of using food as a political weapon:

1. Since the 1930s, the supply of surplus grain has become increasingly concentrated. In the 1930s, the US share of the world grain market was about 15 per cent, in the 1950s about 25 per cent, and in the 1970s more than 50 per cent (Cathie, 1985). Today, the USA is the pre-eminent supplier of grain to the world market, followed at a considerable distance by some few additional countries, notably Argentina, Australia, Canada, and France (table 7.1).

2. Much of the global grain trade has become concentrated in the hands of few private grain companies, several of them US-based, but transnational in their operations (Morgan, 1979).

3. The demand for grain has been rising sharply, previously primarily in Western Europe, but now increasingly also in China, Japan, and especially the USSR (Brown, 1975; Cathie, 1985; Paarlberg, 1979; 1982; see also table 7.1).

4. 'Absolute' scarcity is found in Third-World countries, whereas 'relative' scarcity is found in some richer countries. Owing to the importance of economic strength, this means that the demands of the latter are more readily met than those of the former.

5. For the main supplier, the USA, the trade in grain is taken from surplus production. What is sold on the world market does not directly affect internal consumption (Hadwiger & Talbot, 1982). Moreover, looking at trade in food products as a whole, the USA is more important to the outside world than *vice versa*. Thus, the USA maintains a very considerable level of independence with respect to food trade.

The strong position of the USA *vis-à-vis* food makes the trade in this commodity a potentially useful tool for influencing other countries. Most vulnerable, of course, are those countries facing an 'absolute' scarcity, that is, where shortfalls in harvest have immediate consequences for the survival of the population and where even modest levels of import might constitute the margin between life and death. It is obvious that an absolute food shortage presents a humanitarian problem, that is to say, such a situation would become difficult to exploit for a country imbued with humanitarian traditions. Still, there are some instances in which absolute food shortages have been exploited for political purposes. For example, the USA in 1974 delayed shipments of food to Bangladesh, apparently because Bangladesh had sold jute to Cuba (Rothschild, 1975–1976, page 296). Moreover, the possibility cannot be excluded that political pressures are exerted in less obvious forms, for example, as leverage in negotiations or other more or less unpublicized situations.

Constraints on the use of food as a political weapon are, paradoxically, fewer when the target nation does not depend for its survival upon the food in question. In the case of the USSR, US grain is used primarily for livestock feed for the production of meat (Malish, 1985; Paarlberg, 1982). This means that a reduction in imports does not affect the basic supply of food. Even in the event of complete Soviet isolation from outside grain, domestic wheat production would probably suffice to supply the entire population with an adequate amount of bread. Still, US grain export restrictions to the USSR in 1975 and 1980 caused severe problems for the Soviet economy. Considerable effort had to be devoted by the USSR to finding alternative sources, and purchase prices were probably higher than they would otherwise have been. In the end, however, it appears that the impact on the Soviet consumer was limited.

The US restrictions in 1980 on the sale of grain to the USSR resulted in great distress among US farmers, who feared not only a reduction in prices, but also finding themselves with no buyer for their grain. In time, the USA found alternative uses for this unsold grain, selling some to Mexico (in exchange for oil) and using some in the domestic production of alcohol for fuel (Brown, 1980). Nevertheless, the situation had various domestic political ramifications. This affair suggests the existence of certain limits: too drastic a curtailment of export will affect domestic farmers (through price reductions), whereas too drastic an increase in trade will affect domestic consumers (through price increases). In other words, the use of food as a political tool depends on the harvest prospects in the sanctioning country as well as on the strength of the interests affected by the measure. Moreover, the apparent independence of action even of a rich producer is seriously circumscribed by domestic factors, no matter whether the potential target of food power is rich or poor.

The US grain export restrictions of 1975 and 1980 illustrate an additional problem. A big buyer is an attractive customer. The USSR, through its centralized trading operation, is such a major buyer and is thus able to exert a significant influence on the seller. Even though the USSR must compete with other organizations (notably with those of Japan and of OPEC countries), its strength lies in the huge size of its purchases. This means that the requirement for demand dispersion is also less important than might be anticipated. In fact, the situation of 1972 shows that the reverse can sometimes be true. At that time the suppliers were not united whereas the buyer was, exploiting the rivalry among the different grain companies. The USA could have interrupted the sales, but, in fact, did not do so. There is still some element of dispute over exactly how well informed the US Administration was at the time. However, as 1972 was also the peak year of détente, it cannot be excluded that there was the desire on the part of the USA to reinforce that state of eased relations through the bestowal of economic benefits.

The Soviet experience with US unreliability has resulted in Soviet measures to reduce its dependence on US supplies (Laird & Francisco, 1985; Malish, 1985). Since 1980, the USSR has been spreading its purchases more evenly among the main suppliers. Thus, both buyer and supplier have taken measures to avoid being dependent upon the other, the buyer through increased dispersion, the seller through agreements that limit purchases. Together, these measures contribute to reducing the likelihood of the use of grain as an instrument of power in the relations between the USA and USSR. Nevertheless, the four requirements pointed to above describe the general situation of employing scarce goods for political purposes.

IV. The role of food in conflict formation

The entire issue of conflict formation remains one of the most under-researched areas in the social sciences. Even in the field of conflict research, conflicts are taken as a given and their deeper origins are seldom sought in a rigorous fashion. There is an abundance of ideas on the origin of conflicts, variously placing their origin in the human mind, in the value systems of society, in its economic conditions, in its social systems, or in the ecological system. Thus, trying to work from a scientific consensus is not easy in evaluating the particular role of food or other scarce good in conflict formation.

A reasonable point of departure might be to investigate what happens in crisis situations. Ideally, different types of crisis should be studied and their patterns of conflict compared. Food crises become particularly pertinent issues of analysis in the present context.

The typical food crisis arises from price changes. For the urban consumer, increased prices for staple foods lead to a dramatic reduction in standard of living when income does not increase comparably. Similarly for the rural producer, reduced prices for staple foods also lead to a dramatic reduction in standard of living when input costs are not declining comparably. This suggests that there are certain basic societal incompatibilities that relate to food production: what is good for one segment of society might well be bad for another. The reaction to reduced real income in Poland, the Sudan, Tunisia, and Morocco referred to earlier supports this notion. Thus, national agricultural policies must be formulated bearing in mind the potential for interplay between strong contending interests. The cited examples show that governments can readily fail to do this.

The rural-urban incompatibility alluded to above is a serious source of domestic tension. Such tension at times gives rise to conflict behaviour, that is, to the actual use of force to seek a redirection of a particular grievance. However, such protest is not necessarily easy for the affected parties to express since a considerable number of countries do not allow protests. As a result, the protest might lead to clandestine actions.

In fact, it is possible to divide societies into those in which the urban-rural incompatibility is handled within a framework of balance between the two interests and those in which one or the other of these factions dominates agricultural policies (or even all economic policies). In countries having strong farm organizations, trade unions, and political parties, the incompatibility will probably result in a tug-of-war situation in which one faction or another dominates for only a limited length of time. Another possible outcome under this last circumstance might be a compromise situation in which all of the groups attain some measure of success. It is remarkable to see that in a number of industrialized societies, farmers' parties have skilfully put themselves in the centre of the political spectrum, making use of their position to the benefit of rural interests.

In a number of centrally planned societies, particularly those in which the industrial working class has become the leading force in society, urban or industrial interests seem to predominate. This often means that food prices are kept low in cities and that priority is given to investment in industrial expansion. Rural interests appear to be the priority only in those centrally planned countries where the elimination of starvation or the fight against landed aristocracy has provided at least part of the legitimacy of the regime. Thus, the situation will differ, but the basic incompatibility between consumer and producer remains the same.

There are certainly additional incompatibilities relating to food production, notably over questions of land use, the role of middlemen, the relation between cash-crop and subsistence production, between capitalist and feudal agriculture, between tenants and landowners, between big and small farmers, and between farming for export and the importing of farm products. Some of these, it could be suggested, will become activated at times of food crisis.

In all societies there exist additional cleavages that relate to food production in only a secondary or derivative sense. To these belong relations between capital and labour, among different businesses, among political organizations, among ethnic groups, and among regions. Such incompatibilities could become activated or accentuated during a food crisis.

The most severe food crisis is, of course, one that involves the danger of starvation. It is possible to investigate societies with respect to their conflict patterns before, during, and after a period of starvation. Analyses of food crisis have dealt for the most part with food aid and its impact. The origins of such disasters have also been investigated to a considerable extent. However, the associated conflicts are a part of the problem and need to be analysed more thoroughly.

The African drought in the first half of the 1970s appears to have revealed the significance of one particular social incompatibility that is in part related to food production, the one between nomadic and sedentary populations. In the fairly homogeneous—largely nomadic—societies of Mauritania and Somalia, governmental reaction to the drought was prompt; and the calamity actually seems to have brought about a reduction in intra-state conflicts. By contrast, in the heterogeneous—mixed nomadic and sedentary—societies typical of most of the afflicted countries (governed largely by the sedentary segment), governmental reaction to the drought was slow; and the calamity seems to have brought about an increase in intra-state conflicts. Acute conflicts developed during the period of drought along the nomadic-sedentary cleavage. In fact, in some of the situations it was alleged that the drought provided an opportunity for the dominant sedentary segment to eliminate nomads as such.

In those situations involving neighbouring African states, it was the nomad-dominated societies that seem to have become embroiled in a larger number of conflicts. Indeed, the nomadic societies all became involved in interstate conflicts following a period of acute starvation. It also appears evident that it was the nomadic societies that initiated the conflicts, the target being the neighbouring country. It is, of course, possible that these conflicts might have taken place without the starvation. However, the point is that the increased unity in one country and the decreased cohesion in the neighbouring country provided an opportunity to the former that might have been irresistible. Thus, Somalia, witnessing the obvious disintegration of its neighbour Ethiopia, with which it had had a long-standing feud, launched a military attack in 1977–78 (Hodson *et al.*, 1978). This attack ended in 1978 not only in military failure for Somalia, but also in its political isolation. Analytically, such action could be termed 'opportunistic exploitation'. As a further example of this process, Mauritania in 1976 lined up with Morocco in an attempt to gain permanent control of a part of the neighbouring Western Sahara (see appendix 2, war 11). This action did not succeed for Mauritania and in time led to a dissolution of its internal unity and to major changes in its domestic and foreign policies.

The most interesting aspect of the apparent drought-related conflicts in Africa during the 1970s is the phenomenon of opportunistic exploitation. Opportunistic exploitation appeared to manifest itself in several ways within the afflicted area: in old political foes trying to launch military coups; in peripheral regions trying to increase their strength *vis-à-vis* the central authorities; and even in outside states trying to expand their local influence. Low levels of violence involving no weapons—such as student protests, trade union actions, and church activities—most often appeared to stem directly from the acute drought situation. However, when such violence escalated to the use of arms, this represented the involvement of institutionalized factions such as regional military commands, well-organized liberation movements, or ethnic groups with hierarchical organization. For them it appears that the primary interest in the drought and starvation was the relative weakening of a government, not the human suffering or other causes motivating the non-violent demonstrators. Thus it can be seen that a higher level of conflict behaviour is associated with a relative weakening of central authority, with food shortages *per se* playing only a secondary role.

In summary, an examination of Africa in the 1970s reveals a rather grim picture, but also one that demonstrates that the relationship between food production and armed conflict is a complex one. There is no doubt that a link exists, but it does not simply arise from frustration over a food crisis *per se*; nor does it escalate from a low level of protest to a high level of protest in any simple action-reaction spiral. Rather, the relationship appears to involve matters more directly related to opportunistic power struggles by organized interests. Of course, some of the disastrous consequences of a drought stem from inappropriate development policies being pursued by a country. Thus, the matter has an important political component, and it clearly seems to be in the enlightened self-interest of a regime to pursue development plans that also provide improved living conditions for the 'marginal' groups of the country.

V. Conclusion

The power inherent in food production and food distribution relates closely to the scarcity of food. It is when there is great demand for food internationally that a country with a surplus can make economic and political gains. Within a nation, it is when all of the domestic demands cannot be met that the influence of a group will determine its level of access to food. In fact, in extreme cases the line between domestic and foreign relations will break down. The weakening of central authority invites outside interference. However, it must be noted parenthetically that the strengthening of central authority could under some conditions also lead to such interference.

Food adequacy is at the heart of national security. In countries where food is scarce, the problem of food-related conflict can be reduced on a long-term basis only through increased food production. Agricultural development must therefore receive the highest priority, but this raises the crucial question of what the possibilities are for increasing the domestic production of food. Clearly, some countries might not be in a position to meet their own demands owing to such inherently adverse conditions as low rainfall; or to an unfavourable population/land radio.

Projections suggest that the total number of undernourished in the Third World will increase over the next two decades from the 400 million or so of today to perhaps 600 million (FAO, 1981). Particularly vulnerable are societies in the Far East and Africa. Whereas the Far East might be able to meet its food demands by imports balanced by exports of industrial goods, this appears hardly possible for Africa. Africa's food problems are exacerbated by rapidly growing populations, limited water supplies (see chapter 5), the increasingly high cost of fertilizers, and the paucity of appropriate crop species and varieties (Mooney, 1983).

A long-term programme for a nation to achieve food security must take into consideration the intertwined problems of food production, food consumption, and food politics. To achieve food security might well require a change in the distribution of power within a country, away from the present tilt towards sedentary and especially urban interests. At the international level, the present concentrated distribution of power should give way to either a centralized system within the framework of the United Nations or to a decentralized system. But most important is the need to give equity and justice a chance. Only in recognizing this can food be turned into what it really should be: a human right for everyone.

References

Brown, L. R. 1975. World food prospect. *Science,* Washington, 190:1053–1059.

Brown, L. R. 1980. *Food or fuel: new competition for the world's cropland.* Washington: Worldwatch Institute, Paper No. 35, 44 pp.

Cathie, J. 1985. US and EEC agricultural trade policies: a long-run view of the present conflict. *Food Policy,* Guildford, UK, 10(1):14–28.

FAO. 1981. *Agriculture: toward 2000.* Rome: Food & Agriculture Organization of the United Nations, 134 pp. + 10 tbls.

Fraser, R. (ed.). 1984. Morocco. *Keesing's Contemporary Archives,* Harlow, UK, 30(6):32949–32950.

Fraser, R. (ed.). 1985. Sudan. *Keesings Contemporary Archives,* Harlow, UK, 31(7):33700–33707.

Hadwiger, D. F. & Talbot, R. B. (eds). 1982. Food policy and farm programs. *Proceedings of the Academy of Political Science,* New York, 34(3):1–254.

Higgins, G. M., Kassam, A. H., Naiken, L., Fischer, G., & Shah, M. M. 1982. *Potential population supporting capacities of lands in the developing world.* Rome: Food & Agriculture Organization of the United Nations, 139+6 pp.

Hobsbawm, E. J. 1962. *Age of revolution: Europe 1789–1848.* London: Weidenfeld & Nicolson, 413 pp.

Hobsbawm, E. J. 1975. *Age of capital, 1848–1875.* London: Weidenfeld & Nicolson, 354 pp.

Hodson, H. V. *et al.* 1978. Ethiopia; Somalia. *Annual Register,* London, 220:207–210.

Hodson, H. V. *et al.* 1980. Poland. *Annual Register,* London, 222:109–114.

Hodson, H. V. *et al.* 1981a. Poland, *Annual Register,* London, 223:112–118.

Hodson, H. V. *et al.* 1981b. Sudan. *Annual Register,* London, 223:211–214.

Hodson, H. V. *et al.* 1983. Tunisia. *Annual Register,* London, 225:204–205.

Hodson, H. V. *et al.* 1984. Tunisia. *Annual Register,* London, 226:213–215.

Laird, R. D. & Francisco, R. A. 1985. Interdependence of agricultural trade. In: Jamgotch, N., Jr (ed.). *Sectors of mutual benefit in U.S.-Soviet relations.* Durham, N. Carolina: Duke University Press, 254 pp.: pp. 83–101.

Landes, D. S. 1969. *Unbound Prometheus: technological change and industrial development in Western Europe from 1750 to the present.* Cambridge, UK: Cambridge University Press, 566 pp.

Lane, H. U. (ed.). 1986. *World almanac & book of facts 1986.* New York: Newspaper Enterprise Association, 928 pp.

Malish, A. 1985. Soviet trade in agricultural commodities and technology. In: Parrott, B. (ed.). *Trade, technology, and Soviet-American relations.* Bloomington, Ind.: Indiana University Press, 394 pp.: pp. 203–240.

Mooney, P. R. 1983. Law of the seed: another development and plant genetic resources. *Development Dialogue,* Uppsala, 1983(1–2):1–173.

Morgan, D. 1979. *Merchants of grain.* New York: Viking, 387 pp.

Paarlberg, R. 1979. Failure of food power. In: Fraenkel, R. M. *et al.* (eds).

Role of U.S. agriculture in foreign policy. New York: Praeger, 253 pp.: pp. 39–55.

Paarlberg, R. L. 1982. Food as an instrument of foreign policy. *Proceedings of the Academy of Political Science,* New York, 34(3):25–39.

Rothschild, E. 1975–1976. Food politics. *Foreign Affairs,* New York, 54:285–307.

Wallensteen, P. 1976. Scarce goods as political weapons: the case of food. *Journal of Peace Research,* Oslo, 4:277–298.

8. Human population as a factor in strategic policy and action.

Marcel Leroy
University College of Cape Breton, Nova Scotia

I. Introduction

Competition over scarce resources can lead to interstate rivalry and
even to war. The world-wide demand for natural resources
increases in relation to population growth and rising expectations.
Population trends thus exert an influence on the domestic and
foreign policies of states and are, in turn, affected by them.

This chapter examines population as a factor in strategic policy
and action. Discussed first are the unproven assertions that have
been made about the relationships between demographic factors
and international relations. This is followed by an examination of
the effect of demographic change on the international behaviour of
states and of the strains, whether actual or perceived, that population growth brings to bear on the availability of natural resources. A
model is presented linking demographic factors with international
politics, based upon the interaction between a population and the
natural resources on which it draws. Next examined are the demographic consequences of war, as compared to the effects of non-
military population catastrophes, and the likely role in the future of
population in world politics. Finally, the impact of refugees and
undocumented migrants is discussed, and some conclusions and
recommendations are made.

This chapter builds upon previous work by the author (Leroy,
1976a; 1978).

II. Assumptions about population and international relations

From antiquity to the present, many unproven assertions have been
voiced about the relationships between demographic factors and

international relations. Generally, the context within which demographic phenomena are shaped is not understood; population trends are viewed as irreversible, or at least as not being susceptible to adaptation. When a general decline in fertility was perceived in western Europe in the 1920s (Kuczynski, 1928), a chorus of concern went up. A decline mentality was maintained even though populations began to rise again in the 1930s. An important study of the time predicted a decline in the population of Europe which was to start by 1970 at the latest (Notestein *et al.*, 1944), a forecast that failed to materialize.

Population growth in particular is often seen as resulting in international strain, aggression, and war (e.g., Huxley, 1963, page 78; Kahn, 1961, page 570; Nef, 1950, page 340). When the magnitude of population growth became apparent in the 1960s, popular reaction was not inspired by those who attempted to understand how this was coming about, but rather by those who viewed the trend as irreversible to the point of disaster (e.g., Ehrlich, 1968; Paddock & Paddock, 1967). Nor have policymakers been immune to making such generalizations. When, during the 1970s, public opinion in the USA became alarmed about the world's rapid population growth (see Leroy, 1981), US Department of State officials reflected this view (State, 1980). They saw such fast growth as potentially destabilizing; repercussions were said to include threats to the availability of critical raw materials, to export markets, and even to the national security of the USA.

The obstacles to empirical verification of assertions relating demography to international relations are formidable: not only is there the constraint that human populations cannot be manipulated like fruit flies, but when studying the dynamics of international politics, the possibility for gathering data through experimental situations is even more limited. Moreover, demographic factors are bound to be reflected within societies. International relations, however, operate at three different levels: at the level of the individual decision-maker; at that of the state; and at that of the community of states (Singer, 1961). Thus the task for those analysing the significance of population for international politics is not just limited to assessing the contribution of demographic evolution to societal reality; it also includes weighing internal factors within states against the motivations and beliefs of leaders, and against the constraints and opportunities imposed by the overall political, military, and economic situation in the world.

Although the measurement of population phenomena has now become quite accurate, the ability to interpret demographic trends and place them in a broader socio-economic perspective has not increased nearly as fast. Deterministic and single-factor explanations are nearly always wrong. Nevertheless, rather simple homeostatic models do provide a good starting point in understanding the problem at hand (Leroy, 1978, pages 97–123). The model presented below should be helpful in suggesting how demographic change relates to the use of natural resources as well as to the behaviour of groups, both internally and externally. It is with the perspective that the interaction between a population and its natural-resource base can be affected at either end of the equation—an integrative pespective rather than a reductionist one—that the task of assessing the significance of demographic factors in international interactions is here approached.

III. Population and resources

Many societies, when left undisturbed in the same natural environment for centuries, develop a life-style in which population and resource use remain relatively stable (Bender, 1971; Douglas, 1966). Under such conditions, societies maintained an equilibrium with a high birth rate to match a high death rate, or with birth and death rates both low (Halbwachs, 1946; Nag, 1973). That populations in developing countries have grown rapidly in this century does not refute the existence of regulatory mechanisms for the maintenance of population levels. This rapid growth has come about through the influence of the developed countries, which has resulted both in reductions in mortality rates and increases in birth rates (Polgar, 1971). Obstacles have been presented to such traditional means of fertility control as polygamy, infanticide, and abortion. Social and economic structures have been caused to change to ones that provide incentives for early marriage or high fertility. Old regulatory mechanisms have been breached without new ones becoming operative.

Understanding the reason for the rapid population growth in developing countries may give little comfort to those who deal with the social and environmental stresses to which such growth contributes. But it should point to avenues that could be pursued in the seach for new population-resource equilibria.

How do demographic changes affect the international behaviour of states? Foreign policy, more so than any other aspect of politics, includes many intangibles. From 'national security' to 'national interest' and *'raison d'état'*, policy-makers and observers have developed their own vocabulary to describe decisions for which they did not wish to divulge—or perhaps did not even fully grasp— the motivations and pressures to which they were responding. In a detailed study of six European countries during the half century leading up to World War I, domestic growth (of population and per-capita income), was found to be a strong factor in national expansion (Choucri & North, 1975). Military expenditures and alliances (both influenced by national growth) were also seen as important factors, partly because of the response they evoke from rival powers. It bears pointing out that population growth in these six states did not seem to impede economic growth; both were, in fact, moving ahead more rapidly than had been recorded in the history of pre-industrial Europe.

Before industrialization has occurred, there is perhaps a closer relationship between populations and the resources on which they can draw; this link forms an important basis for the life-styles and cultures of societies. Because of the limited ability to recognize what in the environment constitutes a natural resource and its limits (Firey, 1960; Spoehr, 1956), there is a tendency to regard available resources as being fixed, unless their supply can be increased through new finds or through territorial expansion. Technological innovation can improve the utilization of resources, but the rate of assimilation of innovations is limited (Hägerstrand, 1952; 1967; Rogers, 1962). Population growth thus tends to bring with it a relative strain, either on the amount of available resources, or on the way in which they are utilized.

Various responses are possible to perceived resource limitations. In conditions of subsistence agriculture—practised in most societies in the world until the last century or two, and still in significant portions of the globe today—land scarcity may cause societies to shift from extensive to intensive systems of cultivation (Boserup, 1965). Such changes often are made only reluctantly, however; the greater amount of labour required by intensive agricultural methods demands social changes that a society may not be willing to make (Clark, 1967). In conditions that sustain population increases, certain collective choices have to be made. The cultural inclination and collective experience of the members of society make them more or less willing to adopt certain courses of action.

Population increase thus contributes to straining the relationship between the people and their environment, leading to different patterns of resource use, or to the search for more resources in order to preserve the same system of resource utilization. Seeking to avoid such societal stresses, many have sought to define optimal levels of population (for a critique of such theories since the 1920s, see Leroy [1978, pages 38–41]). Based on traditional economic criteria, the optimal population level would be that at which—with all other factors such as soil, resources, capital, and technology remaining constant—the greatest return per capita would be achieved on a sustained basis (Ferenczi, 1938, pages 42–43). Yet even early discussions on population optima did not restrict the concept to domestic resources. International trade has long been recognized as a factor in determining optimal levels of population (Robbins, 1927).

If population optima are hard to define, and fluctuate with the choice of criteria or as a result of shifts in factors that would be hard to keep constant (such as technology or foreign trade), similar problems surround the term 'overpopulation'. The subjectivity of this concept has been skilfully demonstrated by Harvey (1974, page 272) in explaining the concept that 'overpopulation arises because of the scarcity of resources available for meeting the subsistence needs of the mass of the population' by substituting for it that 'there are too many people in the world because the particular ends we have in view (together with the form of social organization we have) and the materials available in nature, that we have the will and the way to use, are not sufficient to provide us with those things to which we are accustomed'.

Those who have considered population growth to be excessive, such as the Zero Population Growth movement in the USA in the 1970s, are worried that patterns of distribution and the existing social order might be altered in a way that would be less favourable for them than the *status quo*. In the USA, for example, it is those who can be identified most readily as benefiting from the existing socio-political order—Republicans, the middle class, Whites—who have been found most favourably inclined towards policies of population limitation (Barnett, 1970). Birth rates, however, are not easy for governments to manipulate and it is difficult to reduce fertility while maintaining the socio-economic *status quo*. In cases where birth rates have been reduced, this has most often followed major socio-economic changes.

In some instances, significant reductions in population growth have been achieved without major increases in per-capita incomes. In the case of Kerala, India, widespread political participation has resulted in more equal distribution of land, income, and services; and was coupled with higher levels of education, particularly for women (Ratcliffe, 1978). Both mortality and fertility rates have dropped there in comparison to India as a whole. China was able to achieve a dramatic impact on fertility, halving the birth rate in less than 20 years (Lin, 1981). However, this reduction appears to have been achieved more through a high degree of 'political commitment' (Organski *et al.*, 1984, page 122) than through the socio-economic processes that have led to the onset of demographic change in virtually all other cases where substantial fertility reductions have occurred.

One more point should be raised to place the significance of population growth for international politics in its proper perspective. Much has been written about population growth as an impediment to economic development. It was pointed out in the 1960s that growth rates of total income in developing countries were only slightly lower than those in developed countries (4.0 versus 4.4 per cent) (Meade, 1967). That per-capita income went up by less than half (1.5 versus 3.1 per cent) was explained by the more rapid growth in population. But the total picture appears to be somewhat more complex. The pressures brought about by population growth may act as catalysts for bringing about the social transformations that are prerequisites for economic growth (Sauvy, 1959). Innovations may also be more readily accepted under the more competitive conditions existing with high growth rates. It has been suggested that increases in fertility in the USA have often coincided with economic upswings which have led to increased demand for housing, services, and consumer goods (Easterlin, 1968). Perhaps more important, empirical investigation of the relationship between population growth and increase in per-capita income fails to confirm the generally negative association that theoretical analyses have predicted for developing countries. Thus, either no significant association, or a slightly positive link, between population growth and income increases has been reported in several empirical studies of developing countries (Aluko, 1971; Chesnais, 1985; Easterlin, 1967; Weintraub, 1962).

At the heart of demographic change is the family, the building block of society. But reproductive decisions within the family are influenced by the dominant thinking and values of the group of which it is a part. Both fertility and life expectancy are affected by the groups, through the social welfare system or by the medical and other facilities available. Population trends are, furthermore, accompanied by socio-economic phenomena and by specific patterns or changes in resource use. Population trends and the ways in which they are (not necessarily correctly) perceived by decision-makers have a bearing on most elements that affect the international position of states: (*a*) on their economic production, including the capacity to export and the need to import; (*b*) on the availability of persons to their military, and the capacity of the economic apparatus to perform with a certain number or proportion of the population under arms; and (*c*) on the way in which they see themselves and are perceived by foreign populations and decision-makers. Population growth, in particular, is likely to engender increased international participation and attention, in both bilateral and multilateral contacts.

IV. Population and international interactions

It is clear that many factors combine to determine the international behaviour of states. That population variables cannot be studied in isolation is illustrated below by the way in which demographic change relates to the most dramatic of international interactions: war.

Although war has often been claimed to be inevitable, a considerable body of evidence points to the fact that fighting behaviour is learned, various cultures having different attitudes towards it (Bandura, 1973; Mead, 1937; Mead & Metraux, 1965). When groups are culturally inclined to accept violence, and experience desirable outcomes to such actions, aggression may be sanctioned and encouraged by the group. In groups of hunter-gatherers, or in those engaged in subsistence agriculture, this may lead to a recurring pattern of territorial expansion. During the second half of the nineteenth century, the Ibans of Sarawak, Borneo, found themselves in this situation (Vayda, 1969). Their population increase was coupled with raids on their neighbours, the Kayans, in order to gain more agricultural land. They might, of course, have chosen a different response to demographic change, such as agricultural intensification.

Population increase does not always result in a strained ecological balance. In pre-Colombian North America, many Indian tribes practised agriculture and were semi-sedentary. Conflict was ritualized and its scope restricted by the limited mobility of the Indians. The Europeans introduced horses, which increased the range of operations and made it easier to hunt and to intrude upon other territories; and firearms, which increased the numbers of casualties (Newcomb, 1950). The combined effect of these two changes was to introduce instability in group security, subsistence methods, and resource territories. Such instability in turn led to an increase in the scope and frequency of collective conflicts. It could be inferred that human beings fight not because they are biologically impelled, but because they are culturally induced and because their ecological equilibrium is disturbed seriously enough to make substantial change necessary. Demographic factors also have an impact on the capability of states. Not only total population numbers but, more specifically, dependency ratios, labour participation rates, and indices of demographic development such as reproduction rates, give an indication of present and future potential economic and military capability (for a more complete discussion of these factors, see Leroy [1978, pages 21–52]). Factors such as the level of education, efficiency of organization, and capital available per worker, are further qualifiers. Capability at any one time is, of course, only a static contribution to international relations; the main question is how and when that potential is to be used.

Population and international politics: a model

A model can be suggested that links demographic factors with international politics. The starting point in such a scheme would be the interaction between a population and the resource base upon which it draws, including agricultural land, minerals, and technology. This interaction can be considered to be the basis of a chain of events that can ultimately result in a greater international presence, including a desire for greater access to resources and markets, greater competitiveness, and sometimes increased aggressiveness. Indeed, in writing about the causation of war from a societal perspective, it was already concluded more than a half century ago that disruption of the equilibrium among demographic, economic, ecological, and political variables was at its origin (Sorokin, 1928, pages 383–84).

The existing relationship between population and the resource base may be altered through population change (growth or decline) or through a shift in the resource base. In the case of an increase in resource availability (through expansion of agricultural land, exploitation of ground water, mineral finds, improvements in technology or production, etc.), a reduction in external demands can be anticipated; conversely, in the case of a decline (through resource depletion, deterioration of agricultural land, water supplies, etc.), an increase in external demands can be anticipated.

The second phase of the model linking demography with international relations is the societal response to the changed resource conditions. A society's culture forms a screen through which it interprets its environment and chooses its response. An unlimited range of responses is possible here. Shifts in productive techniques, innovations, altered resource utilization, and other changes in internal conditions can accommodate the changed population-resource situation. The group's values, and the capacity of its social structure to accept change, are significant factors here; where these are absent or minimal, a greater proportion of the change in the environmental balance will have to be accommodated through increases in external flows.

The third phase of the model is reached once society's options have been narrowed through cultural choice. Domestic decision-makers must take account of demographic capability factors—dependency ratios, labour participation rates, reproduction rates, and so on—which influence a group's ability to pursue economic and military goals.

The fourth phase of the model concerns domestic political conditions. Different types of political system have varying ways of relating internal conditions to external participation and conflict (Wilkenfeld, 1968). An élite-dominated political system, for example, often uses diversionary war as a means to diffuse domestic demands and social conflicts (Mayer, 1969), whereas pluralistic governments often perpetuate their previous foreign conflict levels, regardless of the amount of domestic conflict (Wilkenfeld, 1972). The level of domestic disturbance created by the shift in the balance or ratio between population and resources is another relevant factor here. Societal frustration and political instability have frequently been linked; low per-capita income, absence of significant growth in per-capita income, inequality of income distribution, and lack of socio-economic mobility have all been found to relate to the level of internal political unrest (Gurr, 1970; Parvin, 1973; Terrell, 1971). Studies investigating the general relationship between domestic and foreign conflict, however, have found domestic instability to have little bearing on a nation's foreign conflict behaviour (Rummel, 1968; 1971; Tanter, 1966). Only in a more detailed analysis of domestic political systems, as suggested above, can domestic conflicts and conditions be linked to international affairs. The degree of militaristic orientation represents a further element that influences the foreign policy output of the societies concerned. Military expenditures, military values, and societal attitudes towards violent solutions are all reflected in foreign policy.

In the fifth and final phase of the model, it is suggested that any foreign policy output will also be influenced by the international system. The general stability or instability of the international situation, and its degree of permissiveness, will influence the type of foreign policy approach that decision-makers can realistically contemplate. Within the competitive environment of international politics, mobility is constantly pursued. Especially when states rank high on some dimensions (e.g., population) but low on others (e.g., per-capita income, access to international resources and markets, international prestige), corrective upward pressure, including aggressiveness, could result from such rank-disequilibrium (Galtung, 1964).

The model of demography and international politics just described offers at least a partial check-list against which any concrete case can be examined. One rather straightforward conclusion is that the often stated assumption of a direct relationship between population pressure and aggressive foreign policy does not hold (see also Leroy, 1976b). During the past century, war seems to have been associated primarily with ascending states, progressing to higher levels of industrialization but not yet fully industrialized, having large and growing populations, possessing limited territory and resources, and enjoying inadequate trade relative to demands (Haas, 1968, page 238; North & Choucri, 1971, page 229; Organski & Organski, 1961, pages 240–42). Processes of causation involved both domestic and systemic (international) elements. The international repercussions of population-resource shifts in certain countries can only be fully appreciated when comparing them to the performance of other states in the same competitive system.

In a thorough and detailed study of the El Salvador-Honduras War of 1969 (see appendix 2, war 8)—a conflict that has most often been blamed on population pressure—Durham (1979, page 165) concluded that certain groups in Honduras had succeeded in 'translating an internal problem of resource competition into an external one'. The author found that changes in access to land had taken place in both El Salvador and Honduras in the years preceding the conflict that had resulted in greater control by ranchers and by farmers producing for export. In the ecological analysis of resource scarcity in that region, distributional changes were found to have been at least as significant as population growth.

An explanation of the El Salvador-Honduras War is further complicated by the likelihood that inequality within a population and population growth are related. In the case of an agrarian society, as population grows the land (its most valued commodity) usually becomes ever more subdivided, while inequality increases (Midlarsky, 1982). Land rents rise with subdivision to the benefit of the landlords, and real wages tend to fall (Harris & Samaraweera, 1984). The circle is completed by the higher birth rate and more rapid growth in population that goes with unequal distribution of income (Repetto, 1979).

Population growth intensifies the struggle for control of resources, especially for land in agrarian societies. Rural competition will increase and income levels will fall unless the urban or industrial sectors are growing and drawing the surplus labour from the agricultural sector. Land-distribution policies could have a mitigating effect on the inequality associated with rural population growth, but in the absence of such policies—and perhaps even in their presence—the stage is set for increasing competition, growing inequality, and continued high fertility.

V. Consequences of war and population decline

Wars, of course, are not only related to population through processes of causality; they also have serious demographic consequences for the societies they affect. Besides civilian and military population losses, there are also changes in the age structure, the latter resulting from a reduction in the birth rate during the war and from higher mortality rates among young adults, particularly males. For example, in the United Kingdom about 5 per cent of all males between the ages of 15 and 49 died in service during World War I (Winter, 1977). During World War II, the smaller cohorts born during 1914–18 were drafted and further decimated. In FR Germany immediately following World War II, the number of 28-year-olds was only 40 per cent of the year-cohort level of males of ages 40 to 45, and less than one-third of the level of males of ages 5 to 10 (Bolte & Kappe, 1967, page 90). Serious sex imbalances also resulted, with excesses of 20 per cent of women over men (Ledermann, 1947).

In spite of such losses, the majority of wars in the Western world cannot be said to have had a demographic function in the regulation of populations in the sense that this might have been the case for primitive societies. Modern warfare destroys a higher percentage of capital and income than of population, so that, in fact, warfare could be said to be a cause of overpopulation (and of poverty), rather than a remedy for it (Oser, 1956). Furthermore, the structure of mortality owing to non-military demographic catastrophes (like epidemics and famines) has been such that it increases the proportion of children and young adults as percentages of all deaths (Jutikkala & Kauppinen, 1971), whereas wars affect primarily the adult age groups. The consequences of famines and epidemics thus drag on longer than those of wars, since depleted cohorts enter the reproductive age group in the following two decades. Furthermore, recuperation time for populations that have suffered from war losses is usually quite short, since fertility tends to rise sharply in the years following the end of a conflict.

It is ironic that, with the record rates of increase in global population apparently barely behind us, many in the industrialized world are now lamenting the decline in fertility that has continued there for at least two decades. Although dire consequences have been predicted for countries with declining fertility, the evidence is more reassuring. In a classic study on population decline it was concluded that in a moderately declining population—with a net reproduction rate of not below 0.8 per cent, as was the case in the United Kingdom in the 1930s and is true now for many countries in both Europe and North America—per-capita income would go up; the increase in the proportion of the population above retirement age would largely be offset by a reduction in the number of young dependents (Reddaway, 1938, pages 229–45). It is not surprising, therefore, that investigation of the impact of ageing on industrialized societies has shown that tax burdens should not increase until the cohorts of the 'baby boom' reach retirement age during the next century; and, moreover, that certain policies might be put in place to soften or avoid such a burden altogether (Ridler, 1984).

Population decline need not (any more than population increase) weaken a country's economic position on the international level. The military consequences may be more debatable, but at least a number of options are open to countries concerned with their defence posture. (The increased duration of compulsory military service in FR Germany indicates one such possibility.) More precarious would be the position of a country that underwent a catastrophic population decline of, let us say, 30 per cent or more (see Le Bras, 1969)—provided its neighbours and enemies did not experience comparable losses. Domestically, such demographic decline has in the past brought about sharply increased social mobility, as a result of vacancies left in all echelons, although sinking to lower strata may be the consequence for children whose upper-class parents died in the crisis (Sorokin, 1942, pages 111–17).

The significant reduction of populations resulting from disasters does not seem to bring about a reduction in the frequency of war (Sorokin, 1928, pages 384–85). For both France and England, the number of years per decade spent in war during the second half of the fourteenth century—following the loss of about one-third of their populations owing to the Black Death—was comparable to the number per decade during the preceding five and a half centuries. For both countries, participation in war during the first half of the fifteenth century reached new peaks, in spite of the fact that population levels were then still substantially below the levels of 1345 (for a fascinating discussion of catastrophic population declines in history, see Sorokin [1942]).

Whereas population losses after a nuclear exchange are certain to fall into the catastrophic range (Heer, 1965), the above comments are nevertheless unlikely to be very relevant if such an event were to take place. Although there would certainly be many opportunities to fill positions, both domestically and internationally, it is unlikely that survivors would do so other than out of necessity for survival; nor would it be appealing to take control of other territories— friendly, neutral, or enemy—that had suffered serious damage or nuclear fall-out. The only possibilities for actual expansion would appear to be in relatively unaffected regions, where local powers might be tempted to extend control over rivals that suddenly found themselves without protection from one of the superpowers. Such regional leaders would most likely be in control of the most populous and best armed countries in their respective subcontinents, but causality for their moves would hardly include any other demographic factors.

VI. Population in future world politics

Although population changes are a major component of the evolution of groups, and of their interaction with the outside world, they do not manifest themselves independently from the environment-resource situation of those societies, nor are they always the basis of such a chain of events. Apart from basic necessities for survival, the quest for resources allows states quite a range of actions. For example, access can be sought beyond a nation's borders by negotiation and trade.

Most resources are not as nearly finite as is often believed. Not only is substitution (e.g., of metals by petrochemical-based products) more common, the long-run course of raw-material prices has tended to go downwards, pointing to greater rather than lesser availability with the passage of time and increases in population (Simon, 1983). Furthermore, long-term trends in consumer spending in industrialized societies—the greatest users of raw materials— suggest a decreasing emphasis on manufactured goods in favour of services and software. Such a trend would make natural resources potentially more available to the developing world. With changes in technology, access to traditional raw materials is likely to improve. The relative oil glut on the world market since 1983 illustrates several of the mechanisms at work: (*a*) a greater incentive and political will to pursue exploration; (*b*) a more rapid development and application of new technologies; and (*c*) a greater emphasis on conservation efforts. The last of these mechanisms has shown that quality of life can be maintained at a high level despite a decline in resource consumption.

Although the population-resource equation is unlikely to precipitate global conflict, differential population growth among various regions of the world is likely to produce substantial shifts in the distribution of power and influence. Recent fertility declines have been more rapid—even in many parts of the developing world—than had been predicted during the past two decades. Yet even if net reproduction rates everywhere in the world were to drop to a value of one, the exact replacement level (i.e., one girl surviving to maturity for each woman who completes the childbearing years), major changes would still occur by the year 2000. Thus, Third-World populations would continue growing for about 50 years after reaching a net reproduction rate of one, because the age distributions are so slanted in favour of young age groups that the next generation of parents will be larger than the present one. An authoritative population forecast for the year 2025 includes the following predictions (UN, 1985, table A-2, medium variant): (*a*) that the USA will have reached 310 million, as compared with Brazil's 250 million and Mexico's 150 million; (*b*) that China will have reached 1500 million and India 1200 million, as compared with the USSR's 370 million and Japan's 130 million; and (*c*) that Indonesia will have reached 260 million, as compared with Australia's 24 million. Moreover, by 2025, Nigeria is predicted to reach 340 million, Bangladesh 220 million, Pakistan 210 million, and the world as a whole 8200 million.

If the Western experience has any relevance, it is the industrializing but not yet fully developed countries with 'personalist' (élite-dominated) governments that are the most war-prone. That description may increasingly fit a fair number of Third-World countries. It is, in fact, among the developing countries that all violent conflicts involving a population factor have taken place (Choucri, 1983, page 19). But even with low levels of external aggressiveness, the increasing numerical preponderance of the Third World—most likely coupled with fairly high conventional military capabilities—will be bound to produce substantial shifts in the distribution of world power. Thus, a major challenge for the world in the next half century will be to distribute access to resources, to markets, and to technology in such a way that development in the Third World can progress sufficiently evenly, both within and among states. Extended capabilities for conflict management at the regional level might facilitate this transition.

Refugees

International politics in the twentieth century can hardly be equated with the spontaneous behaviour and movement of primitive groups. In virtually all settings, the state has succeeded in becoming the sole agent through which groups deal with the outside world. Nevertheless, studies of the behaviour of small groups outside a state setting can yield useful information on how the relationship between people and their environment can become strained. The chaos produced by war results in much human movement beyond the control of the state (Kulischer, 1948). Of special interest here is the movement across international boundaries caused by conditions of environmental adversity or degradation.

There are about 10 million refugees on foreign soil in the world at present as a result of movements across national frontiers (UNHCR, 1984, page 457). They have left their home countries because their subsistence has been placed in jeopardy by environmental degradation, domestic political turmoil, or war. Effective border control is difficult because some of the groups are nomadic by tradition and because national borders often cut across the traditional territories of ethnic groups. Between 1978 and 1980, 700 000 Ethiopian refugees settled in Somalia; during 1980–82 more than 2 million Afghan refugees were registered in Pakistan. In both cases, the presence of such large numbers of refugees in a relatively restricted portion of the host country has precipitated new environmental problems, especially deforestation for construction and fuel and soil erosion owing to overgrazing by livestock (UNHCR, 1984, pages 460–61).

The number of undocumented migrants in the world is estimated at between 10 and 15 million (ICM, 1984). Moreover, the number of illegal migrants entering the industrialized countries has been rising rapidly. For example, the number residing in the USA is thought to be between 3 and 5 million, about half from Mexico (ICM, 1984, page 414). Most of the illegal migrants are in search of better economic conditions, although some have fled, or been expelled, for political reasons. That the refugee problems mentioned above are often caused or at least compounded by government actions is an indication that the state system may not be capable of dealing with a whole range of modern problems including such environmental ones as desertification (Falk, 1983, pages 12–15).

It is possible to envisage population becoming a direct cause of conflict as a result of the mass movement of refugees across a national border. To the extent that such a movement is the result of environmental degradation, the situation should be ameliorated by international agencies, not only helping the refugees themselves, but also providing special assistance to prevent further environmental damage in both of the countries involved. If the mass movement has been deliberately instigated by a government, then the demographic component of such international behaviour is not spontaneous, but rather part of a national strategy. In such cases, it must not be overlooked that population factors may well be an excuse for, rather than a cause of, the action.

VII. Conclusion

Many factors combine to determine the international behaviour of states and population variables cannot be studied in isolation. However, population trends and their perception by decision-makers are shown to be major components of the interaction of groups with the outside world. In the past, domestic growth was a strong factor in national expansion, and even today a normal consequence of population growth is an increase in international interaction.

Constraints on the availability of critical raw materials are an important repercussion of destabilizing population growth. The relationship between a population and its natural-resource base is closely tied to population change and underlies a chain of events which may lead to a greater international presence, to greater competition, and even to increased aggressiveness. The model of demography and international politics described above shows the relation between population pressure and aggressive foreign policy to be less direct than often assumed; the relation must be examined alongside other factors, not least the behaviour of other states.

The populations of developing countries will continue to grow for a further two generations even after their birth rates decline to the replacement level since the age distribution of their populations is skewed sharply towards the young. Contending with such growth will be a major social and environmental challenge to national and international institutions. One need merely consider that the population of Africa is anticipated to grow from 550 million in 1985 to 1600 million by the year 2025 (UN, 1985, table A-1, medium variant) to appreciate the magnitude of the problem.

Population growth has been beneficial in various ways. The psychological stress associated with such growth has led to new socio-cultural systems, promoting needed organizational change (Cohen, 1984). It has led to technological innovations and improved living conditions (Boserup, 1981). Availability of resources and standards of living have more than kept up with the increasing size of the global population (Simon, 1981, page 345). Nevertheless, because of the speed with which the populations of developing countries are growing, some of these mechanisms may fail in the future. The time lag between population growth and an appropriate institutional response to contain the social and environmental stresses it engenders may be too great in some cases to prevent a collapse of domestic and perhaps even international order.

The annual rate of growth of the global population has dropped from 2.06 per cent per year (doubling time, 34 years) in the period 1965–70 to 1.67 per cent per year (doubling time, 42 years) in the period 1980–85 (UN, 1985, table A-1, medium variant). The economic and political returns for policies that continue to reduce population growth hold considerable promise (Demeny, 1984). Making available to the Third World appropriate technical and management tools for its development should stimulate the growth of income (Weizsäcker *et al.*, 1983). To the extent that such aid also reduces domestic and global inequalities, it will decrease the potential for conflict arising from population growth.

In closing, it must be stressed that aggressive foreign policy is not the only option open to states seeking to expand their resource base: negotiation, trade, substitution, and improved technology are the more usual means. Demographic elements relate to conflict situations through a complex set of intermediate variables. It is concluded that whereas the population-resource equation is unlikely to precipitate global conflict directly, differential population growth is likely to produce substantial shifts in the global distribution of power and influence.

References

Aluko, S. A. 1971. Population growth and the level of income: a survey. *Journal of Modern African Studies,* Cambridge, UK, 9:561–575.

Bandura, A. 1973. *Aggression: a social learning analysis.* Englewood Cliffs, New Jersey: Prentice-Hall, 390 pp.

Barnett, L. D. 1970. Political affiliation and attitudes towards population limitation. *Social Biology,* Madison, Wis., 17(2):124–131.

Bender, D. R. 1971. Population and productivity in tropical forest bush fallow agriculture. In: Polgar, S. (ed.). *Culture and population: a collection of current studies.* Cambridge, Mass.: Schenkman, 195 pp.: pp. 32–45.

Bolte, K. M. & Kappe, D. 1967. *Struktur und Entwicklung der Bevölkerung [Structure and development of the populace]* (in German). Opladen, FR Germany: C. W. Leske, 98 pp.

Boserup, E. 1965. *Conditions of agricultural growth: the economics of agrarian change under population pressure.* London: George Allen & Unwin, 124 pp.

Boserup, E. 1981. *Population and technological change.* Chicago: University of Chicago Press, 255 pp.

Chesnais, J. C. 1985. [Economic progress and demographic transition in the poor countries: thirty years of experience (1950–1980)] (in French). *Population,* Paris, 40:11–28.

Choucri, N. 1983. *Population and conflict: new dimensions of population dynamics.* New York: UN Fund for Population Activities, Policy Development Study No. 8, 47 pp.

Choucri, N. & North, R. C. 1975. *Nations in conflict: national growth and international violence.* San Francisco: W. H. Freeman, 356 pp.

Clark, C. 1967. *Population growth and land use.* London: Macmillan, 406 pp.

Cohen, M. N. 1984. Population growth, interpersonal conflict, and organizational response in human history. In: Choucri, N. (ed.). *Multidisciplinary perspectives on population and conflict.* Syracuse, NY: Syracuse University Press, 220 pp.: pp. 27–57.

Demeny, P. 1984. Long-term effects of global population on the international system. In: United Nations (ed.). *Population, resources, environment and development.* New York: UN Department of International Economic & Social Affairs, Population Study No. 90 (ST/ESA/SER.A/90), 534 pp.: pp. 125–143.

Douglas, M. 1966. Population control in primitive groups. *British Journal of Sociology,* Henley-on-Thames, UK, 17:263–273.

Durham, W. H. 1979. *Scarcity and survival in Central America: ecological origins of the Soccer War.* Stanford, Calif.: Stanford University Press, 209 pp.

Easterlin, R. 1967. Effects of population growth on the economic development of developing countries. *Annals of the American Academy of Political & Social Science,* Philadelphia, 369:98–108.

Easterlin, R. A. 1968. *Population, labor force, and long swings in economic growth: the American experience.* New York: Columbia University Press, 298 pp.

Ehrlich, P. R. 1968. *Population bomb.* New York: Ballantine, 201 pp.

Falk, R. A. 1983. *End of world order: essays on normative international relations.* New York: Holmes & Meier, 358 pp.

Ferenczi, I. 1938. *Synthetic optimum of population.* Paris: International Institute of Intellectual Co-operation, 115 pp.

Firey, W. I. 1960. *Man, mind and land: a theory of resource use.* Glencoe, Illinois: Free Press, 256 pp.

Galtung, J. 1964. Structural theory of aggression. *Journal of Peace Research,* Oslo, 1:95–119.

Gurr, T. R. 1970. *Why men rebel.* Princeton, New Jersey: Princeton University Press, 421 pp.

Haas, M. 1968. Social change and national aggressiveness, 1900–1960. In: Singer, J. D. (ed.). *Quantitative international politics: insights and evidence.* New York: Free Press, 394 pp.: pp. 215–244, 359–374.

Hägerstrand, T. 1952. *Propagation of innovation waves.* Lund: University of Lund Studies in Geography, Ser. B, No. 4, 20 pp. + 1 map.

Hägerstrand, T. 1967. *Innovation diffusion as a spatial process.* Chicago: University of Chicago Press, 334 pp.

Halbwachs, M. 1946. [Reflections on a demographic equilibrium: many births, many deaths; few infants, few deaths] (in French). *Annales. Economies, Sociétés, Civilisations,* Paris, 1(4):289–305.

Harris, J. R. & Samaraweera, V. 1984. Economic dimensions of conflict. In: Choucri, N. (ed.). *Multidisciplinary perspectives on population and conflict.* Syracuse, NY: Syracuse University Press, 220 pp.: pp. 123–156.

Harvey, D. 1974. Population, resources, and the ideology of science. *Economic Geography,* Worcester, Mass., 50:256–277.

Heer, D. M. 1965. *After nuclear attack: a demographic inquiry.* New York: Praeger, 405 pp.

Huxley, J. 1963. *Human crisis.* Seattle: University of Washington Press, 88 pp.

ICM (Intergovernmental Committee for Migration). 1984. World-wide situation and problems of undocumented migration. In: United Nations (ed.). *Population distribution, migration and development.* New York:

UN Department of International Economic & Social Affairs, Population Study No. 89 (ST/ESA/SER.A/89), 505 pp.: pp. 409–426.

Jutikkala, E. & Kauppinen, M. 1971. Structure of mortality during catastrophic years in a pre-industrial society. *Population Studies,* London, 25:283–285.

Kahn, H. 1961. *On thermonuclear war.* 2nd ed. Princeton, New Jersey: Princeton University Press, 668 pp.

Kuczynski, R. R. 1928. *Balance of births and deaths. I. Western and northern Europe.* New York: MacMillan, 140 pp.

Kulischer, E. M. 1948. *Europe on the move: war and population changes, 1917–47.* New York: Columbia University Press, 377 pp.

Le Bras, H. 1969. [Return of a population to a stable state after a 'catastrophe'] (in French). *Population,* Paris, 24:861–896.

Ledermann, S. 1947. [German population: present situation and perspectives] (in French). *Population,* Paris, 2:81–92.

Leroy, M. 1976a. Ecological instability, population change, and the causation of war. *Peace & the Sciences,* Vienna, 1976(2):41–51.

Leroy, M. 1976b. Neo-Malthusianism, foreign aid, and international relations. *International Journal,* Toronto, 31(1):26–43.

Leroy, M. 1978. *Population and world politics: the interrelationships between demographic factors and international relations.* Leiden: Martinus Nijhoff, 144 pp.

Leroy, M. 1981. Population ideology in the more developed countries in the 1970's and 1980's. *Proceedings of the International Population Conference,* Manila, 5:737–743.

Lin Fu De. 1981. *Status quo* and prospect of China's population. *Proceedings of the International Population Conference,* Manila, 5:449–457.

Mayer, A. J. 1969. Internal causes and purposes of war in Europe, 1870–1956. *Journal of Modern History,* Chicago, 41:291–303.

Mead, M. (ed.). 1937. *Co-operation and conflict among primitive peoples.* New York: McGraw-Hill, 531 pp.

Mead, M. & Metraux, R. 1965. Anthropology of human conflict. In: McNeil, E. B. (ed.). *Nature of human conflict.* Englewood Cliffs, New Jersey: Prentice-Hall, 315 pp.: pp. 116–138.

Meade, J. E. 1967. Population explosion, the standard of living, and social conflict. *Economic Journal,* Cambridge, UK, 77:233–255.

Midlarsky, M. I. 1982. Scarcity and inequality: prologue to the onset of mass revolution. *Journal of Conflict Resolution,* Beverly Hills, Calif., 26:3–38.

Nag, M. 1973. Anthropology and population: problems and perspectives. *Population Studies,* London, 27:59–68.

Nef, J. U. 1950. *War and human progress: an essay on the rise of industrial civilization.* Cambridge, Mass.: Harvard University Press, 464 pp.

180   *Global resources and international conflict*

Newcomb, W. W., Jr. 1950. Re-examination of the causes of plains warfare. *American Anthropologist,* Washington, 52:317–330.

North, R. C. & Choucri, N. 1971. Population, technology and resources in the future international system. *Journal of International Affairs,* New York, 25:224–237.

Notestein, F. W., Taeuber, I. B., Kirk, D., Coale, A. J., & Kiser, L. K. 1944. *Future population of Europe and the Soviet Union: population projections 1940–1970.* Geneva: League of Nations, 315 pp.

Organski, A. F. K., Kugler, J., Johnson, J. T. & Cohen, Y. 1984. *Births, deaths, and taxes: the demographic and political transitions.* Chicago: University of Chicago Press, 161 pp.

Organski, K. & Organski, A. F. K. 1961. *Population and world power.* New York: Alfred A. Knopf, 263 pp.

Oser, J. 1956. *Must men starve?: the Malthusian controversy.* London: Jonathan Cape, 331 pp.

Paddock, W. & Paddock, P. 1967. *Famine 1975!: America's decision: who will survive?* Boston: Little, Brown, 286 pp.

Parvin, M. 1973. Economic determinants of political unrest: an econometric approach. *Journal of Conflict Resolution,* Beverly Hills, Calif., 17:271–296.

Polgar, S. 1971. Culture, history and population dynamics. In: Polgar, S. (ed.). *Culture and population: a collection of current studies.* Cambridge, Mass.: Schenkman, 195 pp.: pp. 3–8.

Ratcliffe, J. 1978. Social justice and the demographic transition: lessons from India's Kerala State. *International Journal of Health Services,* Farmingdale, NY, 8(1):123–144.

Reddaway, W. B. 1938. *Economics of a declining population.* New York: MacMillan, 270 pp.

Repetto, R. C. 1979. *Economic equality and fertility in developing countries.* Baltimore: Johns Hopkins University Press, 186 pp.

Ridler, N. B. 1984. Population aging: its fiscal impact in selected OECD countries. *Canadian Studies in Population,* Edmonton, Alberta, 11(1):47–60.

Robbins, L. 1927. Optimum theory of population. In: Gregory, T. E. & Dalton, H. (eds). *London essays in economics: in honour of Edwin Cannan.* London: George Routledge, 376 pp.: pp. 103–134.

Rogers, E. M. 1962. *Diffusion of innovations.* New York: Free Press, 367 pp.

Rummel, R. J. 1968. Relationship between national attributes and foreign conflict behavior. In: Singer, J. D. (ed.). *Quantitative international politics: insights and evidence.* New York: Free Press, 394 pp.: pp. 187–214, 359–374.

Rummel, R. J. 1971. Dimensions of conflict within and between states. In:

Gillespie, J. V. & Nesvold, B. A. (eds). *Macro-quantitative analysis: conflict, development, and democratization.* Beverley Hills, Calif.: Sage Publications, 576 pp.: pp. 49–84.

Sauvy, A. 1959. [Demographic investments and economic investments] (in French). *Proceedings of the International Population Conference,* Vienna, 1959:136–141.

Simon, J. L. 1981. *Ultimate resource.* Princeton, New Jersey: Princeton University Press, 415 pp.

Simon, J. L. 1983. Present value of population growth in the western world. *Population Studies,* London, 37:5–21.

Singer, J. D. 1961. Level-of-analysis problem in international relations. *World Politics,* Princeton, New Jersey, 14(1):77–92.

Sorokin, P. A. 1928. *Contemporary sociological theories.* New York: Harper, 758 pp.

Sorokin, P. A. 1942. *Man and society in calamity.* New York: E. P. Dutton, 352 pp.

Spoehr, A. 1956. Cultural differences in the interpretation of natural resources. In: Thomas, W. L., Jr (ed.). *Man's role in changing the face of the earth.* Chicago: University of Chicago Press, 1193 pp.: pp. 93–102.

State, US Dept of. 1980. *International population policy.* Washington: US Department of State, Current Policy No. 171, 5 pp.

Tanter, R. 1966. Dimensions of conflict behavior within and between nations, 1958–60. *Journal of Conflict Resolution,* Beverly Hills, Calif., 10:41–64.

Terrell, L. M. 1971. Social stress, political instability, and levels of military effort. *Journal of Conflict Resolution,* Beverly Hills, Calif., 15:329–346.

UN (United Nations). 1985. *World population prospects: estimates and projections as assessed in 1982.* New York: UN Department of International Economic & Social Affairs, Population Study No. 86 (ST/ESA/SER.A/86), 521 pp.

UNHCR (United Nations High Commissioner for Refugees). 1984. International migration: refugees. In: United Nations (ed.). *Population distribution, migration and development.* New York: UN Department of International Economic & Social Affairs, Population Study No. 89 (ST/ESA/SER.A/89) 505 pp.: pp. 457–467.

Vayda, A. P. 1969. Study of the causes of war, with special reference to head-hunting raids in Borneo. *Ethnohistory,* Tucson, Ariz., 16:211–224.

Weintraub, R. 1962. Birth rate and economic development: an empirical study. *Econometrica,* Evanston, Illinois, 40:812–817.

Weizsäcker, E U.v., Swaminathan, M. S. & Lemma, A. (eds). 1983. *New frontiers in technology application: integration of emerging and traditional technologies.* Dublin: Tycooly, 271 pp.

Wilkenfeld, J. 1968. Domestic and foreign conflict behavior of nations. *Journal of Peace Research,* Oslo, 5:56–69.

Wilkenfeld, J. 1972. Models for the analysis of foreign conflict behavior of states. In: Russett, B. M. (ed.). *Peace, war, and numbers.* Beverly Hills, Calif.: Sage Publications, 352 pp.: pp. 275–298, 321–335.

Winter, J. M. 1977. Britain's 'lost generation' of the First World War. *Population Studies,* London, 31:449–466.

9. An expanded concept of international security

Arthur H. Westing
Stockholm International Peace Research Institute

I. Introduction

The natural resources of the earth, both living and non-living, are most unevenly distributed. Many of them are thus in short supply or even absent in various countries. It is therefore not surprising that a substantial number of our many wars are fought over natural resources, whether or not this is made explicit by the initiating state (see chapter 1). Even when natural resources do not figure prominently as the cause of a war, they are often a contributing factor of some significance.

Demands on the land, fresh waters, and other natural resources of the earth are growing rapidly owing to the rapid increases in human numbers and to the even more rapid increases in human aspirations, the latter in both the developed and developing nations. This dilemma suggests that natural resources have the potential for playing an even more important role as a cause of war in the future than they have in the past. It is especially with this prospect in mind that two major issues are addressed in this chapter: (*a*) means for reducing the likelihood of international conflict over natural resources; and (*b*) environmental measures for strengthening international security. This chapter is thus a complement to the opening chapter in which the relationship between humans and the environment and the prevalence of conflict over resources were discussed (see chapter 1). It draws perforce upon analyses of a number of specific resources presented in the intervening chapters (chapters 2–8) and on the work of others (see appendix 1).

Military actions involving natural resources take one of two major forms: those the object of which is to obtain one or more natural resources and, conversely, those that would deny natural resources to an adversary (see appendix 2). The former include wars of plunder, of aggrandizement, of colonial retention, and of dispute in contested or extra-territorial areas. The latter include wars or strategies of destruction, of attrition, and of siege or blockade. Means for preventing resource wars can be based on some combination of military posture, arms-control or disarmament treaties, commercial (trade) agreements, domestic development, restraints on population growth, and restraints on the use of resources.

II. Towards the prevention of resource wars

The natural resources over which wars might be waged can fall within the domain of a nation (territorial resources), can be international in the sense that they do not respect national boundaries (shared resources), or can be a part of the so-called international commons (extra-territorial resources). Very different problems are associated with these three categories, so that each deserves a separate section.

Territorial resources

Wars that violate the integrity of another state, whether to gain possession of its natural resources or for some other aggressive end, are prohibited by international law and are today ostensibly rejected by the world at large. Indeed, some 60 nations formally condemned recourse to war in becoming parties to the Pact of Paris (signed at Paris in 1928; entry into force, 1929) (Goldblat, 1982, pages 136–37). Today, about 95 per cent of the 170 or so nations are members of the United Nations, which commits them to eschewing wars of aggression (UN, 1968, Charter article 2.4); and there exists an integral (albeit ineffectual) mechanism of conflict resolution (UN, 1968, Charter articles 33–51). Moreover, numerous bilateral and multilateral pacts of non-aggression or mutual assistance are in force.

Disputes over the location of a border between two states can be heightened, or even motivated, by the presence of natural resources in the contested strip, and such disagreements from time to time lead to armed conflict. The International Court of Justice provides one avenue for arbitration (UN, 1968, Charter articles 92–96 and pages 58–87).

In recent years a growing number of coastal states have laid exclusive claim to the natural resources of the ocean contiguous to their coastlines (Borgese & Ginsberg, 1982, pages 564–68). Although these claims vary in width, many extend out to 370 kilometres and thus encompass huge areas. These *de facto* claims have as yet no explicit basis in international law, yet appear to be generally recognized. An elaborate codification of the rules relating to such exclusive economic zones would be legally established were the Law of the Sea Convention of 1982 to come into force (see appendix 6). Among other things, the Convention would provide for the conservation and optimum utilization of the living resources (articles 61–62), for some level of 'equitable' participation by land-locked and geographically disadvantaged states in exploiting the 'surplus' of the living resources (articles 69–71), and for regulations, enforcement, and the resolution of conflicts (various articles).

The Law of the Sea Convention is the product of a lengthy multinational effort under United Nations auspices. It would *inter alia* establish a comprehensive and integrated body of international law for this recent widespread extension of national jurisdiction over natural resources. Since formal adoption of the Convention is foundering because of the unpalatability to the USA and other advanced industrialized nations of other portions (see below), it may be useful to extract the portion devoted to exclusive economic zones for separate early adoption.

It is clear that the prevention of wars that aim at gaining control of territorial resources by plunder, aggrandizement, or similar means are subsumed under the overall efforts of the world community to preserve the sanctity of the sovereign state. Such interstate wars therefore require no further elaboration here. However, before leaving the matter of territorial resources it is important to mention two further matters: (*a*) colonial wars; and (*b*) domestic strife.

Numerous imperial colonies or similar possessions have attempted to secede from their metropolitan states and this has often led to intense warfare. The original acquisition of the possession—often a distant and at the time 'primitive' land—had in most instances been motivated by a desire for its land or other natural resources. And the reluctance to relinquish the possession has generally been based on similar natural-resource motives. Many of these armed attempts to gain independence met with failure in the early decades of this century, but in recent decades most have succeeded. Such wars of national liberation are now widely condoned and even recognized as permissible (UNGA, 1974, article 7); at any rate, relatively few colonies remain.

Political unrest within a country, rioting, and even *coups d'état* in the Third World in recent years have been attributed to shortages of food (see chapter 7). The implicated food deficits in Africa and elsewhere are the result of agricultural development not keeping up with rapidly growing populations, of reduced returns from nutrient-impoverished and eroded land being too heavily farmed or overgrazed or recklessly logged, and of other environmental, political, and social factors (Eckholm, 1982; Sai, 1984). The situation becomes especially acute from time to time in some of the more arid countries during the occasionally recurring years of particularly low rainfall. Many from among the excess rural populations—so-called environmental refugees—migrate to urban centres, where living conditions become increasingly submarginal and chances for gainful employment are slim (see chapter 8; see also El-Hinnawi, 1985). The violent overthrow of the regime in Sudan in 1985 has been attributed in large measure to shortages and accompanying high prices of food (Fraser, 1985). Approaches to alleviating these problems of domestic strife are addressed below.

Shared resources

Natural resources that do not respect national boundaries include fresh waters, ocean fisheries, and the atmosphere. The optimal and equitable utilization of such shared resources requires the establishment of a comprehensive body of law enjoying multilateral if not world-wide acceptance. Codification of this sort is also necessary to prevent disputes or to provide a vehicle for the peaceful resolution of those not prevented. No such codification is as yet in force despite various efforts, including recommendations by the United Nations Environment Programme (UNEP, 1978a; 1978b) and several attempts within the United Nations General Assembly over the past 25 years. Even simple resolutions establishing the principle of 'co-operation in the field of the environment concerning natural resources shared by two or more States' have received only weak support and none from the major powers (UNGA, 1973). One very modest step towards protecting shared resources has been the establishment of transfrontier nature reserves (Thorsell, 1985).

The numerous bodies of fresh water (rivers, lakes, aquifers) that overlap national boundaries (see UN, 1978) are a particular cause for future concern owing especially to the rapidly increasing agricultural and municipal demands for this fundamental resource (see chapter 5). International upstream/downstream conflicts will arise both over allocation of use and over pollution control. Numerous disparate bilateral and regional water treaties exist, but these are often inadequate because they lack an integrated ecological or environmental approach and for other reasons (Biswas, 1983; Caldwell, 1984, pages 112–15, 308–9). An appropriate body of international law on shared bodies of fresh water is sorely needed, but remains an elusive goal.

Most ocean fish live over the continental shelves and thus largely within the rather newly proclaimed exclusive economic zones. Rational management of fish populations that overlap the boundaries of two or more such zones of national jurisdiction over natural resources, or the boundaries between such zones and the ocean beyond any national jurisdiction, requires international co-operation (see chapter 6). Various multilateral treaties exist that deal with a particular species or class of fish (Kiss, 1983; UNEP, 1985), but adoption of the Law of the Sea Convention of 1982 (see appendix 6), or at least the relevant portion of it, would establish an appropriate body of comprehensive international law.

The atmosphere is shared by all the nations of the world and, owing to the air currents, constantly crosses national boundaries. Among a number of serious or potentially serious atmospheric problems (carbon dioxide enrichment, ozone depletion, air-lane crowding, weather modification, etc.), the one now most likely to lead to international conflict is that of noxious pollutants being introduced into the atmosphere by one country and blowing into and causing harm in another. There is usually little of a technical nature that a nation can do domestically to protect itself from foreign air pollution.

International problems associated with air pollution are covered in part by a number of *ad hoc* bilateral and regional agreements as well as by one major multilateral instrument, the Treaty Banning Nuclear Weapon Tests in the Atmosphere, in Outer Space and Under Water (signed at Moscow in 1963; entry into force, also 1963) (Goldblat, 1982, pages 157–58). This Partial Test Ban

Treaty—a public-health and air-quality measure of some significance—is now adhered to by well over 100 nations, including the USA, the USSR, and the United Kingdom, but not China or France (neither of which, however, has carried out atmospheric tests in recent years). An important regional (European) agreement is the Convention on Long-Range Transboundary Air Pollution (signed at Geneva in 1979; entry into force, 1983), which now has 24 or more parties (Kiss, 1983, pages 519–22; UNEP, 1985, pages 168–70).

The atmosphere is another shared natural resource that calls for a comprehensive body of international law if future international conflict is to be avoided or dealt with in a reasonable fashion.

Extra-territorial resources

The ocean beyond any national jurisdiction plus the sea-bed beneath it, perhaps Antarctica plus the surrounding waters south of latitude 60°S, and the moon comprise the major extra-territorial domains that contain natural resources which either are exploitable or else may become so in the future. The upper atmosphere and outer space also deserve at least brief mention. The legal regimes pertaining to the various extra-territorial areas leave much to be desired, suggesting the possibility of future conflicts over the natural resources of these areas. The basic question is whether these areas or their resources can be laid claim to, and perhaps fought over, by individual nations or whether they are to be treated as a common heritage of humankind and managed accordingly for the equitably shared benefit of all.

The extra-territorial ocean, and the sea-bed beneath it, is distributed in three major and several minor basins that together represent more than half the global surface area (Westing, 1980, pages 144–82). The extent of this immense public domain is perhaps 270 million square kilometres, the distance between sea-surface and sea-bed averages about 4 kilometres, and its volume is thus of the order of 10^{18} cubic metres.

The extra-territorial ocean supports a modest population of fish which are widely dispersed and therefore not too readily exploitable (see chapter 6). The sea-bed beneath the extra-territorial ocean is in various regions a treasure trove of minerals, including such strategic ones as manganese and cobalt (Cronan, 1985; Stavridis, 1985;

Waldheim, 1975). The depth of the sea-bed has to date precluded the commercial exploitation of these resources, but the time is not far off. More than 100 nations once declared support for the principle that the resources of the sea-bed beyond the limits of national jurisdiction be exploited for the benefit of humankind as a whole (UNGA, 1970). The Law of the Sea Convention of 1982 would establish this public domain as a common heritage of humankind, at the same time providing for its equitable management for the benefit of all (see appendix 6). However, the advanced industrialized nations of the world—that is, those technically and economically capable of exploiting the resources of the deep sea-bed—have not been interested in supporting such a concept of an equitably shared international commons (see appendix 6, section II).

Antarctica is a huge, largely ice-covered, and essentially uninhabited continent the area of which has been for the most part (*circa* 85 per cent) divided up by the territorial claims (overlapping in three instances) of seven nations: Argentina, Australia, Chile, France, New Zealand, Norway, and the United Kingdom. Moreover, all of these claims have been contested by several major nations, including the USA and the USSR. The territorial disputes have been deferred for a time by the interested parties through the vehicle of the Antarctic Treaty of 1959 (see appendix 4, article IV). This treaty *inter alia* demilitarizes the continent (article I), provides for the preservation of its living resources (article IX.1.f), and permits its 'use' (article IX.1.a). The terrestrial resources are not as yet commercially exploitable, but the associated fishery resources are being harvested by a number of nations within the limitations of two associated treaties: (*a*) the Convention for the Conservation of Antarctic Seals (signed at London in 1972; entry into force, 1978) (Kiss, 1983, pages 38–39, 272–76; UNEP, 1985, page 104); and (*b*) the Convention on the Conservation of Antarctic Marine Living Resources (signed at Canberra in 1980; entry into force, 1982) (UNEP, 1985, pages 174–75). Despite several years of discussion among the parties, no comparable associated treaty that would regulate the exploitation of the terrestrial and offshore mineral resources exists as yet.

It is clear that there is a potential for dispute and even armed conflict over the mineral resources of Antarctica, especially if existing or new territorial claims are exercised in the coming years

(Kimball, 1985; Luard, 1983–1984; Shusterich, 1984). The problem is exacerbated by the limited number of nations that support the treaty—only 32 at present—and the preferential treatment accorded to certain parties—the 16 full members (see appendix 4, section II). In a sense, this group of full members has at least provisionally usurped the decision-making powers over Antarctica, in the process providing for the protection of the living natural resources of the continent, but at the same time not permitting it to become a common heritage of humankind.

The Svalbard archipelago in the Arctic Ocean deserves mention because it is in essence an extra-territorial area. The main island, Spitsbergen, has rich deposits of coal as well as lesser deposits of several other minerals, and its associated waters support a fishery resource. The Spitsbergen Treaty of 1920 has established a legal regime for the archipelago (see appendix 3). The treaty demilitarizes the area (article 9) and provides for the preservation of the fauna and flora of the islands and associated waters (article 2). All parties to the treaty (40 at present; see appendix 3, section II) enjoy access to the area and the right to exploit its natural resources 'on a footing of absolute equality', including specifically equal rights of fishing and hunting (article 2) and of mining (article 3). Norway—which was awarded limited sovereignty over the archipelago—was given the task, on behalf of the parties, of establishing and overseeing the administrative regulations in support of the various stipulations of the treaty (articles 2, 3, 8, 9, etc.). The Svalbard archipelago provides an early example of the management of an international commons, one in which the interested parties (a non-exclusionary group) provide for the orderly utilization of the natural resources involved but not for any sort of equitable sharing of the benefits derived from them.

The moon is the only celestial body that could conceivably become accessible for exploitation in the foreseeable future. At least two multilateral treaties would impinge upon such activity: (*a*) the Outer Space Treaty of 1967 (see appendix 5); and (*b*) the Moon Agreement of 1979 (see appendix 7). The Outer Space Treaty boasts more than 80 parties, including all of the major powers (see appendix 5, section II). The parties have agreed that the moon 'is not subject to national appropriation' by any means (article II). It further commits the parties to the 'use' of the moon 'for the benefit and in the interests of all countries, irrespective of their degree of economic or scientific development' and that the moon 'shall be the province of all mankind', for 'use by all States without discrimination of any kind' (article I). The treaty demilitarizes the moon (article IV) and forbids 'harmful contamination' (article IX).

The more recent Moon Agreement repeats in essence all of the strictures quoted above from the Outer Space Treaty, but adds that 'due regard shall be paid to the interests of present and future generations as well as to the need to promote higher standards of living and conditions of economic and social progress and development' (article 4) and also that measures be taken 'to prevent the disruption of the existing balance of its environment' (article 7). However, in its most important innovation, the Agreement proclaims that 'the moon and its natural resources are the common heritage of mankind' and goes on to provide for the establishment of 'an international régime . . . to govern the exploitation of the natural resources of the moon', the purposes of which include 'an equitable sharing by all States Parties in the benefits derived from those resources' (article 11). As is noted above with respect to the Law of the Sea Convention of 1982, the notion of a common heritage of humankind that is coupled with provisions for equitable sharing by all parties appears to be unacceptable to any major power (see appendix 7, section II). A legal analysis of the 'common heritage' principle with special reference to the moon can be found elsewhere (Halket *et al.*, 1982–1983).

The upper atmosphere and outer space contain a number of extra-territorial resources of limited extent and thus subject to dispute. Of particular concern are (*a*) the communication portion of the electromagnetic spectrum (frequency range, *circa* $10 \times 10^3 - 300 \times 10^9$ hertz) and (*b*) the geostationary (geosynchronous) satellite orbit (in the equatorial plane at an altitude of *circa* 36 000 kilometres). The current status of these resources, how they are managed, and existing mechanisms for conflict resolution are discussed elsewhere (Jackson, 1980; Smith, 1983).

In conclusion, it is well known that extra-territorial resources are highly vulnerable to destructive exploitation unless they are managed within the framework of an enlightened, comprehensive system of international regulation. Such destruction has come to be referred to as the 'tragedy of the commons' (Hardin, 1968; Hardin & Baden, 1977). Thus, withholding support for such codification for the management of the natural resources of the ocean beyond any national jurisdiction or of the moon will not only prevent the establishment of effective mechanisms for conflict resolution, but will also lead to the extinction or exhaustion of the resources.

III. Towards the establishment of a secure globe

The concept of national security is generally considered to refer to the security of a nation from being attacked by a potential enemy. States, of course, have the legitimate and necessary function—indeed, obligation—to protect their citizens from such a threat. And to this end most states maintain at least some sort of military establishment. However, it is not sufficient for states merely to ensure for everyone (to lean upon the *Universal Declaration of Human Rights*) 'life, liberty and security of person', but in addition to ensure for each citizen 'a standard of living adequate for the health and well-being of himself and of his family, including food, clothing [and] housing' and even 'a social and international order in which the rights . . . can be fully realized' (UNGA, 1948, articles 3, 25, 28).

There is, in fact, a growing recognition that threats to national and international security extend beyond external military threats (Behar, 1985; Gordon, 1978; Romulo *et al.*, 1982; Thorsson *et al.*, 1982; Ullman, 1983–1984). Indeed, it has even been specifically recognized that such threats can arise from agricultural, natural-resource, and other environmental problems (Barnett, 1984; Brown, 1977; Purcell, 1982; Weinstein, 1985). The adverse effects of soil erosion, of water and air pollution, of harvesting renewable resources faster than their rates of renewal, of the rising demands for land, fresh water, fuels, and minerals, and of the accelerated rates of extinction of flora and fauna are all among the threats to national or international security in the expanded sense that have been identified as being of particular concern.

It is abundantly clear that many nations, regions, and the world as a whole are faced with serious environmental problems, various of which are becoming increasingly severe (Brown *et al.*, 1985; Holdgate *et al.*, 1982). Thus, any local, national, or multinational actions that come to grips with these problems—whether these be governmental, intergovernmental, or non-governmental—will serve to reduce the threat to national and international security in the expanded sense. Moreover, it is clear that concerted actions of an international nature are often specifically called for because, as is noted, many of the problems are not confined to single countries, and also because some of the problems have progressed too far or are too complex to be dealt with by the intellectual or material resources of any one nation (IUCN, 1980).

In considering the extent to which an amelioration of environmental problems would lead to a reduced threat of military action and to fewer wars, it is convenient to make a distinction between the living and non-living resources. There is, however, one principle that transcends this distinction: the concept that the earth and many of its most important natural resources constitute a common heritage of humankind that must be prudently and equitably managed for the benefit of all. If this concept of common heritage combined with shared benefits were embraced by the nations of the world, many potential threats to national and global security would become either moot or more readily soluble; and the likelihood of international conflict would be correspondingly reduced.

As to the living, renewable resources, the guiding principle must be, in the words of the *World Charter for Nature*, that such resources 'shall not be utilized in excess of their natural capacity for regeneration' (UNGA, 1982, principle II.10.d). In terms of human ecology, the carrying capacity must not be transgressed, even to the point that the 'sanctity of life' must give way before the 'sanctity of the carrying capacity' (Hardin, 1985, page 172). As stressed above, in order that this crucial aim be achieved without international conflict for those living resources that overlap national boundaries—and especially for those living resources that are found in international commons such as the extra-territorial ocean—agreed norms of conduct and associated codification are required, as embodied, for example, in the Law of the Sea Convention of 1982 (see appendix 6).

Within individual nations, especially within the many impoverished ones of the Third World, it is most important that population numbers (which are in some instances rising rapidly) be brought into balance on a long-term (sustained) basis with the capacities to produce food and wood (which are in some instances falling rapidly). In addition to the ecological and social or humanitarian benefits to be derived from such an achievement, the balance is likely to reduce domestic political turmoil and the number of violent changes of regime that occur so often in the developing countries.

Thus, high priority must be given to instituting: (*a*) programmes of soil reclamation and improvement; (*b*) appropriate farm practices and technologies (including those of fish culture); (*c*) programmes of range management and forest management built around restoration and sustained yield of forage and wood; and (*d*) equitable distribution of, or access to, the nation's domestic land and water resources.

Among the non-living resources, the case of fresh waters has already been addressed in a prior section. Suffice it to say here that further conflict over shared fresh waters—regarding both equitable allocation and contaminants (water quality)—is imminent in various parts of the world in the absence of a relevant body of international law. And it could almost go without saying that nations must be able to bring into balance their demands for fresh water with the availability of that precious and often limited commodity.

For mineral fuels and non-fuel minerals, a strategy of sustained self-sufficiency is applicable only to the world as a whole. A large number of countries must depend upon external sources (i.e., international trade) for many if not most of their oil and other mineral needs. It is thus evident that strategies for mineral security and the avoidance of conflicts over these resources are complex and at best not fully adequate (Blechman, 1985; Maull, 1984; Vogely, 1982; see also chapters 2–4). Suggestions that can be made, most of them quite obvious, include: (*a*) the establishment of favourable international trade relations; (*b*) the parsimonious utilization of minerals not domestically available; (*c*) the use of (and continued research and development for) substitutes from available materials; and (*d*) the stockpiling of emergency supplies for use during temporary disruptions of supply. With respect to the energy resources, it has been shown, at least for the USA, that the present situation is vulnerable to disruption and disaster (Lovins & Lovins, 1982). It was suggested that greater national security could be achieved by decentralization and greater reliance on a variety of non-renewable and renewable sources of energy, although not including nuclear energy.

It is perhaps fortunate for other states that the two superpowers are sufficiently well endowed with oil and, it seems, all other strategic minerals to be able to overcome interruptions of any foreign supply for extended periods of national emergency—

preoccupied as they are with military might and the associated need for ready access to huge quantities of natural resources in time of war.

Reference was made earlier to the state's obligation, *inter alia*, to provide national military security. Any defensive military posture established by a state to that end must be as non-offensive and non-provocative as possible (Barnaby & Boeker,1982; Galtung, 1982; 1984). One important component in providing such military security is for a nation to become as invulnerable as possible to enemy blockade or attack. Conforming to such a strategy provides one more motivation for a nation to become self-sufficient in the production of its staple foods, or potentially so. Moreover, such agricultural self-reliance should be independently achieved (or readily achievable) in as many subdivisions of the country as is feasible (Eide, 1975).

IV. Conclusion

Civilization is rooted in nature, an environment which has shaped human culture and influenced all scientific and artistic achievement. Indeed, humans are a part of nature, and life depends on the uninterrupted functioning of natural systems. It is thus inescapable that any concept of international security must in the last analysis be based on this obligate relationship of humankind with its environment. As has been recommended to the world community of nations by the United Nations Environment Programme (UNEP, 1978b, principle 1): 'It is necessary for States to co-operate in the field of the environment concerning the conservation and harmonious utilization of natural resources shared by two or more States. Accordingly, it is necessary that consistent with the concept of equitable utilization of shared natural resources, States co-operate with a view to controlling, preventing, reducing or eliminating adverse environmental effects which may result from the utilization of such resources. Such co-operation is to take place on an equal footing and taking into account the sovereignty, rights and interests of the States concerned.'

The global scarcity or uneven distribution of some of the natural resources upon which humans depend has often led to violent conflict. The attempt to eliminate competition over such resources as a source of international conflict must take several forms: (*a*) for the living natural resources (whether national, shared, or extra-territorial), an inviolate balance must be established between harvesting and natural regeneration; (b) for all natural resources that overlap national boundaries, formal mechanisms under international auspices must be established for equitable sharing; and (c) for all extra-territorial natural resources it must be accepted that they constitute a common heritage of humankind, and bodies of international law must be established accordingly that provide for their equitable sharing for the benefit of all.

The scarcity and degraded condition of crop lands, range (grazing) lands, and forest lands in many countries of the world has often led to serious medical and social problems, to political unrest, and to domestic violence and strife. In some developing countries these problems are of such magnitude and urgency that their alleviation and ultimate solution require the widest possible international co-operation and support. United Nations agencies might well be the avenue through which both material aid and the sharing of knowledge and skills could be channelled.

The attempt to eliminate such environmental calamities as a source of domestic, or even wider, conflict must again take several forms: (a) for the degraded soils, an urgent programme of rehabilitation must be established; (b) for the over-used grazing lands and forest lands, a rigorous management regime must be established that limits intensity of exploitation to a level which permits regeneration; and (c) a long-term balance must be achieved between the production of staple foods and other necessities of life, such as wood, on the one hand and the size of the population on the other—such balance to be achieved on a national and even local level.

The dimensions of the social and ecological problems facing humankind today are formidable, indeed. And the human record in dealing with major problems, whether real or perceived, does not provide much cause for optimism, as can be so amply demonstrated (e.g., Janis, 1982; Tuchman, 1984). But nevertheless, recognition of a problem is the first step to overcoming it. It is thus heartening to realize that at least 110 nations have been persuaded that (UNGA, 1982): 'Competition for scarce resources creates conflicts, whereas the conservation of nature and natural resources contributes to justice and the maintenance of peace and cannot be achieved until [humankind] learns to live in peace and to forsake war and armaments.'

References

Barnaby, F. & Boeker, E. 1982. *Defence without offence: non-nuclear defence for Europe*. Bradford, UK: Bradford University, School of Peace Studies Paper No. 8, 60 pp.

Barnett, R. W. 1984. *Beyond war: Japan's concept of comprehensive national security*. New York: Pergamon Press, 155 pp.

Behar, N. 1985. Non-military aspects of mutual security: regional and global issues. *Bulletin of Peace Proposals*, Oslo, 16:363–373.

Biswas, A. K. 1983. Shared natural resources: future conflicts or peaceful development? In: Dupuy, R.-J. (ed.). *Settlement of disputes on the new natural resources*. Hague: Martinus Nijhoff, 487 pp.: pp. 197–215.

Blechman, B. M. 1985. *National security and strategic minerals: an analysis of U.S. dependence on foreign sources of cobalt*. Boulder, Colorado: Westview Press, 96 pp.

Borgese, E. M. & Ginsburg, N. (eds). 1982. *Ocean yearbook. III*. Chicago: University of Chicago Press, 581 pp.

Brown, L. R. 1977. *Redefining national security*. Washington: Worldwatch Institute Paper No. 14, 46 pp.

Brown, L. R. *et al.* 1985. *State of the world 1985*. New York: W. W. Norton, 301 pp.

Caldwell, L. K. 1984 *International environmental policy: emergence and dimensions*. Durham, N. Carolina: Duke University Press, 368 pp.

Cronan, D. 1985. Wealth of sea-floor minerals. *New Scientist*, London, 106(1459):34–38.

Eckholm, E. P. 1982. *Down to earth: environment and human needs*. New York: W. W. Norton, 238 pp.

Eide, A. 1975. Planting every inch. *Ceres*, Rome, 8(1):50–53.

El-Hinnawi, E. 1985. *Environmental refugees*. Nairobi: UN Environment Programme, 41 pp.

Fraser, R. (ed.). 1985. Sudan. *Keesing's Contemporary Archives*, Harlow, UK, 31(7):33700–33707.

Galtung, J. 1982. *Environment, development and military activity: towards alternative security doctrines*. Oslo: Universitetsforlaget, 143 pp.

Galtung, J. 1984. *There are alternatives!: four roads to peace and security*. Nottingham, UK: Spokesman, 221 pp.

Goldblat, J. 1982. *Agreements for arms control: a critical survey*. London: Taylor & Francis, 387 pp. [a SIPRI BOOK].

Gordon, L. 1978. *International stability and North–South relations*. Muscatine, Iowa: Stanley Foundation, Occasional Paper No. 17, 35 pp.

Halket, T. D., Leister, V., Savage, E. A., Lephart, J. V., & Miller, A. 1982–1983. Report on the proposed agreement governing the activities of states on the moon and other celestial bodies. *Jurimetrics Journal*, Chicago, 23(3):259–277.

Hardin, G. 1968. Tragedy of the commons. *Science*, Washington, 162:1243–1248.

Hardin, G. & Baden, J. (eds). 1977. *Managing the commons*. San Francisco: W. H. Freeman, 294 pp.

Hardin, G. 1985. Human ecology: the subversive, conservative science. *American Zoologist*, USA, 25:469–476.

Holdgate, M. W., Kassas, M., & White, G. F. (eds). 1982. *World environment 1972–1982: a report by the United Nations Environment Programme*. Dublin: Tycooly, 637 pp.

IUCN (International Union for Conservation of Nature & Natural Resources). 1980. *World conservation strategy: living resource conservation for sustainable development*. Gland, Switzerland: IUCN, portfolio (unpaginated).

Jackson, C. L. 1980. Allocation of the radio spectrum. *Scientific American*, New York, 242(2):30–35,130.

Janis, I. L. 1982. *Groupthink: psychological studies of policy decisions and fiascoes*. 2nd ed. Boston: Houghton Mifflin, 351 pp.

Kimball, L. 1985. Antarctica: testing the great experiment. *Environment*, Washington, 27(7):14–17, 26–30.

Kiss, A. C. (ed.). 1983. *Selected multilateral treaties in the field of the environment*. Nairobi: United Nations Environment Programme, Reference Series No. 3, 525 pp.

Lovins, A. B. & Lovins, L. H. 1982. *Brittle power: energy strategy for national security*. Andover, Mass.: Brick House, 486 pp.

Luard, E. 1983–1984. Who owns the Antarctic? *Foreign Affairs*, New York, 62:1175–1193.

Maull, H. W. 1984. *Raw materials, energy and Western security*. London: Macmillan, 413 pp.

Purcell, A. H. 1982. *Resource optimization and world peace*. Muscatine, Iowa: Stanley Foundation, Occasional Paper No. 30, 22 pp.

Romulo, C. P. *et al.* 1982. *Relationship between disarmament and international security*. New York: UN Department of Political & Security Council Affairs, Disarmament Study Series No. 8 (A/36/567), 55 pp.

Sai, F. T. 1984. Population factor in Africa's development dilemma. *Science*, Washington, 226:801–805.

Shusterich, K. M. 1984. Antarctic treaty system: history, substance, and speculation. *International Journal*, Toronto, 39:800–827.

Smith, D. D. 1983. Conflict resolution in outer space: international law and policy. In: Dupuy, R.-J. (ed.). *Settlement of disputes on the new natural resources*. Hague: Martinus Nijhoff, 487 pp.: pp. 243–277.

Stavridis, J. 1985. Resource wars. *U.S. Naval Institute Proceedings*, Annapolis, Maryland, 111(1):72–77.

Thorsell, J. 1985. Parks that promote peace. *WWF News*, Gland, Switzerland, 1985(38):2.

Thorsson, I. *et al.* 1982. *Relationship between disarmament and develop-ment.* New York: UN Department of Political & Security Council Affairs, Disarmament Study Series No. 5 (A/36/536), 189 pp.

Tuchman, B. W. 1984. *March of folly: from Troy to Vietnam.* New York: Alfred A. Knopf, 447 pp. + 24 pl.

Ullman, R. H. 1983–1984. Redefining security. *International Security,* Cambridge, Mass., 8(1):129–153.

UN (United Nations). 1968. *Charter of the United Nations and statute of the International Court of Justice.* New York: United Nations, 87 pp.

UN (United Nations). 1978. Register of international rivers. *Water Supply & Management,* Oxford, 2(1):1–58 + 5 maps.

UNEP (United Nations Environment Programme). 1978a. *Co-operation in the field of the environment concerning natural resources shared by two or more states.* Nairobi: UN Environment Programme, Decision No. 6/14 of 24 May 1978, 1 p.

UNEP (United Nations Environment Programme). 1978b. *Draft principles of conduct in the field of the environment for the guidance of states in the conservation and harmonious utilization of natural resources shared by two or more states.* Nairobi: UN Environment Programme, Document No. UNEP/GC.6/17 of 10 March 1978, 3+14 pp.

UNEP (United Nations Environment Programme). 1985. *Register of international treaties and other agreements in the field of the environment.* Nairobi: UN Environment Programme, Document No. UNEP/GC/ INFORMATION/11/REV.1, 209 pp.

UNGA (United Nations General Assembly). 1948. *Universal declaration of human rights.* New York: UN General Assembly Resolution No. 217(III)A of 10 December 1948, 3 pp.

UNGA (United Nations General Assembly). 1970. *Declaration of principles governing the sea-bed and the ocean floor, and the subsoil thereof, beyond the limits of national jurisdiction.* New York: UN General Assembly Resolution No. 2749 (XXV) of 17 December 1970, 2 pp.

UNGA (United Nations General Assembly). 1973. *Co-operation in the field of the environment concerning natural resources shared by two or more States.* New York: UN General Assembly Resolution No. 3129 (XXVIII) of 13 December 1973, 1 p.

UNGA (United Nations General Assembly). 1974. *Definition of aggres-sion.* New York: UN General Assembly Resolution No. 3314 (XXIX) of 14 December 1974, 6 pp.

UNGA (United Nations General Assembly). 1982. *World charter for nature.* New York: UN General Assembly Resolution No. 37/7 of 28 October 1982, 5 pp.

Vogely, W. A. 1982. International security implications of materials and energy resource depletion. In: Teich, A. H. & Thornton, R. (eds).

Science, technology, and the issues of the eighties: policy outlook. Boulder, Colorado: Westview Press, 290 pp.: pp. 233–251.

Waldheim, K. 1975. *Economic implications of sea-bed mining in the international area.* New York: UN General Assembly, Document No. A/CONF.62/37 of 18 February 1975, 17 pp.

Weinstein, J. M. 1985. Nonmilitary threats to Soviet national security. *Naval War College Review*, Newport, Rhode Island, 38(4):28–40.

Westing, A. H. 1980. *Warfare in a fragile world: military impact on the human environment.* London: Taylor & Francis, 249 pp. [a SIPRI book].

Appendix 1: Global resources and international conflict: select bibliography

Arthur H. Westing
Stockholm International Peace Research Institute

Arad, R. W. & Arad, U. B. 1979. Scarce natural resources and potential conflict. In: Arad, R. W. *et al. Sharing global resources.* New York: McGraw-Hill, 220 pp.: pp. 23–104.

Arbatov, A. & Amirov, I. 1984. Raw material problems in interstate conflicts. *International Affairs,* Moscow, 1984(8):65–73,103.

Archer, C. & Scrivener, D. 1982–1983. Frozen frontiers and resource wrangles: conflict and cooperation in northern waters. *International Affairs,* London, 59:59–76.

Brown, L. R. 1977. *Redefining national security.* Washington: Worldwatch Institute, Paper No. 14, 46 pp.

Bullis, L. H. (ed.). 1981. *Congressional handbook on U.S. materials import dependency/vulnerability.* Washington: US House of Representatives, Committee on Banking, Finance & Urban Affairs Print No. 97–6, 405 pp.

Caldwell, L. K. 1985. *US interests and the global environment.* Muscatine, Iowa: Stanley Foundation, Occasional Paper No. 35, 25 pp.

Castle, E. N. & Price, K. A. (eds). 1983. *U.S. interests and global natural resources: energy, minerals, food.* Washington: Resources for the Future, 147 pp.

Choucri, N. 1983. *Population and conflict: new dimensions of population dynamics.* New York: UN Fund for Population Activities, Policy Development Study No. 8, 47 pp.

Choucri, N. (ed.). 1984. *Multidisciplinary perspectives on population and conflict.* Syracuse, NY: Syracuse University Press, 220 pp.

Choucri, N. & North, R. C. 1975. *Nations in conflict: national growth and international violence.* San Francisco: W. H. Freeman, 356 pp.

Colinvaux, P. 1980. *Fates of nations: a biological theory of history.* New York: Simon & Schuster, 384 pp.

Cooley, J. K. 1984. War over water. *Foreign Policy,* Washington, 1984(54):3–26.

Dupuy, R.-J. (ed.). 1983. *Settlement of disputes on the new natural resources.* Hague: Martinus Nijhoff, 487 pp.

Durham, W. H. 1979. *Scarcity and survival in Central America: ecological origins of the Soccer War.* Stanford, Calif.: Stanford University Press, 209 pp.

Falk, R. A. 1971. *This endangered planet: prospects and proposals for human survival.* New York: Random House, 496 pp.

Frolov, I. 1982. *Global problems and the future of mankind.* Moscow: Progress Publishers, 311 pp.

Galtung, J. 1982. *Environment, development and military activity: towards alternative security doctrines.* Oslo: Universitetsforlaget, 143 pp.

Hargreaves, D. & Fromson, S. 1983. *World index of strategic minerals: production, exploitation and risk.* Aldershot, UK: Gower, 300 pp.

Heinebäck, B. 1974. *Oil and security.* Stockholm: Almqvist & Wiksell, 197 pp. [a SIPRI book].

Hveem, H. & Malnes, R. 1980. *Military use of natural resources: the case for conversion and control.* Oslo: International Peace Research Institute, Publication No. S-29/80, 138 pp.

Inozemtsev, N. N. (ed.). 1984. *Global problems of our age.* Moscow: Progress Publishers, 328 pp.

Kemp, G. 1977–1978. Scarcity and strategy. *Foreign Affairs,* New York, 56:396–414.

LeCuyer, J. A. 1977. Food as a component of national defense strategy. *Parameters,* Carlisle Barracks, Pennsylvania, 7(4):56–70.

Leroy, M. 1978. *Population and world politics: the interrelationships between demographic factors and international relations.* Leiden: Martinus Nijhoff, 144 pp.

Levin, A. L. 1977. *Protecting the human environment: procedures and principles for preventing and resolving international controversies.* New York: UN Institute for Training and Research, 131 pp.

Lovins, A. B. & Lovins, L. H. 1982. *Brittle power: energy strategy for national security.* Andover, Mass.: Brick House, 486 pp.

Luard, E. 1983–1984. Who owns the Antarctic? *Foreign Affairs,* New York, 62:1175–1193.

Maull, H. W. 1984. *Raw materials, energy and Western security.* London: Macmillan, 413 pp.

McCartan, B. 1985. Resource wars: the myth of American mineral vulnerability. *Defense Monitor,* Washington, 14(9):1–8.

McNaugher, T. L. 1985. *Arms and oil: U.S. military strategy and the Persian Gulf.* Washington: Brookings Institution, 226 pp.

Miller, J. A., Fine, D. I. & McMichael, R. D. (eds). 1980. *Resource war in 3-D: dependency, diplomacy, defense.* Pittsburgh: World Affairs Council of Pittsburgh, 109 pp.

Mitchell, B. 1976. Politics, fish, and international resource management: the British-Icelandic cod war. *Geographical Review,* New York, 66:127–138.

Mitchell, B. 1977. Resources in Antarctica: potential for conflict. *Marine Policy,* Guildford, UK, 1:91–101.

Nincic, M. 1985. *How war might spread to Europe.* London: Taylor & Francis, 109 pp. [a SIPRI book].

Purcell, A. H. 1982. *Resource optimization and world peace.* Muscatine, Iowa: Stanley Foundation, Occasional Paper No. 30, 22 pp.

Shafer, M. 1982. Mineral myths. *Foreign Policy,* Washington, 1982(47):154–171.

Solem, K. E. 1976. Energy resources and global strategic planning. *Impact of Science on Society,* Paris, 26:77–90.

Sprout, H. & Sprout, M. 1957. Environmental factors in the study of international politics. *Journal of Conflict Resolution,* Beverly Hills, Calif., 1:309–328.

Sprout, H. & Sprout, M. 1957. Environmental factors in the study of *with special reference to international politics.* Princeton, New Jersey: Princeton University Press, 236 pp.

Timberlake, L. & Tinker, J. 1984. *Environment and conflict.* London: International Institute for Environment and Development, Earthscan Briefing Document No. 40, 88 pp. + 6 pl.

Ullman, R. H. 1983–1984. Redefining security. *International Security,* Cambridge, Mass., 8(1):129–153.

Vogely, W. A. 1982. International security implications of materials and energy resource depletion. In: Teich, A. H. & Thornton, R. (eds). *Science, technology, and the issues of the eighties: policy outlook.* Boulder, Colo.: Westview Press, 290 pp.: pp. 233–251.

Wallensteen, P. 1976. Scarce goods as political weapons: the case of food. *Journal of Peace Research,* Oslo, 4:277–298.

Wallerstein, M. B. 1980. *Food for war—food for peace: United States food aid in a global context.* Cambridge, Mass.: MIT Press, 312 pp.

Weinstein, J. M. 1985. Nonmilitary threats to Soviet national security. *Naval War College Review,* Newport, Rhode Island, 38(4):28–40.

Westing, A. H. 1980. *Warfare in a fragile world: military impact on the human environment.* London: Taylor & Francis, 249 pp. [a SIPRI book],

Wionczek, M. S. 1983. Energy and international security in the 1980s: realities or misperceptions? *Third World Quarterly,* London, 5:839–847.

Appendix 2. Wars and skirmishes involving natural resources: a selection from the twentieth century[1]

Arthur H. Westing
Stockholm International Peace Research Institute

1. World War I of 1914–18

(*a*) *Particulars:* Primarily in the northern hemisphere, primarily Europe, but also Asia, Africa, etc.; primarily in the temperate habitat. An interstate war, July 1914–November 1918; fatality class 7.

(*b*) *Description:* A complex of several more or less distinct wars that can in simple terms be summarized as an unsuccessful war by the Central Powers—i.e., Germany, Austria-Hungary, Turkey, Bulgaria, etc.— against the Allies—i.e., France, the United Kingdom, Russia, Italy, the USA, Belgium, Portugal, Serbia, Montenegro (the last two now part of Yugoslavia), Greece, Romania, Japan, etc.

(*c*) *Natural resource aspect:* Among the causes of World War I were population pressures in central Europe, territorial rivalries (e.g., over the iron-rich Lorraine region, now a part of France), a desire by Germany to gain access to oil, and conflicts over colonies or spheres of influence in resource-rich Africa, eastern Asia, Pacific Ocean islands, etc.

(*d*) *References:* Eckes (1979, pages 3–25, 277–80), Leith (1931, pages 139–49), McNeill (1982, pages 307–17), and Russett (1981–1982).

[1]This compilation is a revision of an earlier work (Westing, 1980, pages 195–97). The wars are located as to hemisphere, land mass, and habitat (Westing, 1980, page 21). They are categorized as interstate, colonial, or civil (intrastate). Fatalities are presented in accordance with the concept of Richardson (1960, pages 4–12). In order to determine the fatality class into which a war falls, the base-ten logarithm of the total number of direct fatalities, both civil and military, is taken and then rounded to the nearest whole number. By way of example, a war of fatality class 5 would be any for which this number of fatalities is in the neighbourhood of 10^5 (100 000), or, more specifically, falls between $10^{4.5}$ (31 623) and $10^{5.5}$ (316 228). The use of such broad logarithmic classes is a reflection of the uncertainty that must be associated with fatality information on most wars—an uncertainty, moreover, that is assumed to increase exponentially as the magnitude of the war increases.

2. Chaco War of 1932–35

(*a*) *Particulars:* In the southern hemisphere, in South America; in the tropical habitat. An interstate war, July 1932–June 1935; fatality class 5.

(*b*) *Description:* Successful war by Paraguay against Bolivia, primarily in order to annex the Gran Chaco wilderness area.

(*c*) *Natural resource aspect:* The Gran Chaco was thought (incorrectly) to contain oil.

(*d*) *Reference:* Zook (1960).

3. World War II of 1939–45

(*a*) *Particulars:* Primarily in the northern hemisphere, in Europe, Asia, Africa, Pacific Ocean islands, Atlantic Ocean islands, etc.; primarily in the temperate and tropical habitats, but also in the desert and arctic habitats. An interstate war, September 1939–August 1945; fatality class 8.

(*b*) *Description:* A complex of several dozen more or less distinct wars, all more or less closely connected in some supportive or opposing fashion with wars of conquest by Germany and Japan; summarized in its simplest terms as an unsuccessful war of aggrandizement by the Axis—i.e., Germany (under Hitler), Austria (annexed by Germany), Italy, Japan, Hungary, Bulgaria, Romania, Finland, etc.—against the Allies—i.e., France, the United Kingdom, Poland, the USSR, Belgium, the USA, China, Czechoslovakia, Greece, the Netherlands, Yugoslavia, Norway, etc.

(*c*) *Natural resource aspect:* A need of added living space (*Lebensraum*) was one of the justifications given by Germany (1937 population density, 190 persons per square kilometre) for pursuing the war; Japan's expansionist tendencies were motivated in large part by its paucity of indigenous natural resources; Germany annexed the iron-rich Lorraine region of north-eastern France and the agriculturally flourishing and iron-rich Ukraine region of the USSR (only to lose them again at the end of the war); Germany made large-scale use of slave labour imported from Poland, the USSR, etc.; Germany pillaged the Polish timber resource; in 1944 the USSR annexed from Finland the nickel-rich Petsamo (now Pechenga) territory on the Barents Sea.

(*d*) *References:* Boldt & Queneau (1967, page 70), Eckes (1979, pages 57–87, 283–88), Hankins (1938), Kamenetsky (1960–1961), Kruszewski (1940), and UN War Crimes Commission (1948, page 496).

4. Algerian War of Independence of 1954–62

(*a*) *Particulars:* In the northern hemisphere, in Africa; largely in the desert habitat. A colonial war, November 1954–March 1962; fatality class 6.

(*b*) *Description:* Successful attempt by Algeria to gain its independence from France.

(*c*) *Natural resource aspect:* France was reluctant to lose Algeria partly because of its rich oil deposits.

(*d*) *Reference:* Horne (1977, pages 241–42).

5. Congo Civil War of 1960–64

(*a*) *Particulars:* In the southern hemisphere, in Africa; in the tropical habitat. A civil war, July 1960–January 1964; fatality class 5.

(*b*) *Description:* Internal turmoil following independence from Belgium that evolved into an unsuccessful attempt by Katanga (now Shaba) Province to secede from the newly independent Republic of the Congo (Zaire since 1971), the latter being helped by United Nations forces. (In March 1977 and again in May 1978 Katangese who had found refuge in Angola launched invasions of Zaire, i.e., of Shaba Province, reportedly with the support of Cuba and other states. These were repulsed by Zaire with the assistance of a number of African and other states, notably Belgium and France.)

(*c*) *Natural resource aspect:* The secession was in large part fomented by Belgian and other foreign interests so as to protect their investments in copper and other minerals (Katanga having rich deposits of copper, uranium, chromium, cobalt, tin, iron, gold, etc.).

(*d*) *References:* Lefever (1965) and Young (1978–1979).

6. Third Arab-Israeli War of 1967

(*a*) *Particulars:* The 'Six-Day' War; in the northern hemisphere, in Asia (Middle East); in the desert habitat. An interstate war, June 1967; fatality class 4.

(*b*) *Description:* Conquest by Israel of portions of Egypt (Sinai Peninsula), Jordan (West Bank and Old Jerusalem), and Syria (Golan Heights), including also the closing by Israel of the Suez Canal and the opening of the Straits of Tiran to the Gulf of Aqaba (thereby restoring access for itself from the port of Elat to the Indian Ocean).

(*c*) *Natural resource aspect:* An important cause of the war was the struggle for the waters of the Jordan and other rivers in the area. The oil deposits of the Sinai Peninsula may have constituted another of the attractions of this region to Israel, the deposits apparently sufficient to supply one-tenth of Israel's needs.

(*d*) *References:* Cooley (1984) and Safran (1969, pages 317–82).

7. Nigerian Civil War of 1967–70

(*a*) *Particulars:* In the northern hemisphere, in Africa; in the tropical habitat. A civil war, June 1967–January 1970; fatality class 6.

(*b*) *Description:* Unsuccessful attempt by the south-eastern (so-called Eastern) region—which proclaimed itself the independent republic of Biafra—to secede from Nigeria.

(*c*) *Natural resource aspect:* The government was reluctant to lose Biafra in large part owing to its rich deposits of oil.

(*d*) *References:* Cervenka (1971) and Nafziger (1972).

8. El Salvador-Honduras War of 1969

(*a*) *Particulars:* The 'Football' or 'Soccer' War; in the northern hemisphere, in North (Central) America; in the tropical habitat. An interstate war, July 1969; fatality class 3.

(*b*) *Description:* Invasion of sparsely populated Honduras by densely populated El Salvador, the latter evacuating Honduras following mediation by the Organization of American States (OAS).

(*c*) *Natural resource aspect:* El Salvador (1969 population density, 158 persons per square kilometre, growth rate, 3.7 per cent, giving a doubling time of 19 years) invaded neighbouring Honduras (1969 population density, 22 persons per square kilometre) primarily (*i*) to prevent Honduras from expelling its unauthorized immigrants from El Salvador (who amounted to perhaps 12 per cent of the Honduran population), and (*ii*) to force it to accept immigrants in the future. El Salvador largely attained its first goal, but not its second one.

(*d*) *Reference:* Durham (1979).

9. Anglo-Icelandic Clash of 1972–73

(*a*) *Particulars:* The 'Cod' War; in the northern hemisphere, an Atlantic Ocean island; in the arctic habitat. An interstate war, July 1972–September 1973; fatality class 0.

(*b*) *Description:* In 1972 Iceland unilaterally extended its coastal fishing rights from 22 to 93 kilometres; the United Kingdom (with the support of the International Court of Justice) refused to recognize this extension, but British trawlers and a frigate were driven away by Icelandic gunboats.

(*c*) *Natural resource aspect:* Iceland (which has been described as 'a rock surrounded by fish') was protecting its access to a natural resource vital to its national economy. (In 1975 the fishing limits were once again extended, this time to 370 kilometres.)

(*d*) *Reference:* Mitchell (1976).

10. Paracel (Hsi-sha) Island Clash of 1974

(*a*) *Particulars:* In the northern hemisphere, a Pacific Ocean (South China Sea) island group (16°30′N, 112°15′E); in the tropical habitat. An interstate war, January 1974; fatality class 1.

(*b*) *Description:* The islands were occupied by Japan during World War II but passed to China in 1945; the islands were also claimed by South Viet Nam which manned a small garrison there until 1974, when it was attacked and driven away by Chinese armed forces.

(*c*) *Natural resource aspect:* The islands are believed to be underlain by rich deposits of oil, presumably one of the chief reasons for the interest shown in them.

(*d*) *References:* Harrison (1977, pp. 189–213, 299–301), Heinebäck (1974, pages 133–35), and Park (1978).

11. Western Sahara Revolt of 1976–

(*a*) *Particulars:* In the nothern hemisphere, in Africa; in the desert habitat. A civil war, February 1976–; fatality class 4.

(*b*) *Description:* Ongoing attempt by insurgents (Frente Polisario) to create an independent nation (the Democratic Saharan Arab Republic) out of the former Spanish (Western) Sahara, which in early 1976 had been partitioned by Spain between Morocco (two-thirds) and Mauritania (one-third), both portions of which have been under the control of Morocco since 1980.

(*c*) *Natural resource aspect:* The region in question contains rich phosphate deposits—a major reason why Morocco (and Mauritania as well until 1980) has been reluctant to relinquish it.

(*d*) *References:* Damis (1983), Hodges (1983), and Kilgore (1981).

12. Falkland/Malvinas Conflict of 1982

(*a*) *Particulars:* In the southern hemisphere, an Atlantic Ocean island group (59°W,52°S); in the temperate habitat. An interstate war, April–June 1982; fatality class 3.

(*b*) *Description:* An unsuccessful attempt by Argentina to gain/regain possession of the islands from the United Kingdom by military force, the ownership of which has been claimed by both states for more than 150 years.

(*c*) *Natural resource aspect:* The attractiveness of the islands to both sides can be attributed in part to a desire to control the fishery resources of the surrounding waters, as well as any offshore oil deposits that might be discovered. Moreover, Argentina considers its claim to the island group to strengthen its claim to a segment of Antarctica and thus to the natural resources.

(*d*) *References:* Fuchs (1985), Goldblat & Millán (1983), and Hoffmann & Hoffmann (1984, page 123–26).

References

Boldt, J. R., Jr & Queneau, P. 1967. *Winning of nickel: its geology, mining, and extractive metallurgy.* Princeton, New Jersey: D. Van Nostrand, 487 pp. + pl.

Cervenka, Z. 1971. *Nigerian War 1967–1970: history of the war, selected bibliography and documents.* Frankfurt a.M.: Bernard & Graefe Verlag für Wehrwesen, 459 pp.

Cooley, J. K. 1984. War over water. *Foreign Policy,* Washington, 1984(54):3–26.

Damis, J. 1983. *Conflict in northwest Africa: the Western Sahara dispute.* Stanford, Calif.: Hoover Institution Press, 196 pp.

Durham, W. H. 1979. *Scarcity and survival in Central America: ecological origins of the Soccer War.* Stanford, Calif.: Stanford University Press, 209 pp.

Eckes, A. E. Jr. 1979. *United States and the global struggle for minerals.* Austin: University of Texas Press, 353 pp.

Fuchs, V. 1985. Falkland Islands and Antarctica. *NATO's Sixteen Nations,* Brussels, 30(4):26–30.

Goldblat, J. & Millán, V. 1983. Falklands/Malvinas Conflict: a spur to arms build-ups. *SIPRI Yearbook,* London, 1983:467–527.

Hankins, F. H. 1938. Pressure of population as a cause of war. *Annals of the American Academy of Political & Social Science,* Philadelphia, 198:101–108.

Harrison, S. S. 1977. *China, oil and Asia: conflict ahead?* New York: Columbia University Press, 317 pp.

Heinebäck, B. 1974. *Oil and security.* Stockholm: Almqvist & Wiksell, 197 pp. [a SIPRI book].

Hodges, T. 1983. *Western Sahara: the roots of a desert war.* Westport, Conn.: Lawrence Hill, 388 pp. + 16 pl.

Hoffmann, F. L. & Hoffmann, O. M. 1984. *Sovereignty in dispute: the Falklands/Malvinas, 1493–1982.* Boulder, Colorado: Westview Press, 194 pp.

Horne, A. 1977. *Savage war of peace: Algeria 1954–1962.* London: Macmillan, 604 pp. + 40 pl.

Kamenetsky, I. 1960–1961. *Lebensraum* in Hitler's war plan: the theory and the Eastern European reality. *American Journal of Economics & Sociology,* New York, 20:313–326.

Kilgore, A. 1981. Phosphate links with desert war. *South*, London, 1981(4):72–73.

Kruszewski, C. 1940. Germany's *Lebensraum*. *American Political Science Review*, Washington, 34:964–975.

Lefever, E. W. 1965. *Crisis in the Congo: a United Nations force in action.* Washington: Brookings Institution, 215 pp.

Leith, C. K. 1931. *World minerals and world politics.* New York: McGraw-Hill, 213 pp.

McNeill, W. H. 1982. *Pursuit of power: technology, armed force, and society since A.D. 1000.* Chicago: University of Chicago Press, 405 pp.

Mitchell, B. 1976. Politics, fish, and international resource management: the British-Icelandic cod war. *Geographical Review*, New York, 66:127–138.

Nafziger, E. W. 1972. Economic aspects of the Nigerian Civil War. In: Higham, R. (ed.). *Civil wars in the twentieth century*. Lexington: University of Kentucky Press, 260 pp.: pp. 184–202, 252–254.

Park, C.-H. 1978. South China Sea disputes: who owns the islands and the natural resources? *Ocean Development & International Law*, New York, 5:27–59.

Richardson, L. F. 1969. *Statistics of deadly quarrels.* Pittsburgh: Boxwood Press, 373 pp. + 2 tables.

Russett, B. 1981–1982. Security and the resources scramble: will 1984 be like 1914? *International Affairs*, London, 58:42–58.

Safran, N. 1969. *From war to war: the Arab-Israeli confrontation, 1948–1967.* New York: Pegasus, 464 pp.

UN War Crimes Commission. 1948. *History of the United Nations War Crimes Commission and the development of the laws of war.* London: His Majesty's Stationery Office, 592 pp.

Westing, A. H. 1980. *Warfare in a fragile world: military impact on the human environment.* London: Taylor & Francis, 249 pp. [a SIPRI book].

Young, C. 1978–1979. *Zaire: the unending crisis. Foreign Affairs*, New York, 57:169–185.

Zook, D. H., Jr. 1960. *Conduct of the Chaco War.* New York: Bookman, 280 pp.

Appendix 3. Spitsbergen Treaty of 1920

I. Text

The Treaty Regulating the Status of Spitsbergen and Conferring the Sovereignty on Norway was signed at Paris on 9 February 1920 and (France, the Depositary, having received the requisite nine ratifications) entered into force on 14 August 1925. The parties to the Treaty are given in section II below. The text of the Treaty follows (League of Nations, 1920–1921):

[The USA, the United Kingdom (also on behalf of Canada, Australia, New Zealand, South Africa, and India), Denmark, France, Italy, Japan, Norway, the Netherlands, and Sweden] . . . have agreed as follows:

Article 1.

The High Contracting Parties undertake to recognise, subject to the stipulations of the present Treaty, the full and absolute sovereignty of Norway over the Archipelago of Spitsbergen, comprising, with Bear Island or Beeren-Eiland, all the islands situated between 10° and 35° longitude East of Greenwich and between 74° and 81° latitude North, especially West Spitsbergen, North-East Land, Barents Island, Edge Island, Wiche Islands, Hope Island or Hopen-Eiland, and Prince Charles Foreland, together with all islands great or small and rocks appertaining thereto.

Article 2.

Ships and nationals of all the High Contracting Parties shall enjoy equally the rights of fishing and hunting in the territories specified in article 1 and in their territorial waters.

Norway shall be free to maintain, take or decree suitable measures to ensure the preservation and, if necessary, the re-constitution of the fauna and flora of the said regions, and their territorial waters; it being clearly understood that these measures shall always be applicable equally to the nationals of all the High Contracting Parties without any exemption, privilege or favour whatsoever, direct or indirect to the advantage of any one of them.

Occupiers of land whose rights have been recognised in accordance with the terms of Articles 6 and 7 will enjoy the exclusive right of hunting on their own land: (1) in the neighbourhood of their habitations, houses, stores, factories and installations, constructed for the purpose of developing their property, under conditions laid down by the local police regulations; (2) within a radius of 10 kilometres round the head-quarters of their place of business or works; and in both cases, subject always to the observance of regulations made by the Norwegian Government in accordance with the conditions laid down in the present Article.

Article 3.

The nationals of all the High Contracting Parties shall have equal liberty of access and entry for any reason or object whatever to the waters, fjords and ports of the territories specified in Article 1; subject to the observance of local laws and regulations, they may carry on there without impediment all maritime, industrial, mining and commercial operations on a footing of absolute equality.

They shall be admitted under the same conditions of equality to the exercise and practice of all maritime, industrial, mining or commercial enterprises both on land and in the territorial waters, and no monopoly shall be established on any account or for any enterprise whatever.

Notwithstanding any rules relating to coasting trade which may be in force in Norway, ships of the High Contracting Parties going to or coming from the territories specified in Article 1 shall have the right to put into Norwegian ports on their outward or homeward voyage for the purpose of taking on board or disembarking passengers or cargo going to or coming from the said territories, or for any other purpose.

It is agreed that in every respect and especially with regard to exports, imports and transit traffic, the nationals of all the High Contracting Parties, their ships and goods shall not be subject to any charges or restrictions whatever which are not borne by the nationals, ships or goods which enjoy in Norway the treatment of the most favoured nation; Norwegian nationals, ships or goods being for this purpose assimilated to those of the other High Contracting Parties, and not treated more favourably in any respect.

No charge or restriction shall be imposed on the exportation of any goods to the territories of any of the Contracting Powers other or more onerous than on the exportation of similar goods to the territory of any other Contracting Power (including Norway) or to any other destination.

Article 4.

All public wireless telegraphy stations established or to be established by or with the authorisation of, the Norwegian Government within the territories referred to in Article 1 shall always be open on a footing of absolute equality to communiations from ships of all flags and from nationals of the High Contracting Parties, under the conditions laid down in the Wireless Telegraphy Convention of July 5th, 1912, or in the subsequent International Convention which may be concluded to replace it.

Subject to international obligations arising out of a state of war, owners of landed property shall always be at liberty to establish and use for their own purposes wireless telegraphy installations, which shall be free to communicate on private business with fixed or moving wireless stations, including those on board ships and aircraft.

Article 5.

The High Contracting Parties recognise the utility of establishing an international meteorological station in the territories specified in Article 1, the organisation of which shall form the subject of a subsequent Convention.

Conventions shall also be concluded laying down the conditions under which scientific investigations may be conducted in the said territories.

Article 6.

Subject to the provisions of the present Article, acquired rights of nationals of the High Contracting Parties shall be recognised.

Claims arising from taking possession or from occupation of land before the signature of the present Treaty shall be dealt with in accordance with the Annex hereto [not included here], which will have the same force and effect as the present Treaty.

Article 7.

With regard to methods of acquisition, enjoyment and exercise of the right of ownership of property, including mineral rights, in the territories specified in Article 1, Norway undertakes to grant to all nationals of the High Contracting Parties treatment based on complete equality and in conformity with the stipulations of the present Treaty.

Expropriation may be resorted to only on grounds of public utility and on payment of proper compensation.

Article 8.

Norway undertakes to provide for the territories specified in Article 1 mining regulations which, especially from the point of view of imposts, taxes or charges of any kind, and of general or particular labour conditions, shall exclude all privileges, monopolies or favours for the benefit of the State or of the nationals of any one of the High Contracting Parties, including Norway, and shall guarantee to the paid staff of all categories the remuneration and protection necessary for their physical, moral and intellectual welfare.

Taxes, dues and duties levied shall be devoted exclusively to the said territories and shall not exceed what is required for the object in view.

So far, particularly, as the exportation of minerals is concerned, the Norwegian Government shall have the right to levy an export duty which shall not exceed 1% of the maximum value of the minerals exported up to 100,000 tons [tonnes], and beyond that quantity the duty will be proportionately diminished. The value shall be fixed at the end of the navigation season by calculating the average free on board price obtained.

Three months before the date fixed for their coming into force, the draft mining regulations shall be communicated by the Norwegian Government to the other Contracting Powers. If during this period one or more of the said Powers propose to modify these regulations before they are applied, such proposals shall be communicated by the Norwegian Government to the other Contracting Powers in order that they may be submitted to examination and the decision of a Commission composed of one representative of each of the said Powers. This Commission shall meet at the invitation of the Norwegian Government and shall come to a decision within a period of three months from the date of its first meeting. Its decisions shall be taken by a majority.

Article 9.

Subject to the rights and duties resulting from the admission of Norway to the League of Nations, Norway undertakes not to create nor to allow the establishment of any naval base in the territories specified in Article 1 and not to construct any fortification in the said territories, which may never be used for warlike purposes.

Article 10.

Until the recognition by the High Contracting Parties of a Russian Government shall permit Russia to adhere to the present Treaty, Russian nationals and companies shall enjoy the same rights as nationals of the High Contracting Parties.

Claims in the territories specified in Article 1 which they may have to put forward shall be presented under the conditions laid down in the present Treaty (Article 6 and Annex) through the intermediary of the Danish

Government, who declare their willingness to lend their good offices for this purpose.

The present Treaty, of which the French and English texts are both authentic, shall be ratified.

Ratifications shall be deposited at Paris as soon as possible.

Powers of which the seat of the Government is outside Europe may confine their action to informing the Government of the French Republic, through their diplomatic representative at Paris, that their ratification has been given, and in this case they shall transmit the instrument as soon as possible.

The present Treaty will come into force, in so far as the stipulations of Article 8 are concerned, from the date of its ratification by all the signatory Powers; and in all other respects on the same date as the mining regulations provided for in that Article.

Third Powers will be invited by the Government of the French Republic to adhere to the present Treaty duly ratified. This adhesion shall be effected by a communication addressed to the French Government, which will undertake to notify the other Contracting Parties.

In witness whereof the above named Plenipotentiaries have signed the present Treaty.

Done at Paris, the ninth day of February, 1920, in duplicate, one copy to be transmitted to the Government of His Majesty the King of Norway, and one deposited in the archives of the French Republic; authenticated copies will be transmitted to the other Signatory Powers.

. . .

II. Parties

As of January 1986, the Spitsbergen Treaty of 1920 has accumulated a total of 40 parties. Of the five permanent members of the United Nations Security Council, four have become parties, that is, France, the United Kingdom, the USA, and the USSR, but not China.[1] A list of the 40 parties to the Treaty as of January 1986, together with the year of joining, follows (Delbrück, 1984, page 976; augmented by information from the Depositary):

Afghanistan (1925), Albania (1930), Argentina (1927), Australia [1925], Austria (1930), Belgium (1925), Bulgaria (1925), Canada [1925], Chile (1928), Czechoslovakia (1930), Denmark (1925), Dominican Republic (1927), Egypt (1925), Finland (1925), France (1925), German DR (1974), Germany, FR (1925), Greece (1925), Hungary (1927), India [1925],

[1]China became a party to the 1920 Spitsbergen Treaty in 1925, but present day China (the People's Republic of China) has not recognized this treaty. It can be added that Taiwan (the Republic of China) has not recognized it either.

Ireland (1976), Italy (1925), Japan (1925), Monaco (1925), Netherlands (1925), New Zealand [1925], Norway (1925), Poland (1931), Portugal (1927), Romania (1925), Saudi Arabia (1925), South Africa [1925], Spain (1925), Sweden (1925), Switzerland (1925), United Kingdom (1925), USA (1925), USSR (1935), Venezuela (1928), and Yugoslavia (1925).

References

Delbrück, J. (ed.). 1984. *Friedensdokumente aus fünf Jahrhunderten [Peace documents from five centuries]* (in German). Kehl, FR Germany: N. P. Engel, 1625 pp.

League of Nations. 1920–1921. Treaty concerning the Archipelago of Spitsbergen. *League of Nations Treaty Series*, Geneva, 2:7–19.

Appendix 4. Antarctic Treaty of 1959

I. Text

The Antarctic Treaty was signed at Washington on 1 December 1959 and (the USA, the Depositary, having received the requisite 12 ratifications) entered into force on 23 June 1961. The parties to the Treaty are given in section II below. The text of the Treaty follows (Goldblat, 1982, pages 150–153):

The Governments of Argentina, Australia, Belgium, Chile, the French Republic, Japan, New Zealand, Norway, the Union of South Africa, the Union of Soviet Socialist Republics, the United Kingdom of Great Britain and Northern Ireland, and the United States of America.

Recognizing that it is in the interest of all mankind that Antarctica shall continue forever to be used exclusively for peaceful purposes and shall not become the scene or object of international discord;

Acknowledging the substantial contributions to scientific knowledge resulting from international cooperation in scientific investigation in Antarctica;

Convinced that the establishment of a firm foundation for the continuation and development of such cooperation on the basis of freedom of scientific investigation in Antarctica as applied during the International Geophysical Year [1957–58] accords with the interests of science and the progress of all mankind;

Convinced also that a treaty ensuring the use of Antarctica for peaceful purposes only and the continuance of international harmony in Antarctica will further the purposes and principles embodied in the Charter of the United Nations;

Have agreed as follows:

Article I

1. Antarctica shall be used for peaceful purposes only. There shall be prohibited, *inter alia,* any measures of a military nature, such as the establishment of military bases and fortifications, the carrying out of military maneuvers, as well as the testing of any type of weapons.

2. The present Treaty shall not prevent the use of military personnel of equipment for scientific research or for any other peaceful purpose.

Article II

Freedom of scientific investigation in Antarctica and cooperation toward that end, as applied during the International Geophysical Year, shall continue subject to the provisions of the present Treaty.

Article III

1. In order to promote international cooperation in scientific investigation in Antarctica, as provided for in Article II of the present Treaty, the Contracting Parties agree that, to the greatest extent feasible and practicable:

(*a*) Information regarding plans for scientific programs in Antarctica shall be exchanged to permit maximum economy and efficiency of operations;

(*b*) scientific personnel shall be exchanged in Antarctica between expeditions and stations;

(*c*) scientific observations and results from Antarctica shall be exchanged and made freely available.

2. In implementing this Article, every encouragement shall be given to the establishment of cooperative working relations with those Specialized Agencies of the United Nations and other international organizations having a scientific or technical interest in Antarctica.

Article IV

1. Nothing contained in the present Treaty shall be interpreted as:

(*a*) a renunciation by any Contracting Party of previously asserted rights of or claims to territorial sovereignty in Antarctica;

(*b*) a renunciation or diminution by any Contracting Party of any basis of claim to territorial sovereignty in Antarctica which it may have whether as a result of its activities or those of its nationals in Antarctica, or otherwise;

(*c*) prejudicing the position of any Contracting Party as regards its recognition or non-recognition of any other State's right of or claim or basis of claim to territorial sovereignty in Antarctica.

2. No acts or activities taking place while the present Treaty is in force shall constitute a basis for asserting, supporting or denying a claim to territorial sovereignty in Antarctica or create any rights of sovereignty in Antarctica. No new claim, or enlargement of an existing claim, to territorial sovereignty in Antarctica shall be asserted while the present Treaty is in force.

Article V

1. Any nuclear explosions in Antarctica and the disposal there of radioactive waste material shall be prohibited.

2. In the event of the conclusion of international agreements concerning the use of nuclear energy, including nuclear explosions and the disposal of radioactive waste material, to which all of the Contracting Parties whose representatives are entitled to participate in the meetings provided for under Article IX are parties, the rules established under such agreements shall apply in Antarctica.

Article VI

The provisions of the present Treaty shall apply to the area south of 60° South Latitude, including all ice shelves, but nothing in the present Treaty shall prejudice or in any way affect the rights, or the exercise of the rights, of any State under international law with regard to the high seas within that area.

Article VII

1. In order to promote the objectives and ensure the observance of the provisions of the present Treaty, each Contracting Party whose representatives are entitled to participate in the meetings referred to in Article IX of the Treaty shall have the right to designate observers to carry out any inspection provided for by the present Article. Observers shall be nationals of the Contracting Parties which designate them. The names of observers shall be communicated to every other Contracting Party having the right to designate observers, and like notice shall be given of the termination of their appointment.

2. Each observer designated in accordance with the provisions of paragraph 1 of this Article shall have complete freedom of access at any time to any or all areas of Antarctica.

3. All areas of Antarctica, including all stations, installations and equipment within those areas, and all ships and aircraft at points of discharging or embarking cargoes or personnel in Antarctica, shall be open at all times to inspection by any observers designated in accordance with paragraph 1 of this Article.

4. Aerial observation may be carried out at any time over any or all areas of Antarctica by any of the Contracting Parties having the right to designate observers.

5. Each Contracting Party shall, at the time when the present Treaty

enters into force for it, inform the other Contracting Parties, and thereafter shall give them notice in advance, of

(*a*) all expeditions to and within Antarctica, on the part of its ships or nationals, and all expeditions to Antarctica organized in or proceeding from its territory;

(*b*) all stations in Antarctica occupied by its nationals; and

(*c*) any military personnel or equipment intended to be introduced by it into Antarctica subject to the conditions prescribed in paragraph 2 of Article I of the present Treaty.

Article VIII

1. In order to facilitate the exercise of their functions under the present Treaty, and without prejudice to the respective positions of the Contracting Parties relating to jurisdiction over all other persons in Antarctica, observers designated under paragraph 1 of Article VII and scientific personnel exchanged under subparagraph 1 (*b*) of Article III of the Treaty, and members of the staffs accompanying any such persons, shall be subject only to the jurisdiction of the Contracting Party of which they are nationals in respect of all acts or omissions occurring while they are in Antarctica for the purpose of exercising their functions.

2. Without prejudice to the provisions of paragraph 1 of this Article, and pending the adoption of measures in pursuance of subparagraph 1 (*e*) of Article IX, the Contracting Parties concerned in any case of dispute with regard to the exercise of jurisdiction in Antarctica shall immediately consult together with a view to reaching a mutually acceptable solution.

Article IX

1. Representatives of the Contracting Parties named in the preamble to the present Treaty shall meet at the City of Canberra within two months after the date of entry into force of the Treaty, and thereafter at suitable intervals and places, for the purpose of exchanging information, consulting together on matters of common interest pertaining to Antarctica, and formulating and considering, and recommending to their Governments, measures in furtherance of the principles and objectives of the Treaty, including measures regarding:

(*a*) use of Antarctica for peaceful purposes only;

(*b*) facilitation of scientific research in Antarctica;

(*c*) facilitation of international scientific cooperation in Antarctica;

(*d*) facilitation of the exercise of the rights of inspection provided for in Article VII of the Treaty;

(*e*) questions relating to the exercise of jurisdiction in Antarctica;

(*f*) preservation and conservation of living resources in Antarctica.[1]

2. Each Contracting Party which has become a party to the present Treaty by accession under Article XIII shall be entitled to appoint representatives to participate in the meetings referred to in paragraph 1 of the present Article, during such time as that Contracting Party demonstrates its interest in Antarctica by conducting substantial scientific research activity there, such as the establishment of a scientific station or the despatch of a scientific expedition.

3. Reports from the observers referred to in Article VII of the present Treaty shall be transmitted to the representatives of the Contracting Parties participating in the meetings referred to in paragraph 1 of the present Article.

4. The measures referred to in paragraph 1 of this Article shall become effective when approved by all the Contracting Parties whose representatives were entitled to participate in the meetings held to consider those measures.

5. Any or all of the rights established in the present Treaty may be exercised as from the date of entry into force of the Treaty whether or not any measures facilitating the exercise of such rights have been proposed, considered or approved as provided in this Article.

Article X

Each of the Contracting Parties undertakes to exert appropriate efforts, consistent with the Charter of the United Nations, to the end that no one engages in any activity in Antarctica contrary to the principles or purposes of the present Treaty.

Article XI

1. If any dispute arises between two or more of the Contracting Parties concerning the interpretation or application of the present Treaty, those Contracting Parties shall consult among themselves with a view to having the dispute resolved by negotiation, inquiry, mediation, conciliation, arbitration, judicial settlement or other peaceful means of their own choice.

---

[1] Article IX.1(f) has led to the consummation of two further treaties: (*a*) the Convention for the Conservation of Antarctic Seals, which was signed at London on 1 June 1972 and entered into force on 11 March 1978 (Kiss, 1983, pages 38–39, 272–76); and (*b*) the Convention on the Conservation of Antarctic Marine Living Resources, which was signed at Canberra on 20 May 1980 and entered into force on 7 April 1982 (UNEP, 1985, pages 174–75).

2. Any dispute of this character not so resolved shall, with the consent, in each case, of all parties to the dispute, be referred to the International Court of Justice for settlement; but failure to reach agreement on reference to the International Court shall not absolve parties to the dispute from the responsibility of continuing to seek to resolve it by any of the various peaceful means referred to in paragraph 1 of this Article.

Article XII

1. (*a*) The present Treaty may be modified or amended at any time by unanimous agreement of the Contracting Parties whose representatives are entitled to participate in the meetings provided for under Article IX. Any such modification or amendment shall enter into force when the depositary Government has received notice from all such Contracting Parties that they have ratified it.

(*b*) Such modification or amendment shall thereafter enter into force as to any other Contracting Party when notice of ratification by it has been received by the depositary Government. Any such Contracting Party from which no notice of ratification is received within a period of two years from the date of entry into force of the modification or amendment in accordance with the provisions of subparagraph 1 (*a*) of this Article shall be deemed to have withdrawn from the present Treaty on the date of expiration of such period.

2. (*a*) If after the expiration of thirty years from the date of entry into force of the present Treaty, any of the Contracting Parties whose representatives are entitled to participate in the meetings provided for under Article IX so requests by a communication addressed to the depositary Government, a Conference of all the Contracting Parties shall be held as soon as practicable to review the operation of the Treaty.

(*b*) Any modification or amendment to the present Treaty which is approved at such a Conference by a majority of the Contracting Parties there represented, including a majority of those whose representatives are entitled to participate in the meetings provided for under Article IX, shall be communicated by the depositary Government to all the Contracting Parties immediately after the termination of the Conference and shall enter into force in accordance with the provisions of paragraph 1 of the present Article.

(*c*) If any such modification or amendment has not entered into force in accordance with the provisions of subparagraph 1 (*a*) of this Article within a period of two years after the date of its communication to all the Contracting Parties, any Contracting Party may at any time after the expiration of that period give notice to the depositary Government of its withdrawal from the present Treaty; and such withdrawal shall take effect two years after the receipt of the notice by the depositary Government.

Article XIII

1. The present Treaty shall be subject to ratification by the signatory States. It shall be open for accession by any State which is a Member of the United Nations, or by any other State which may be invited to accede to the Treaty with the consent of all the Contracting Parties whose representatives are entitled to participate in the meetings provided for under Article IX of the Treaty.

2. Ratification of or accession to the present Treaty shall be effected by each State in accordance with its constitutional processes.

3. Instruments of ratification and instruments of accession shall be deposited with the Government of the United States of America, hereby designated as the depositary Government.

4. The depositary Government shall inform all signatory and acceding States of the date of each deposit of an instrument of ratification or accession, and the date of entry into force of the Treaty and of any modification or amendment thereto.

5. Upon the deposit of instruments of ratification by all the signatory States, the present Treaty shall enter into force for those States and for States which have deposited instruments of accession. Thereafter the Treaty shall enter into force for any acceding State upon the deposit of its instrument of accession.

6. The present Treaty shall be registered by the depositary Government pursuant to Article 102 of the Charter of the United Nations.

Article XIV

The present Treaty, done in the English, French, Russian and Spanish languages, each version being equally authentic, shall be deposited in the archives of the Government of the United States of America, which shall transmit duly certified copies thereof to the Governments of the signatory and acceding States.

II. Parties

As of January 1986, the Antarctic Treaty of 1959 has accumulated a total of 32 parties, of which 16 are full ('consultative') parties and 16 are limited ('non-consultative') parties. Of the five permanent members of the United Nations Security Council, all have become full parties, that is, China, France, the United Kingdom, the USA, and the USSR. Lists of the 16 full and 16 limited parties to the Treaty as of January 1986, together with the year of joining, follow (Goldblat & Ferm, 1985; augmented by information from the Depositary):

1. *Full ('consultative') parties:* Argentina (1961), Australia (1961), Belgium (1961), Chile (1961), China (limited 1983; full 1985), France (1961), Germany, FR (limited 1979; full 1981), India (limited 1983; full 1983), Japan (1961), New Zealand (1961), Norway (1961), Poland (limited 1961; full 1977), South Africa (1961), United Kingdom (1961), USA (1961), and USSR (1961).

2. *Limited ('non-consultative') parties:* Brazil (1975), Bulgaria (1978), Cuba (1984), Czechoslovakia (1962), Denmark (1965), Finland (1984), German DR (1974), Hungary (1984), Italy (1981), Netherlands (1967), Papua New Guinea (1981), Peru (1981), Romania (1971), Spain (1982), Sweden (1984), and Uruguay (1980).

References

Goldblat, J. 1982. *Agreements for arms control: a critical survey.* London: Taylor & Francis, 387 pp. [a SIPRI book].

Goldblat, J. & Ferm, R. 1985. Major multilateral arms control agreements. *SIPRI Yearbook,* London, 1985:499–526,

Kiss, A. C. (ed.). 1983. *Selected multilateral treaties in the field of the environment.* Nairobi: United Nations Environment Programme, Reference Series No. 3, 525 pp.

UNEP (United Nations Environment Programme). 1985. *Register of international treaties and other agreements in the field of the environment.* Nairobi: UN Environment Programme, Document No. UNEP/GC/INFORMATION/11/REV.1, 209 pp.

Appendix 5. Outer Space Treaty of 1967

I. Text

The Treaty on Principles Governing the Activities of States in the Exploration and Use of Outer Space, including the Moon and other Celestial Bodies was signed at London, Moscow, and Washington on 27 January 1967 and (the United Kingdom, the USSR, and the USA, the Depositaries, having received the requisite five ratifications) entered into force on 10 October 1967. The parties to the Treaty are given in section II below. The text of the Treaty follows (Goldblat, 1982, pages 159–162):

The States Parties to this Treaty,

Inspired by the great prospects opening up before mankind as a result of man's entry into outer space,

Recognizing the common interest of all mankind in the progress of the exploration and use of outer space for peaceful purposes,

Believing that the exploration and use of outer space should be carried on for the benefit of all peoples irrespective of the degree of their economic or scientific development,

Desiring to contribute to broad international co-operation in the scientific as well as the legal aspects of the exploration and use of outer space for peaceful purposes,

Believing that such co-operation will contribute to the development of mutual understanding and to the strengthening of friendly relations between States and peoples,

Recalling resolution 1962 (XVIII), entitled "Declaration of Legal Principles Governing the Activities of States in the Exploration and Use of Outer Space", which was adopted unanimously by the United Nations General Assembly on 13 December 1963,

Recalling resolution 1884 (XVIII), calling upon States to refrain from placing in orbit around the earth any objects carrying nuclear weapons or any other kinds of weapons of mass destruction or from installing such weapons on celestial bodies, which was adopted unanimously by the United Nations General Assembly on 17 October 1963,

Taking account of United Nations General Assembly resolution 110 (II) of 3 November 1947, which condemned propaganda designed or likely to provoke or encourage any threat to the peace, breach of the peace or act of aggression, and considering that the aforementioned resolution is applicable to outer space,

Convinced that a Treaty on Principles Governing the Activities of States in the Exploration and Use of Outer Space, including the Moon and Other Celestial Bodies, will further the Purposes and Principles of the Charter of the United Nations,

Have agreed on the following:

Article I

The exploration and use of outer space, including the moon and other celestial bodies, shall be carried out for the benefit and in the interests of all countries, irrespective of their degree of economic or scientific development, and shall be the province of all mankind.

Outer space, including the moon and other celestial bodies, shall be free for exploration and use by all States without discrimination of any kind, on a basis of equality and in accordance with international law, and there shall be free access to all areas of celestial bodies.

There shall be freedom of scientific investigation in outer space, including the moon and other celestial bodies, and States shall facilitate and encourage international co-operation in such investigation.

Article II

Outer space, including the moon and other celestial bodies, is not subject to national appropriation by claim of sovereignty, by means of use or occupation, or by any other means.

Article III

States Parties to the Treaty shall carry on activities in the exploration and use of outer space, including the moon and other celestial bodies, in accordance with international law, including the Charter of the United Nations, in the interest of maintaining international peace and security and promoting international co-operation and understanding.

Article IV

States Parties to the Treaty undertake not to place in orbit around the earth any objects carrying nuclear weapons or any other kinds of weapons of mass destruction, install such weapons on celestial bodies, or station such weapons in outer space in any other manner.

The moon and other celestial bodies shall be used by all States Parties to the Treaty exclusively for peaceful purposes. The establishment of military bases, installations and fortifications, the testing of any type of weapons and the conduct of military manoeuvres on celestial bodies shall be forbidden. The use of military personnel for scientific research or for any other peaceful purposes shall not be prohibited. The use of any equipment or facility necessary for peaceful exploration of the moon and other celestial bodies shall also not be prohibited.

Article V

States Parties to the Treaty shall regard astronauts as envoys of mankind in outer space and shall render to them all possible assistance in the event of accident, distress, or emergency landing on the territory of another State Party or on the high seas. When astronauts make such landing, they shall be safely and promptly returned to the State of registry of their space vehicle.

In carrying on activities in outer space and on celestial bodies, the astronauts of one State Party shall render all possible assistance to the astronauts of other States Parties.

States Parties to the Treaty shall immediately inform the other States Parties to the Treaty or the Secretary-General of the United Nations of any phenomena they discover in outer space, including the moon and other celestial bodies, which could constitute a danger to the life or health of astronauts.

Article VI

States Parties to the Treaty shall bear international responsibility for national activities in outer space, including the moon and other celestial bodies, whether such activities are carried on by government agencies or by non-governmental entities, and for assuring that national activities are carried out in conformity with the provisions set forth in the present Treaty. The activities of non-governmental entities in outer space, including the moon and other celestial bodies, shall require authorization and continuing supervision by the appropriate State party to the Treaty. When activities are carried on in outer space, including the moon and other celestial bodies, by an international organization, responsibility for compliance with this Treaty shall be borne both by the international organization and by the States Parties to the Treaty participating in such organization.

Article VII

Each State Party to the Treaty that launches or procures the launching of an object into outer space, including the moon and other celestial bodies, and each State Party from whose territory or facility an object is launched, is internationally liable for damage to another State Party to the Treaty or to its natural or juridical persons by such object or its component parts on the Earth, in the air space or in outer space, including the moon and other celestial bodies.

Article VIII

A State Party to the Treaty on whose registry an object launched into outer space is carried shall retain jurisdiction and control over such object, and over any personnel thereof, while in outer space or on a celestial body. Ownership of objects launched into outer space, including objects landed or constructed on a celestial body, and of their component parts, is not affected by their presence in outer space or on a celestial body or by their return to the Earth. Such objects or component parts found beyond the limits of the State Party to the Treaty on whose registry they are carried shall be returned to that State Party, which shall, upon request, furnish identifying data prior to their return.

Article IX

In the exploration and use of outer space, including the moon and other celestial bodies, States Parties to the Treaty shall be guided by the principle of co-operation and mutual assistance and shall conduct all their activities in outer space, including the moon and other celestial bodies, with due regard to the corresponding interests of all other States Parties to the Treaty. States Parties to the Treaty shall pursue studies of outer space, including the moon and other celestial bodies, and conduct exploration of them so as to avoid their harmful contamination and also adverse changes in the environment of the Earth resulting from the introduction of extraterrestrial matter and, where necessary, shall adopt appropriate measures for this purpose. If a State Party to the Treaty has reason to believe that an activity or experiment planned by it or its nationals in outer space, including the moon and other celestial bodies, would cause potentially harmful interference with activities of other States Parties in the peaceful exploration and use of outer space, including the moon and other celestial bodies, it shall undertake appropriate international consultations before proceeding with any such activity or experiment. A State Party to the Treaty which has reason to believe that an activity or experiment planned by another State Party in outer space, including the moon and other celestial bodies, would cause potentially harmful interference with activities in the peaceful exploration and use of outer space, including the moon and other celestial bodies, may request consultation concerning the activity or experiment.

Article X

In order to promote international cooperation in the exploration and use of outer space, including the moon and other celestial bodies, in conformity with the purposes of this Treaty, the States Parties to the Treaty shall consider on a basis of equality any requests by other States Parties to the Treaty to be afforded an opportunity to observe the flight of space objects launched by these States.

The nature of such an opportunity for observation and the conditions under which it could be afforded shall be determined by agreement between the States concerned.

Article XI

In order to promote international cooperation in the peaceful exploration and use of outer space, States Parties to the Treaty conducting activities in outer space, including the moon and other celestial bodies, agree to inform the Secretary-General of the United Nations as well as the public and the international scientific community, to the greatest extent feasible and practicable, of the nature, conduct, locations and results of such activities. On receiving the said information, the Secretary-General of the United Nations should be prepared to disseminate it immediately and effectively.

Article XII

All stations, installations, equipment and space vehicles on the moon and other celestial bodies shall be open to representatives of other States Parties to the Treaty on a basis of reciprocity. Such representatives shall give reasonable advance notice of a projected visit, in order that appropriate consultations may be held and that maximum precautions may be taken to assure safety and to avoid interference with normal operations in the facility to be visited.

Article XIII

The provisions of this Treaty shall apply to the activities of States Parties to the Treaty in the exploration and use of outer space, including the moon and other celestial bodies, whether such activities are carried on by a single State Party to the Treaty or jointly with other States, including cases where they are carried on within the framework of international inter-governmental organizations.

Any practical questions arising in connexion with activities carried on by international inter-governmental organizations in the exploration and use of outer space, including the moon and other celestial bodies, shall be resolved by the States Parties to the Treaty either with the appropriate international organization or with one or more States members of that international organization, which are Parties to this Treaty.

Article XIV

1. This Treaty shall be open to all States for signature. Any State which does not sign this Treaty before its entry into force in accordance with paragraph 3 of this Article may accede to it at any time.

2. This Treaty shall be subject to ratification by signatory States. Instruments of ratification and instruments of accession shall be deposited with the Governments of the United Kingdom of Great Britain and Northern Ireland, the Union of Soviet Socialist Republics and the United States of America, which are hereby designated the Depositary Governments.

3. This Treaty shall enter into force upon the deposit of instruments of ratification by five Governments including the Governments designated as Depositary Governments under this Treaty.

4. For States whose instruments of ratification or accession are deposited subsequent to the entry into force of this Treaty, it shall enter into force on the date of the deposit of their instruments of ratification or accession.

5. The Depositary Governments shall promptly inform all signatory and acceding States of the date of each signature, the date of deposit of each instrument of ratification of and accession to this Treaty, the date of its entry into force and other notices.

6. This Treaty shall be registered by the Depositary Governments pursuant to Article 102 of the Charter of the United Nations.

Article XV

Any State Party to the Treaty may propose amendments to this Treaty. Amendments shall enter into force for each State Party to the Treaty accepting the amendments upon their acceptance by a majority of the States Parties to the Treaty and thereafter for each remaining State Party to the Treaty on the date of acceptance by it.

Article XVI

Any State Party to the Treaty may give notice of its withdrawal from the Treaty one year after its entry into force by written notification to the

Depositary Governments. Such withdrawal shall take effect one year from the date of receipt of this notification.

Article XVII

This Treaty, of which the English, Russian, French, Spanish and Chinese texts are equally authentic, shall be deposited in the archives of the Depositary Governments. Duly certified copies of this Treaty shall be transmitted by the Depositary Governments to the Governments of the signatory and acceding States.

II. Parties

As of January 1986, the Outer Space Treaty of 1967 has accumulated a total of 83 parties (this sum not including Byelorussia and the Ukraine, both constituent republics of the USSR). Of the five permanent members of the United Nations Security Council, all have become parties, that is, China, France, the United Kingdom, the USA, and the USSR. A list of the 83 parties to the Treaty as of January 1986, together with the year of joining, follows (Goldblat & Ferm, 1985; augmented by information from the Depositaries):

Argentina (1969), Australia (1967), Austria (1968), Bahamas (1976), Barbados (1968), Belgium (1973), Brazil (1969), Bulgaria (1967), Burkina Faso (1968), Burma (1970), Canada (1967), Chile (1981), China (1983), Cuba (1977), Cyprus (1972), Czechoslovakia (1967), Denmark (1967), Dominican Republic (1968), Ecuador (1969), Egypt (1967), El Salvador (1969), Fiji (1972), Finland (1967), France (1970), German DR (1967), Germany, FR (1971), Greece (1971), Guinea-Bissau (1976), Hungary (1967), Iceland (1968), India (1982), Iraq (1968), Ireland (1968), Israel (1977), Italy (1972), Jamaica (1970), Japan (1967), Korea, Rep. (1967), Kuwait (1972), Laos (1972), Lebanon (1969), Libya (1968), Madagascar (1968), Mali (1968), Mauritius (1969), Mexico (1968), Mongolia (1967), Morocco (1967), Nepal (1967), Netherlands (1969), New Zealand (1968), Niger (1967), Nigeria (1967), Norway (1969), Pakistan (1968), Papua New Guinea (1980), Peru (1979), Poland (1968), Romania (1968), San Marino (1968), Saudi Arabia (1976), Seychelles (1978), Sierra Leone (1967), Singapore (1976), South Africa (1968), Spain (1968), Sweden (1967), Switzerland (1969), Syria (1968), Taiwan (1970), Thailand (1968), Tonga (1971), Tunisia (1968), Turkey (1968), Uganda (1968), United Kingdom (1967), Uruguay (1970), USA (1967), USSR (1967), Venezuela (1970), Viet Nam (1980), Yemen, PDR (1979), and Zambia (1973).

References

Goldblat, J. 1982. *Agreements for arms control: a critical survey.* London: Taylor & Francis, 387 pp. [a SIPRI book].
Goldblat, J. & Ferm, R. 1985. Major multilateral arms control agreements. *SIPRI Yearbook,* London, 1985:499–526.

Appendix 6. Law of the Sea Convention of 1982

I. Text

The United Nations Convention of the Law of the Sea was signed at Montego Bay, Jamaica on 10 December 1982, but (the United Nations Secretary-General, the Depositary, having not received the requisite 60 ratifications) has not entered into force.[1] The potential parties to the Convention are given in section II below. The text of the Convention is lengthy (17 parts with 320 articles plus 9 annexes with 126 articles) and only excerpts relevant to this book are included here, that is, all of part V (articles 55–75 plus annex 1), most of part VII, section 1 (articles 86–90), all of part VII, section 2 (articles 116–20), and all of part XV (articles 279–99). Thus, many of the internal cross-references are not included here. The relevant excerpts follow (UN, 1983):

. . .

PART V. EXCLUSIVE ECONOMIC ZONE

Article 55

Specific legal régime of the exclusive economic zone

The exclusive economic zone is an area beyond and adjacent to the territorial sea, subject to the specific legal régime established in this Part, under which the rights and jurisdiction of the coastal State and the rights and freedoms of other States are governed by the relevant provisions of this Convention.

[1]The Law of the Sea Convention of 1982 emerged from the Third United Nations Conference on the Law of the Sea, New York, etc., 1973–82 (UNCLOS-III). UNCLOS-I, Geneva, 1958 led to the consummation of four treaties (Oda, 1972, pages 3–26): (a) the Convention on the Territorial Sea and the Contiguous Zone, which was signed at Geneva on 29 April 1958 and entered into force on 10 September 1964; (b) the Convention on the High Seas, which was signed at Geneva on 29 April 1958 and entered into force on 30 September 1962; (c) the Convention on Fishing and Conservation of the Living Resources of the High Seas, which was signed àt Geneva on 29 April 1958 and entered into force on 20 March 1966; and (d) the Convention on the Continental Shelf, which was signed at Geneva on 29 April 1958 and entered into force on 10 June 1964. UNCLOS-II, Geneva, 1960 had no tangible outcome.

Article 56

Rights, jurisdiction and duties of the coastal State in the exclusive economic zone

1. In the exclusive economic zone, the coastal State has:

(*a*) sovereign rights for the purpose of exploring and exploiting, conserving and managing the natural resources, whether living or non-living, of the waters superjacent to the sea-bed and of the sea-bed and its subsoil, and with regard to other activities for the economic exploitation and exploration of the zone, such as the production of energy from the water, currents and winds;

(*b*) jurisdiction as provided for in the relevant provisions of this Convention with regard to:

(i) the establishment and use of artificial islands, installations and structures;

(ii) marine scientific research;

(iii) the protection and preservation of the marine environment;

(*c*) other rights and duties provided for in this Convention.

2. In exercising its rights and performing its duties under this Convention in the exclusive economic zone, the coastal State shall have due regard to the rights and duties of other States and shall act in a manner compatible with the provisions of this Convention.

3. The rights set out in this article with respect to the sea-bed and subsoil shall be exercised in accordance with Part VI.

Article 57

Breadth of the exclusive economic zone

The exclusive economic zone shall not extend beyond 200 nautical miles [370 kilometres] from the baselines from which the breadth of the territorial sea is measured.

Article 58

Rights and duties of other States in the exclusive economic zone.

1. In the exclusive economic zone, all States, whether coastal or landlocked, enjoy, subject to the relevant provisions of this Convention, the freedoms referred to in article 87 of navigation and overflight and of the laying of submarine cables and pipelines, and other internationally lawful uses of the sea related to these freedoms, such as those associated with the operation of ships, aircraft and submarine cables and pipelines, and compatible with the other provisions of this Convention.

2. Articles 88 to 115 and other pertinent rules of international law apply to the exclusive economic zone in so far as they are not incompatible with this Part.

3. In exercising their rights and performing their duties under this Convention in the exclusive economic zone, States shall have due regard to the rights and duties of the coastal State and shall comply with the laws and regulations adopted by the coastal State in accordance with the provisions of this Convention and other rules of international law in so far as they are not incompatible with this Part.

Article 59

Basis for the resolution of conflicts regarding the attribution of rights and jurisdiction in the exclusive economic zone

In cases where this Convention does not attribute rights or jurisdiction to the coastal State or to other States within the exclusive economic zone, and a conflict arises between the interests of the coastal State and any other State or States, the conflict should be resolved on the basis of equity and in the light of all the relevant circumstances, taking into account the respective importance of the interests involved to the parties as well as to the international community as a whole.

Article 60

Artificial islands, installations and structures in the exclusive economic zone

1. In the exclusive economic zone, the coastal State shall have the exclusive right to construct and to authorize and regulate the construction operation and use of:

(*a*) artificial islands;

(*b*) installations and structures for the purposes provided for in article 56 and other economic purposes;

(*c*) installations and structures which may interfere with the exercise of the rights of the coastal State in the zone.

2. The coastal State shall have exclusive jurisdiction over such artificial islands, installations and structures, including jurisdiction with regard to customs, fiscal, health, safety and immigration laws and regulations.

3. Due notice must be given of the construction of such artificial islands, installations or structures, and permanent means for giving warning of their presence must be maintained. Any installations or structures which are abandoned or disused shall be removed to ensure safety of navigation, taking into account any generally accepted international standards established in this regard by the competent international organization.

Such removal shall also have due regard to fishing, the protection of the marine environment and the rights and duties of other States. Appropriate publicity shall be given to the depth, position and dimensions of any installations or structures not entirely removed.

4. The coastal State may, where necessary, establish reasonable safety zones around such artificial islands, installations and structures in which it may take appropriate measures to ensure the safety both of navigation and of the artificial islands, installations and structures.

5. The breadth of the safety zones shall be determined by the coastal State, taking into account applicable international standards. Such zones shall be designed to ensure that they are reasonably related to the nature and function of the artificial islands, installations or structures, and shall not exceed a distance of 500 metres around them, measured from each point of their outer edge, except as authorized by generally accepted international standards or as recommended by the competent international organization. Due notice shall be given of the extent of safety zones.

6. All ships must respect these safety zones and shall comply with generally accepted international standards regarding navigation in the vicinity of artificial islands, installations, structures and safety zones.

7. Artificial islands, installations and structures and the safety zones around them may not be established where interference may be caused to the use of recognized sea lanes essential to international navigation.

8. Artificial islands, installations and structures do not possess the status of islands. They have no territorial sea of their own, and their presence does not affect the delimitation of the territorial sea, the exclusive economic zone or the continental shelf.

Article 61

Conservation of the living resources

1. The coastal State shall determine the allowable catch of the living resources in its exclusive economic zone.

2. The coastal State, taking into account the best scientific evidence available to it, shall ensure through proper conservation and management measures that the maintenance of the living resources in the exclusive economic zone is not endangered by over-exploitation. As appropriate, the coastal State and competent international organizations, whether subregional, regional or global, shall co-operate to this end.

3. Such measures shall also be designed to maintain or restore populations of harvested species at levels which can produce the maximum sustainable yield, as qualified by relevant environmental and economic factors, including the economic needs of coastal fishing communities and

the special requirements of developing States, and taking into account fishing patterns, the interdependence of stocks and any generally recommended international minimum standards, whether subregional, regional or global.

4. In taking such measures the coastal State shall take into consideration the effects on species associated with or dependent upon harvested species with a view to maintaining or restoring populations of such associated or dependent species above levels at which their reproduction may become seriously threatened.

5. Available scientific information, catch and fishing effort statistics, and other data relevant to the conservation of fish stocks shall be contributed and exchanged on a regular basis through competent international organizations, whether subregional, regional or global, where appropriate and with participation by all States concerned, including States whose nationals are allowed to fish in the exclusive economic zone.

Article 62

Utilization of the living resources

1. The coastal States shall promote the objective of optimum utilization of the living resources in the exclusive economic zone without prejudice to article 61.

2. The coastal State shall determine its capacity to harvest the living resources of the exclusive economic zone. Where the coastal State does not have the capacity to harvest the entire allowable catch, it shall, through agreements or other arrangements and pursuant to the terms, conditions, laws and regulations referred to in paragraph 4, give other States access to the surplus of the allowable catch, having particular regard to the provisions of articles 69 and 70, especially in relation to the developing States mentioned therein.

3. In giving access to other States to its exclusive economic zone under this article, the coastal State shall take into account all relevant factors, including, *inter alia,* the significance of the living resources of the area to the economy of the coastal State concerned and its other national interests, the provisions of articles 69 and 70, the requirements of developing States in the subregion or region in harvesting part of the surplus and the need to minimize economic dislocation in States whose nationals have habitually fished in the zone or which have made substantial efforts in research and identification of stocks.

4. Nationals of other States fishing in the exclusive economic zone shall comply with the conservation measures and with the other terms and conditions established in the laws and regulations of the coastal State.

These laws and regulations shall be consistent with this Convention and may relate, *inter alia*, to the following:

(*a*) licensing of fishermen, fishing vessels and equipment, including payment of fees and other forms of remuneration, which, in the case of developing coastal States, may consist of adequate compensation in the field of financing, equipment and technology relating to the fishing industry;

(*b*) determining the species which may be caught, and fixing quotas of catch, whether in relation to particular stocks or groups of stocks or catch per vessel over a period of time or to the catch by nationals of any State during a specified period;

(*c*) regulating seasons and areas of fishing, the types, sizes and amount of gear, and the types, sizes and number of fishing vessels that may be used;

(*d*) fixing the age and size of fish and other species that may be caught;

(*e*) specifying information required of fishing vessels, including catch and effort statistics and vessel position reports;

(*f*) requiring, under the authorization and control of the coastal State, the conduct of specified fisheries research programmes and regulating the conduct of such research, including the sampling of catches, disposition of samples and reporting of associated scientific data;

(*g*) the placing of observers or trainees on board such vessels by the coastal State;

(*h*) the landing of all or any part of the catch by such vessels in the ports of the coastal State;

(*i*) terms and conditions relating to joint ventures or other co-operative arrangements;

(*j*) requirements for the training of personnel and the transfer of fisheries technology, including enhancement of the coastal State's capability of undertaking fisheries research;

(*k*) enforcement procedures.

5. Coastal States shall give due notice of conservation and management laws and regulations.

Article 63

Stocks occurring within the exclusive economic zones of two or more coastal States or both within the exclusive economic zone and in an area beyond and adjacent to it

1. Where the same stock or stocks of associated species occur within the exclusive economic zones of two or more coastal States, these States shall seek, either directly or through appropriate subregional or regional organizations, to agree upon the measures necessary to co-ordinate and

ensure the conservation and development of such stocks without prejudice to the other provisions of this Part.

2. Where the same stock or stocks of associated species occur both within the exclusive economic zone and in an area beyond and adjacent to the zone, the coastal State and the States fishing for such stocks in the adjacent area shall seek, either directly or through appropriate subregional or regional organizations, to agree upon the measures necessary for the conservation of these stocks in the adjacent area.

Article 64

Highly migratory species

1. The coastal State and other States whose nationals fish in the region for the highly migratory species listed in Annex I [included here] shall co-operate directly or through appropriate international organizations with a view to ensuring conservation and promoting the objective of optimum utilization of such species throughout the region, both within and beyond the exclusive economic zone. In regions for which no appropriate international organization exists, the coastal State and other States whose nationals harvest these species in the region shall co-operate to establish such an organization and participate in its work.

2. The provisions of paragraph 1 apply in addition to the other provisions of this Part.

Article 65

Marine mammals

Nothing in this Part restricts the right of a coastal State or the competence of an international organization, as appropriate, to prohibit, limit or regulate the exploitation of marine mammals more strictly than provided for in this Part. States shall co-operate with a view to the conservation of marine mammals and in the case of cetaceans shall in particular work through the appropriate international organizations for their conservation, management and study.

Article 66

Anadromous stocks

1. States in whose rivers anadromous stocks originate shall have the primary interest in and responsibility for such stocks.

2. The State of origin of anadromous stocks shall ensure their conserva-

tion by the establishment of appropriate regulatory measures for fishing in all waters landward of the outer limits of its exclusive economic zone and for fishing provided for in paragraph 3(b). The State of origin may, after consultations with the other States referred to in paragraphs 3 and 4 fishing these stocks, establish total allowable catches for stocks originating in its rivers.

3. (*a*) Fisheries for anadromous stocks shall be conducted only in waters landward of the outer limits of exclusive economic zones, except in cases where this provision would result in economic dislocation for a State other than the State of origin. With respect to such fishing beyond the outer limits of the exclusive economic zone, States concerned shall maintain consultations with a view to achieving agreement on terms and conditions of such fishing giving due regard to the conservation requirements and the needs of the State of origin in respect of these stocks.

(*b*) The State of origin shall co-operate in minimizing economic disloca-tion in such other States fishing these stocks, taking into account the normal catch and the mode of operations of such States, and all the areas in which such fishing has occurred.

(*c*) States referred to in subparagraph (b), participating by agreement with the State of origin in measures to renew anadromous stocks, particu-larly by expenditures for that purpose, shall be given special consideration by the State of origin in the harvesting of stocks originating in its rivers.

(*d*) Enforcement of regulations regarding anadromous stocks beyond the exclusive economic zone shall be by agreement between the State of origin and the other States concerned.

4. In cases where anadromous stocks migrate into or through the waters landward of the outer limits of the exclusive economic zone of a State other than the State of origin, such State shall co-operate with the State of origin with regard to the conservation and management of such stocks.

5. The State of origin of anadromous stocks and other States fishing these stocks shall make arrangements for the implementation of the provisions of this article, where appropriate, through regional organizations.

Article 67

Catadromous species

1. A coastal State in whose waters catadromous species spend the greater part of their life cycle shall have responsibility for the management of these species and shall ensure the ingress and egress of migrating fish.

2. Harvesting of catadromous species shall be conducted only in waters landward of the outer limits of exclusive economic zones. When conducted

in exclusive economic zones, harvesting shall be subject to this article and the other provisions of this Convention concerning fishing in these zones.

3. In cases where catadromous fish migrate through the exclusive economic zone of another State, whether as juvenile or maturing fish, the management, including harvesting, of such fish shall be regulated by agreement between the State mentioned in paragraph 1 and the other State concerned. Such agreement shall ensure the rational management of the species and take into account the responsibilities of the State mentioned in paragraph 1 for the maintenance of these species.

Article 68

Sedentary species

This part does not apply to sedentary species as defined in article 77, paragraph 4 [i.e., organisms which, at the harvestable stage, either are immobile on or under the sea-bed or are unable to move except in constant physical contact with the sea-bed or the subsoil].

Article 69

Right of land-locked States

1. Land-locked States shall have the right to participate, on an equitable basis, in the exploitation of an appropriate part of the surplus of the living resources of the exclusive economic zones of coastal States of the same subregion or region, taking into account the relevant economic and geographical circumstances of all the States concerned and in conformity with the provisions of this article and of articles 61 and 62.

2. The terms and modalities of such participation shall be established by the States concerned through bilateral, subregional or regional agreements taking into account, *inter alia*:

(*a*) the need to avoid effects detrimental to fishing communities or fishing industries of the coastal State;

(*b*) the extent to which the land-locked State, in accordance with the provisions of this article, is participating or is entitled to participate under existing bilateral, subregional or regional agreements in the exploitation of living resources of the exclusive economic zones of other coastal States;

(*c*) the extent to which other land-locked States and geographically disadvantaged States are participating in the exploitation of the living resources of the exclusive economic zone of the coastal State and the consequent need to avoid a particular burden for any single coastal State or a part of it;

(*d*) the nutritional needs of the populations of the respective States.

3. When the harvesting capacity of a coastal State approaches a point which would enable it to harvest the entire allowable catch of the living resources in its exclusive economic zone, the coastal State and other States concerned shall co-operate in the establishment of equitable arrangements on a bilateral, subregional or regional basis to allow for participation of developing land-locked States of the same subregion or region in the exploitation of the living resources of the exclusive economic zones of coastal States of the subregion or region, as may be appropriate in the circumstances and on terms satisfactory to all parties. In the implementation of this provision the factors mentioned in paragraph 2 shall also be taken into account.

4. Developed land-locked States shall, under the provisions of this article, be entitled to participate in the exploitation of living resources only in the exclusive economic zones of developed coastal States of the same subregion or region having regard to the extent to which the coastal State, in giving access to other States to the living resources of its exclusive economic zone, has taken into account the need to minimize detrimental effects on fishing communities and economic dislocation in States whose nationals have habitually fished in the zone.

5. The above provisions are without prejudice to arrangements agreed upon in subregions or regions where the coastal States may grant to land-locked States of the same subregion or region equal or preferential rights for the exploitation of the living resources in the exclusive economic zones.

Article 70

Right of geographically disadvantaged States

1. Geographically disadvantaged States shall have the right to participate, on an equitable basis, in the exploitation of an appropriate part of the surplus of the living resources of the exclusive economic zones of coastal States of the same subregion or region, taking into account the relevant economic and geographical circumstances of all the States concerned and in conformity with the provisions of this article and of articles 61 and 62.

2. For the purposes of this Part, 'geographically disadvantaged States' means coastal States, including States bordering enclosed or semi-enclosed seas, whose geographical situation makes them dependent upon the exploitation of the living resources of the exclusive economic zones of other States in the subregion or region for adequate supplies of fish for the nutritional purposes of their populations or parts thereof, and coastal States which can claim no exclusive economic zones of their own.

3. The terms and modalities of such participation shall be established by

the States concerned through bilateral, subregional or regional agreements taking into account, *inter alia*:

(*a*) the need to avoid effects detrimental to fishing communities or fishing industries of the coastal State;

(*b*) the extent to which the geographically disadvantaged State, in accordance with the provisions of this article, is participating or is entitled to participate under existing bilateral, subregional or regional agreements in the exploitation of living resources of the exclusive economic zones of other coastal States;

(*c*) the extent to which other geographically disadvantaged States and landlocked States are participating in the exploitation of the living resources of the exclusive economic zone of the coastal State and the consequent need to avoid a particular burden for any single coastal State or a part of it;

(*d*) the nutritional needs of the populations of the respective States.

4. When the harvesting capacity of a coastal State approaches a point which would enable it to harvest the entire allowable catch of the living resources in its exclusive economic zone, the coastal State and other States concerned shall co-operate in the establishment of equitable arrangements on a bilateral, subregional or regional basis to allow for participation of developing geographically disadvantaged States of the same subregion or region in the exploitation of the living resources of the exclusive economic zones of coastal States of the subregion or region, as may be appropriate in the circumstances and on terms satisfactory to all parties. In the implementation of this provision the factors mentioned in paragraph 3 shall also be taken into account.

5. Developed geographically disadvantaged States shall, under the provisions of this article, be entitled to participate in the exploitation of living resources only in the exclusive economic zones of developed coastal States of the same subregion or region having regard to the extent to which the coastal State, in giving access to other States to the living resources of its exclusive economic zone, has taken into account the need to minimize detrimental effects on fishing communities and economic dislocation in States whose nationals have habitually fished in the zone.

6. The above provisions are without prejudice to arrangements agreed upon in subregions or regions where the coastal States may grant to geographically disadvantaged States of the same subregion or region equal or preferential rights for the exploitation of the living resources in the exclusive economic zones.

Article 71

Non-applicability of articles 69 and 70

The provisions of articles 69 and 70 do not apply in the case of a coastal State whose economy is overwhelmingly dependent on the exploitation of the living resources of its exclusive economic zone.

Article 72

Restrictions on transfer of rights

1. Rights provided under articles 69 and 70 to exploit living resources shall not be directly or indirectly transferred to third States or their nationals by lease or licence, by establishing joint ventures or in any other manner which has the effect of such transfer unless otherwise agreed by the States concerned.

2. The foregoing provision does not preclude the States concerned from obtaining technical or financial assistance from third States or international organizations in order to facilitate the exercise of the rights pursuant to articles 69 and 70, provided that it does not have the effect referred to in paragraph 1.

Article 73

Enforcement of laws and regulations of the coastal State

1. The coastal State may, in the exercise of its sovereign rights to explore, exploit, conserve and manage the living rsources in the exclusive economic zone, take such measures, including boarding, inspection, arrest and judicial proceedings, as may be necessary to ensure compliance with the laws and regulations adopted by it in conformity with this Convention.

2. Arrested vessels and their crews shall be promptly released upon the posting of reasonable bond or other security.

3. Coastal State penalties for violations of fisheries laws and regulations in the exclusive economic zone may not include imprisonment, in the absence of agreements to the contrary by the States concerned, or any other form of corporal punishment.

4. In cases of arrest or detention of foreign vessels the coastal State shall promptly notify the flag State, through appropriate channels, of the action taken and of any penalties subsequently imposed.

Article 74

Delimitation of the exclusive economic zone between States with opposite or adjacent coasts

1. The delimitation of the exclusive economic zone between States with opposite or adjacent coasts shall be effected by agreement on the basis of international law, as referred to in Article 38 of the Statute of the International Court of Justice,[2] in order to achieve an equitable solution.

2. If no agreement can be reached within a reasonable period of time, the States concerned shall resort to the procedures provided for in Part XV.

3. Pending agreement as provided for in paragraph 1, the States concerned, in a spirit of understanding and co-operation, shall make every effort to enter into provisional arrangements of a practical nature and, during this transitional period, not to jeopardize or hamper the reaching of the final agreement. Such arrangements shall be without prejudice to the final delimitation.

4. Where there is an agreement in force between the States concerned, questions relating to the delimitation of the exclusive economic zone shall be determined in accordance with the provisions of that agreement.

Article 75

Charts and lists of geographical co-ordinates

1. Subject to this Part, the outer limit lines of the exclusive economic zone and the lines of delimitation drawn in accordance with article 74 shall be shown on charts of a scale or scales adequate for ascertaining their position. Where appropriate, lists of geographical co-ordinates of points, specifying the geodetic datum, may be substituted for such outer limit lines or lines of delimitation.

2. The coastal State shall give due publicity to such charts or lists of geographical co-ordinates and shall deposit a copy of each such chart or list with the Secretary-General of the United Nations.

. . .

[2]International Court of Justice (the Hague) statute article 38 (UN, 1968, pages 75-76, 83): 1. The Court, whose function is to decide in accordance with international law such disputes as are submitted to it, shall apply: a. international conventions, whether general or particular, establishing rules expressly recognized by the contesting states; b. international custom, as evidence of a general practice accepted as law; c. the general principles of law recognized by civilized nations; d. subject to the provisions of Article 59 [The decision of the Court has no binding force except between the parties and in respect of that particular case], judicial decisions and the teachings of the most highly qualified publicists of the various nations, as subsidiary means for the determination of rules of law. 2. This provision shall not prejudice the power of the Court to decide a case *ex aequo et bono*, if the parties agree thereto.

PART VII. HIGH SEAS

Section 1. General Provisions

Article 86

Application of the provisions of this Part

The provisions of this Part apply to all parts of the sea that are not included in the exclusive economic zone, in the territorial sea or in the internal waters of a State, or in the archipelagic waters of an archipelagic State. This article does not entail any abridgement of the freedoms enjoyed by all States in the exclusive economic zone in accordance with article 58.

Article 87

Freedom of the high seas

1. The high seas are open to all States, whether coastal or land-locked. Freedom of the high seas is exercised under the conditions laid down by this Convention and by other rules of international law. It comprises, *inter alia,* both for coastal and land-locked States:

(*a*) freedom of navigation;

(*b*) freedom of overflight;

(*c*) freedom to lay submarine cables and pipelines, subject to Part VI;

(*d*) freedom to construct artificial islands and other installations permitted under international law, subject to Part VI;

(*e*) freedom of fishing, subject to the conditions laid down in section 2;

(*f*) freedom of scientific research, subject to Parts VI and XIII.

2. These freedoms shall be exercised by all States with due regard for the interests of other States in their exercise of the freedom of the high seas, and also with due regard for the rights under this Convention with respect to activities in the Area.

Article 88

Reservation of the high seas for peaceful purposes

The high seas shall be reserved for peaceful purposes.

Article 89

Invalidity of claims of sovereignty over the high seas

No State may validly purport to subject any part of the high seas to its sovereignty.

Article 90

Right of navigation

Every State, whether coastal or land-locked, has the right to sail ships flying its flag on the high seas.

. . .

Section 2. Conservation and Management of the Living Resources of the High Seas

Article 116

Right to fish on the high seas

All States have the right for their nationals to engage in fishing on the high seas subject to:

(*a*) their treaty obligations;

(*b*) the rights and duties as well as the interests of coastal States provided for, *inter alia,* in article 63, paragraph 2, and articles 64 to 67; and

(*c*) the provisions of this section.

Article 117

Duty of States to adopt with respect to their nationals measures for the conservation of the living resources of the high seas

All States have the duty to take, or to co-operate with other States in taking, such measures for their respective nationals as may be necessary for the conservation of the living resources of the high seas.

Article 118

Co-operation of States in the conservation and management of living resources

States shall co-operate with each other in the conservation and management of living resources in the areas of the high seas. States whose nationals exploit identical living resources, or different living resources in the same area, shall enter into negotiations with a view to taking the measures necessary for the conservation of the living resources concerned. They shall, as appropriate, co-operate to establish subregional or regional fisheries organizations to this end.

Article 119

Conservation of the living resources of the high seas

1. In determining the allowable catch and establishing other conservation measures for the living resources in the high seas, States shall:

(*a*) take measures which are designed, on the best scientific evidence available to the States concerned, to maintain or restore populations of harvested species at levels which can produce the maximum sustainable yield, as qualified by relevant environmental and economic factors, including the special requirements of developing States, and taking into account fishing patterns, the interdependence of stocks and any generally recommended international minimum standards, whether subregional, regional or global;

(*b*) take into consideration the effects on species associated with or dependent upon harvested species with a view to maintaining or restoring populations of such associated or dependent species above levels at which their reproduction may become seriously threatened.

2. Available scientific information, catch and fishing effort statistics, and other data relevant to the conservation of fish stocks shall be contributed and exchanged on a regular basis through competent international organizations, whether subregional, regional or global, where appropriate and with participation by all States concerned.

3. States concerned shall ensure that conservation measures and their implementation do not discriminate in form or in fact against the fishermen of any State.

Article 120

Marine mammals

Article 65 also applies to the conservation and management of marine mammals in the high seas.

. . .

PART XV. SETTLEMENT OF DISPUTES

Section 1. General Provisions

Article 279

Obligation to settle disputes by peaceful means

States Parties shall settle any dispute between them concerning the interpretation of this Convention by peaceful means in accordance with

Article 2, paragraph 3, of the Charter of the United Nations and, to this end, shall seek a solution by the means indicated in Article 33, paragraph 1, of the Charter.[3]

Article 280

Settlement of disputes by any peaceful means chosen by the parties

Nothing in this Part impairs the right of any States Parties to agree at any time to settle a dispute between them concerning the interpretation or application of this Convention by any peaceful means of their own choice.

Article 281

Procedure where no settlement has been reached by the parties

1. If the States Parties which are parties to a dispute concerning the interpretation or application of this Convention have agreed to seek settlement of the dispute by a peaceful means of their own choice, the procedures provided for in this Part apply only where no settlement has been reached by recourse to such means and the agreement between the parties does not exclude any further procedure.

2. If the parties have also agreed on a time-limit, paragraph 1 applies only upon the expiration of that time-limit.

Article 282

Obligations under general, regional or bilateral agreements

If the States Parties which are parties to a dispute concerning the interpretation or application of this Convention have agreed, through a general, regional or bilateral agreement or otherwise, that such dispute shall, at the request of any party to the dispute, be submitted to a procedure that entails a binding decision, that procedure shall apply in lieu of the procedures provided for in this Part, unless the parties to the dispute otherwise agree.

---

[3]United Nations (New York) charter article 2.3 (UN, 1968, page 4): All Members shall settle their international disputes by peaceful means in such a manner that international peace and security, and justice, are not endangered.

Article 33.1 (UN, 1968, page 19): The parties to any dispute, the continuance of which is likely to endanger the maintenance of international peace and security, shall, first of all, seek a solution by negotiation, enquiry, mediation, conciliation, arbitration, judicial settlement, resort to regional agencies or arrangements, or other peaceful means of their own choice.

Article 283

Obligation to exchange views

1. When a dispute arises between States Parties concerning the interpretation or application of this Convention, the parties to the dispute shall proceed expeditiously to an exchange of views regarding its settlement by negotiation or other peaceful means.

2. The parties shall also proceed expeditiously to an exchange of views where a procedure for the settlement of such a dispute has been terminated without a settlement or where a settlement has been reached and the circumstances require consultation regarding the manner of implementing the settlement.

Article 284

Conciliation

1. A State Party which is a party to a dispute concerning the interpretation or application of this Convention may invite the other party or parties to submit the dispute to conciliation in accordance with the procedure under Annex V, section 1, or another conciliation procedure.

2. If the invitation is accepted and if the parties agree upon the conciliation procedure to be applied, any party may submit the dispute to that procedure.

3. If the invitation is not accepted or the parties do not agree upon the procedure, the conciliation proceedings shall be deemed to be terminated.

4. Unless the parties otherwise agree, when a dispute has been submitted to conciliation, the proceedings may be terminated only in accordance with the agreed conciliation procedure.

Article 285

Application of this section to disputes submitted pursuant to Part XI

This section applies to any dispute which pursuant to Part XI, section 5, is to be settled in accordance with procedures provided for in this Part. If an entity other than a State Party is a party to such a dispute, this section applies *mutatis mutandis*.

Section 2. Compulsory Procedures Entailing Binding Decisions

Article 286

Application of procedures under this section

Subject to section 3, any dispute concerning the interpretation or application of this Convention shall, where no settlement has been reached by recourse to section 1, be submitted at the request of any party to the dispute to the court or tribunal having jurisdiction under this section.

Article 287

Choice of procedure

1. When signing, ratifying or acceding to this Convention or at any time thereafter, a State shall be free to choose, by means of a written declaration, one or more of the following means for the settlement of disputes concerning the interpretation or application of this Convention:

(*a*) the International Tribunal for the Law of the Sea established in accordance with Annex VI;

(*b*) the International Court of Justice;

(*c*) an arbitral tribunal constituted in accordance with Annex VII;

(*d*) a special arbitral tribunal constituted in accordance with Annex VIII for one or more of the categories of disputes specified therein.

2. A declaration made under paragraph 1 shall not affect or be affected by the obligation of a State Party to accept the jurisdiction of the Sea-Bed Disputes Chamber of the International Tribunal for the Law of the Sea to the extent and in the manner provided for in Part XI, section 5.

3. A State Party, which is a party to a dispute not covered by a declaration in force, shall be deemed to have accepted arbitration in accordance with Annex VII.

4. If the parties to a dispute have accepted the same procedure for the settlement of the dispute, it may be submitted only to that procedure, unless the parties otherwise agree.

5. If the parties to a dispute have not accepted the same procedure for the settlement of the dispute, it may be submitted only to arbitration in accordance with Annex VII, unless the parties otherwise agree.

6. A declaration made under paragraph 1 shall remain in force until three months after notice of revocation has been deposited with the Secretary-General of the United Nations.

7. A new declaration, a notice of revocation or the expiry of a declaration does not in any way affect proceedings pending before a court or

tribunal having jurisdiction under this article, unless the parties otherwise agree.

8. Declarations and notices referred to in this article shall be deposited with the Secretary-General of the United Nations, who shall transmit copies thereof to the States Parties.

Article 288

Jurisdiction

1. A court or tribunal referred to in article 287 shall have jurisdiction over any dispute concerning the interpretation or application of this Convention which is submitted to it in accordance with this Part.

2. A court or tribunal referred to in article 287 shall also have jurisdiction over any dispute concerning the interpretation or application of an international agreement related to the purposes of this Convention, which is submitted to it in accordance with the agreement.

3. The Sea-Bed Disputes Chamber of the International Tribunal for the Law of the Sea established in accordance with Annex VI, and any other chamber or arbitral tribunal referred to in Part XI, section 5, shall have jurisdiction in any matter which is submitted to it in accordance therewith.

4. In the event of a dispute as to whether a court or tribunal has jurisdiction, the matter shall be settled by decision of that court or tribunal.

Article 289

Experts

In any dispute involving scientific or technical matters, a court or tribunal exercising jurisdiction under this section may, at the request of a party or *proprio motu,* select in consultation with the parties no fewer than two scientific or technical experts chosen preferably from the relevant list prepared in accordance with Annex VIII, article 2, to sit with the court or tribunal but without the right to vote.

Article 290

Provisional measures

1. If a dispute has been duly submitted to a court or tribunal which considers that *prima facie* it has jurisdiction under this Part or Part XI, section 5, the court or tribunal may prescribe any provisional measures which it considers appropriate under the circumstances to preserve the

respective rights of the parties to the dispute or to prevent serious harm to the marine environment, pending the final decision.

2. Provisional measures may be modified or revoked as soon as the circumstances justifying them have changed or ceased to exist.

3. Provisional measures may be prescribed, modified or revoked under this article only at the request of a party to the dispute and after the parties have been given an opportunity to be heard.

4. The court or tribunal shall forthwith give notice to the parties to the dispute, and to such other States Parties as it considers appropriate, of the prescription, modification or revocation or provisional measures.

5. Pending the constitution of an arbitral tribunal to which a dispute is being submitted under this section, any court or tribunal agreed upon by the parties or, failing such agreement within two weeks from the date of the request for provisional measures, the International Tribunal for the Law of the Sea or, with respect to activities in the Area, the Sea-Bed Disputes Chamber, may prescribe, modify or revoke provisional measures in accordance with this article if it considers that *prima facie* the tribunal which is to be constituted would have jurisdiction and that the urgency of the situation so requires. Once constituted, the tribunal to which the dispute has been submitted may modify, revoke or affirm those provisional measures, acting in conformity with paragraphs 1 to 4.

6. The parties to the dispute shall comply promptly with any provisional measures prescribed under this article.

Article 291

Access

1. All the dispute settlement procedures specified in this Part shall be open to States Parties.

2. The dispute settlement procedures specified in this Part shall be open to entities other than States Parties only as specifically provided for in this Convention.

Article 292

Prompt release of vessels and crews

1. Where the authorities of a State Party have detained a vessel flying the flag of another State Party and it is alleged that the detaining State has not complied with the provisions of this Convention for the prompt release of the vessel or its crew upon the posting of a reasonable bond or other financial security, the question of release from detention may be submitted to any court or tribunal agreed upon by the parties or, failing such

agreement within 10 days from the time of detention, to a court or tribunal accepted by the detaining State under article 287 or to the International Tribunal for the Law of the Sea, unless the parties otherwise agree.

2. The application for release may be made only by or on behalf of the flag State of the vessel.

3. The court or tribunal shall deal without delay with the application for release and shall deal only with the question of release, without prejudice to the merits of any case before the appropriate domestic forum against the vessel, its owner or its crew. The authorities of the detaining State remain competent to release the vessel or its crew at any time.

4. Upon the posting of the bond or other financial security determined by the court or tribunal, the authorities of the detaining State shall comply promptly with the decision of the court or tribunal concerning the release of the vessel or its crew.

Article 293

Applicable law

1. A court or tribunal having jurisdiction under this section shall apply this Convention and other rules of international law not incompatible with this Convention.

2. Paragraph 1 does not prejudice the power of the court or tribunal having jurisdiction under this section to decide a case *ex aequo et bono,* if the parties so agree.

Article 294

Preliminary proceedings

1. A court or tribunal provided for in article 287 to which an application is made in respect of a dispute referred to in article 297 shall determine at the request of a party, or may determine *proprio motu,* whether the claim constitutes an abuse of legal process or whether *prima facie* it is well founded. If the court or tribunal determines that the claim constitutes an abuse of legal process or is *prima facie* unfounded, it shall take no further action in the case.

2. Upon receipt of the application, the court or tribunal shall immediately notify the other party or parties of the application, and shall fix a reasonable time-limit within which they may request it to make a determination in accordance with paragraph 1.

3. Nothing in this article affects the right of any party to a dispute to make preliminary objections in accordance with the applicable rules of procedure.

Article 295

Exhaustion of local remedies

Any dispute between States Parties concerning the interpretation or application of this Convention may be submitted to the procedures provided for in this section only after local remedies have been exhausted where this is required by international law.

Article 296

Finality and binding force of decisions

1. Any decision rendered by a court or tribunal having jurisdiction under this section shall be final and shall be complied with by all the parties to the dispute.

2. Any such decision shall have no binding force except between the parties and in respect of that particular dispute.

Section 3. Limitations and Exceptions to Applicability of Section 2

Article 297

Limitations on applicability of section 2

1. Disputes concerning the interpretation or application of this Convention with regard to the exercise by a coastal State of its sovereign rights or jurisdiction provided for in this Convention shall be subject to the procedures provided for in section 2 in the following cases:

(*a*) when it is alleged that a coastal State has acted in contravention of the provisions of this Convention in regard to the freedoms and rights of navigation, overflight or the laying of submarine cables and pipelines, or in regard to other internationally lawful uses of the sea specified in article 58;

(*b*) when it is alleged that a State in exercising the aforementioned freedoms, rights or uses has acted in contravention of this Convention or of laws or regulations adopted by the coastal State in conformity with this Convention and other rules of international law not incompatible with this Convention; or

(*c*) when it is alleged that a coastal State has acted in contravention of specified international rules and standards for the protection and preservation of the marine environment which are applicable to the coastal State and which have been established by this Convention or through a competent international organization or diplomatic conference in accordance with this Convention.

2. (*a*) Disputes concerning the interpretation or application of the provisions of this Convention with regard to marine scientific research shall be settled in accordance with section 2, except that the coastal State shall not be obliged to accept the submission to such settlement of any dispute arising out of:

(i) the exercise by the coastal State of a right or discretion in accordance with article 246; or

(ii) a decision by the coastal State to order suspension or cessation of a research project in accordance with article 253.

(*b*) A dispute arising from an allegation by the researching State that with respect to a specific project the coastal State is not exercising its rights under articles 246 and 253 in a manner compatible with this Convention shall be submitted, at the request of either party, to conciliation under Annex V, section 2, provided that the conciliation commission shall not call in question the exercise by the coastal State of its discretion to designate specific areas as referred to in article 246, paragraph 6, or of its discretion to withhold consent in accordance with article 246, paragraph 5.

3. (*a*) Disputes concerning the interpretation or application of the provisions of this Convention with regard to fisheries shall be settled in accordance with section 2, except that the coastal State shall not be obliged to accept the submission to such settlement of any dispute relating to its sovereign rights with respect to the living resources in the exclusive economic zone or their exercise, including its discretionary powers for determining the allowable catch, its harvesting capacity, the allocation of surpluses to other States and the terms and conditions established in its conservation and management laws and regulations.

(*b*) Where no settlement has been reached by recourse to section 1 of this Part, a dispute shall be submitted to conciliation under Annex V, section 2, at the request of any party to the dispute, when it is alleged that:

(i) a coastal State has manifestly failed to comply with its obligations to ensure through proper conservation and management measures that the maintenance of the living resources in the exclusive economic zone is not seriously endangered;

(ii) a coastal State has arbitrarily refused to determine, at the request of another State, the allowable catch and its capacity to harvest living resources with respect to stocks which that other State is interested in fishing; or

(iii) a coastal State has arbitrarily refused to allocate to any State, under articles 62, 69 and 70 and under the terms and conditions established by the coastal State consistent with this Convention, the whole or part of the surplus it has declared to exist.

(*c*) In no case shall the conciliation commission substitute its discretion for that of the coastal State.

(*d*) The report of the conciliation commission shall be communicated to the appropriate international organizations.

(*e*) In negotiating agreements pursuant to articles 69 and 70, States Parties, unless they otherwise agree, shall include a clause on measures which they shall take in order to minimize the possibility of a disagreement concerning the interpretation or application of the agreement, and on how they should proceed if a disagreement nevertheless arises.

Article 298

Optional exceptions to applicability of section

1. When signing, ratifying or acceding to this Convention or at any time thereafter, a State may, without prejudice to the obligations arising under section 1, declare in writing that it does not accept any one or more of the procedures provided for in section 2 with respect to one or more of the following categories of disputes:

(*a*) (i) disputes concerning the interpretation or application of articles 15, 74 and 83 relating to sea boundary delimitations, or those involving historic bays or titles, provided that a State having made such a declaration shall, when such a dispute arises subsequent to the entry into force of this Convention and where no agreement within a reasonable period of time is reached in negotiations between the parties, at the request of any party to the dispute, accept submission of the matter to conciliation under Annex V, section 2; and provided further that any dispute that necessarily involves the concurrent consideration of any unsettled dispute concerning sovereignty or other rights over continental or insular land territory shall be excluded from such submission;

(ii) after the conciliation commission has presented its report, which shall state the reasons on which it is based, the parties shall negotiate an agreement on the basis of that report; if these negotiations do not result in an agreement, the parties shall, by mutual consent, submit the question to one of the procedures provided for in section 2, unless the parties otherwise agree;

(iii) this subparagraph does not apply to any sea boundary dispute finally settled by an arrangement between the parties, or to any such dispute which is to be settled in accordance with a bilateral or multilateral agreement binding upon those parties;

(*b*) disputes concerning military activities, including military activities by government vessels and aircraft engaged in non-commercial service, and disputes concerning law enforcement activities in regard to the exercise of sovereign rights or jurisdiction excluded from the jurisdiction of a court or tribunal under article 297, paragraph 2 or 3;

(c) disputes in respect of which the Security Council of the United Nations is exercising the functions assigned to it by the Charter of the United Nations, unless the Security Council decides to remove the matter from its agenda or calls upon the parties to settle it by the means provided for in this Convention.

2. A State Party which has made a declaration under paragraph 1 may at any time withdraw it, or agree to submit a dispute excluded by such declaration to any procedure specified in this Convention.

3. A State Party which has made a declaration under paragraph 1 shall not be entitled to submit any dispute falling within the excepted category of disputes to any procedure in this Convention as against another State Party, without the consent of that party.

4. If one of the States Parties has made a declaration under paragraph 1(a), any other State Party may submit any dispute falling within an excepted category against the declarant party to the procedure specified in such declaration.

5. A new declaration, or the withdrawal of a declaration, does not in any way affect proceedings pending before a court or tribunal in accordance with this article, unless the parties otherwise agree.

6. Declarations and notices of withdrawal of declarations under this article shall be deposited with the Secretary-General of the United Nations, who shall transmit copies thereof to the States Parties.

Article 299

Right of the parties to agree upon a procedure

1. A dispute excluded under article 297 or excepted by a declaration made under article 298 from the dispute settlement procedures provided for in section 2 may be submitted to such procedures only by agreement of the parties to the dispute.

2. Nothing in this section impairs the right of the parties to the dispute to agree to some other procedure for the settlement of such dispute or to reach an amicable settlement.

. . .

Annex 1. High Migratory Species

[cf. article 64]

1. Albacore tuna: *Thunnus alalunga*.
2. Bluefin tuna: *Thunnus thynnus*.

3. Bigeye tuna: *Thunnus obesus*
4. Skipjack tuna: *Katsuwonus pelamis.*
5. Yellowfin tuna: *Thunnus albacares.*
6. Blackfin tuna: *Thunnus atlanticus.*
7. Little tuna: *Ethynnus alletteratus; Euthynnus affinis.*
8. Southern bluefin tuna: *Thunnus maccoyii.*
9. Frigate mackerel: *Auxis thazard; Auxis rochei.*
10. Pomfrets: Family *Bramidae.*
11. Marlins: *Tetrapturus angustirostris; Tetrapturus belone; Tetrapturus pfluegeri; Tetrapturus albidus; Tetrapturus audax; Tetrapturus georgei; Makaira mazara; Makaira indica; Makaira nigricans.*
12. Sail-fishes: *Istiophorus platypterus; Istiophorus albicans.*
13. Swordfish: *Xiphias gladius.*
14. Sauries: *Scomberesox saurus; Cololabis saira; Cololabis adocetus; Scomberesox saurus scombroides.*
15. Dolphin: *Coryphaena hippurus; Coryphaena equiselis.*
16. Oceanic sharks: *Hexanchus griseus; Cetorhinus maximus; Family Alopiidae; Rhincodon typus; family Carcharhinidae; Family Sphyrnidae; Family Isurida.*
17. Cetaceans: Family *Physeteridae;* Family *Balaenopteridae;* Family *Balaenidae;* Family *Eschrichtiidae;* Family *Monodontidae;* Family *Ziphiidae;* Family *Delphinidae.*
. . .

II. Potential parties

As of January 1986, the Law of the Sea Convention of 1982 has accumulated a total of 24 potential parties (this sum not including Namibia, which is not an independent state). Of the five permanent members of the United Nations Security Council, none has become a potential party, that is, not China, France, the United Kingdom, the USA, or the USSR. A list of the 24 potential parties to the Convention as of January 1986, together with the year of commitment, follows (information from the Depositary):

Bahamas (1983), Bahrain (1985), Belize (1983), Cameroon (1985), Cuba (1984), Egypt (1983), Fiji (1982), Gambia (1984), Ghana (1983), Guinea (1985), Iceland (1985), Iraq (1985), Ivory Coast (1984), Jamaica (1983), Mali (1985), Mexico (1983), Philippines (1984), Sta Lucia (1985), Senegal (1984), Sudan (1985), Tanzania (1985), Togo (1985), Tunisia (1985), and Zambia (1983).

References

Oda, S. 1972. *International law of the ocean development: basic documents.* Leiden: Sijthoff, 519 pp.

UN (United Nations). 1968. *Charter of the United Nations and statute of the International Court of Justice.* New York: United Nations, 87 pp.

UN (United Nations). 1983. *Law of the Sea: official text of the United Nations Convention on the Law of the Sea with annexes and index.* New York: United Nations, 224 pp.

Appendix 7. Moon Agreement of 1979

I. Text

The Agreement Governing the Activities of States on the Moon and Other Celestial Bodies was signed at New York on 18 December 1979 and (the United Nations Secretary-General, the Depositary, having received the requisite five ratifications) entered into force on 11 July 1984. The parties to the Agreement are given in section II below. The text of the Agreement follows (UNGA, 1979):

The States Parties to this Agreement,

Noting the achievements of States in the exploration and use of the moon and other celestial bodies,

Recognizing that the moon, as a natural satellite of the earth, has an important role to play in the exploration of outer space,

Determined to promote on the basis of equality the further development of co-operation among States in the exploration and use of the moon and other celestial bodies,

Desiring to prevent the moon from becoming an area of international conflict,

Bearing in mind the benefits which may be derived from the exploitation of the natural resources of the moon and other celestial bodies,

Recalling the Treaty on Principles Governing the Activities of States in the Exploration and Use of Outer Space, including the Moon and Other Celestial Bodies, the Agreement on the Rescue of Astronauts, the Return of Astronauts and the Return of Objects Launched into Outer Space, the Convention on International Liability for Damage Caused by Space Objects, and the Convention on Registration of Objects Launched into Outer Space,

Taking into account the need to define and develop the provisions of these international instruments in relation to the moon and other celestial bodies, having regard to further progress in the exploration and use of outer space,

Have agreed on the following:

Article 1

1. The provisions of this Agreement relating to the moon shall also apply to other celestial bodies within the solar system, other than the earth,

except in so far as specific legal norms enter into force with respect to any of these celestial bodies.

2. For the purposes of this Agreement reference to the moon shall include orbits around or other trajectories to or around it.

3. This Agreement does not apply to extraterrestrial materials which reach the surface of the earth by natural means.

Article 2

All activities on the moon, including its exploration and use, shall be carried out in accordance with international law, in particular the Charter of the United Nations, and taking into account the Declaration on Principles of International Law concerning Friendly Relations and Co-operation among States in accordance with the Charter of the United Nations, adopted by the General Assembly on 24 October 1970, in the interest of maintaining international peace and security and promoting international co-operation and mutual understanding, and with due regard to the corresponding interests of all other States Parties.

Article 3

1. The moon shall be used by all States Parties exclusively for peaceful purposes.

2. Any threat or use of force or any other hostile act or threat of hostile act on the moon is prohibited. It is likewise prohibited to use the moon in order to commit any such act or to engage in any such threat in relation to the earth, the moon, spacecraft, the personnel of spacecraft or man-made space objects.

3. States Parties shall not place in orbit around or other trajectory to or around the moon objects carrying nuclear weapons or any other kinds of weapons of mass destruction or place or use such weapons on or in the moon.

4. The establishment of military bases, installations and fortifications, the testing of any type of weapons and the conduct of military manoeuvres on the moon shall be forbidden. The use of military personnel for scientific research or for any other peaceful purposes shall not be prohibited. The use of any equipment or facility necessary for peaceful exploration and use of the moon shall also not be prohibited.

Article 4

1. The exploration and use of the moon shall be the province of all mankind and shall be carried out for the benefit and in the interests of all

countries, irrespective of their degree of economic or scientific development. Due regard shall be paid to the interests of present and future generations as well as to the need to promote higher standards of living and conditions of economic and social progress and development in accordance with the Charter of the United Nations.

2. States Parties shall be guided by the principle of cooperation and mutual assistance in all their activities concerning the exploration and use of the moon. International cooperation in pursuance of this Agreement should be as wide as possible and make take place on a multilateral basis, on a bilateral basis or through international intergovernmental organizations.

Article 5

1. States Parties shall inform the Secretary-General of the United Nations as well as the public and the international scientific community, to the greatest extent feasible and practicable, of their activities concerned with the exploration and use of the moon. Information on the time, purposes, locations, orbital parameters and duration shall be given in respect of each mission to the moon as soon as possible after launching, while information on the results of each mission, including scientific results, shall be furnished upon completion of the mission. In the case of a mission lasting more than sixty days, information on conduct of the mission, including any scientific results, shall be given periodically, at thirty-day intervals. For missions lasting more than six months, only significant additions to such information need be reported thereafter.

2. If a State Party becomes aware that another State Party plans to operate simultaneously in the same area of or in the same orbit around or trajectory to or around the moon, it shall promptly inform the other State of the timing of and plans for its own operations.

3. In carrying out activities under this Agreement, States Parties shall promptly inform the Secretary-General, as well as the public and the international scientific community, of any phenomena they discover in outer space, including the moon, which could endanger human life or health, as well as of any indication of organic life.

Article 6

1. There shall be freedom of scientific investigation on the moon by all States Parties without discrimination of any kind, on the basis of equality and in accordance with international law.

2. In carrying out scientific investigations and in futherance of the provisions of this Agreement, the States Parties shall have the right to collect on and remove from the moon samples of its mineral and other

substances. Such samples shall remain at the disposal of those States Parties which caused them to be collected and may be used by them for scientific purposes. States Parties shall have regard to the desirability of making a portion of such samples available to other interested States Parties and the international scientific community for scientific investigation. States Parties may in the course of scientific investigations also use mineral and other substances of the moon in quantities appropriate for the support of their missions.

3. States Parties agree on the desirability of exchanging scientific and other personnel on expeditions to or installations on the moon to the greatest extent feasible and practicable.

Article 7

1. In exploring and using the moon, States Parties shall take measures to prevent the disruption of the existing balance of its environment, whether by introducing adverse changes in that environment, by its harmful contamination through the introduction of extra-environmental matter or otherwise. States Parties shall also take measures to avoid harmfully affecting the environment of the earth through the introduction of extraterrestrial matter or otherwise.

2. States Parties shall inform the Secretary-General of the United Nations of the measures being adopted by them in accordance with paragraph 1 of this article and shall also, to the maximum extent feasible, notify him in advance of all placements by them of radioactive materials on the moon and of the purposes of such placements.

3. States Parties shall report to other States Parties and to the Secretary-General concerning areas of the moon having special scientific interest in order that, without prejudice to the rights of other States Parties, consideration may be given to the designation of such areas as international scientific preserves for which special protective arrangements are to be agreed upon in consultation with the competent bodies of the United Nations.

Article 8

1. States Parties may pursue their activities in the exploration and use of the moon anywhere on or below its surface, subject to the provisions of this Agreement.

2. For these purposes States Parties may, in particular:

(*a*) Land their space objects on the moon and launch them from the moon;

(*b*) Place their personnel, space vehicles, equipment, facilities, stations and installations anywhere on or below the surface of the moon.

Personnel, space vehicles, equipment, facilities, stations and installations may move or be moved freely over or below the surface of the moon.

3. Activities of States Parties in accordance with paragraphs 1 and 2 of this article shall not interfere with the activities of other States Parties on the moon. Where such interference may occur, the States Parties concerned shall undertake consultations in accordance with article 15, paragraphs 2 and 3, of this Agreement.

Article 9

1. States Parties may establish manned and unmanned stations on the moon. A State Party establishing a station shall use only that area which is required for the needs of the station and shall immediately inform the Secretary-General of the United Nations of the location and purposes of that station. Subsequently, at annual intervals that State shall likewise inform the Secretary-General whether the station continues in use and whether its purposes have changed.

2. Stations shall be installed in such a manner that they do not impede the free access to all areas of the moon of personnel, vehicles and equipment of other States Parties conducting activities on the moon in accordance with the provisions of this Agreement or of article I of the Treaty on Principles Governing the Activities of States in the Exploration and Use of Outer Space, including the Moon and Other Celestial bodies.

Article 10

1. States Parties shall adopt all practicable measures to safeguard the life and health of persons on the moon. For this purpose they shall regard any person on the moon as an astronaut within the meaning of article V of the Treaty on Principles Governing the Activities of States in the Exploration and Use of Outer Space, including the Moon and Other Celestial Bodies and as part of the personnel of a spacecraft within the meaning of the Agreement on the Rescue of Astronauts, the Return of Astronauts and the Return of Objects Launched into Outer Space.

2. States Parties shall offer shelter in their stations, installations, vehicles and other facilities to persons in distress on the moon.

Article 11

1. The moon and its natural resources are the common heritage of mankind, which finds its expression in the provisions of this Agreement, in particular in paragraph 5 of this article.

2. The moon is not subject to national appropriation by any claim of sovereignty, by means of use or occupation, or by any other means.

3. Neither the surface nor the subsurface of the moon, nor any part thereof or natural resources in place, shall become property of any State, international intergovernmental or non-governmental organization, national organization or non-governmental entity or of any natural person. The placement of personnel, space vehicles, equipment, facilities, stations and installations on or below the surface of the moon, including structures connected with its surface or subsurface, shall not create a right of ownership over the surface or the subsurface of the moon or any areas thereof. The foregoing provisions are without prejudice to the international régime referred to in paragraph 5 of this article.

4. States Parties have the right to exploration and use of the moon without discrimination of any kind, on the basis of equality and in accordance with international law and the provisions of this Agreement.

5. States Parties to this Agreement hereby undertake to establish an international régime, including appropriate procedures, to govern the exploitation of the natural resources of the moon as such exploitation is about to become feasible. This provision shall be implemented in accordance with article 18 of this Agreement.

6. In order to facilitate the establishment of the international régime referred to in paragraph 5 of this article, States Parties shall inform the Secretary-General of the United Nations as well as the public and the international scientific community, to the greatest extent feasible and practicable, of any natural resources they may discover on the moon.

7. The main purposes of the international régime to be established shall include:

(*a*) The orderly and safe development of the natural resources of the moon;

(*b*) The rational management of those resources;

(*c*) The expansion of opportunities in the use of those resources;

(*d*) An equitable sharing by all States Parties in the benefits derived from those resources, whereby the interests and needs of the developing countries, as well as the efforts of those countries which have contributed either directly or indirectly to the exploration of the moon, shall be given special consideration.

8. All the activities with respect to the natural resources of the moon shall be carried out in a manner compatible with the purposes specified in paragraph 7 of this article and the provisions of article 6, paragraph 2, of this Agreement.

Article 12

1. States Parties shall retain jurisdiction and control over their personnel, space vehicles, equipment, facilities, stations and installations on the

moon. The ownership of space vehicles, equipment, facilities, stations and installations shall not be affected by their presence on the moon.

2. Vehicles, installations and equipment or their component parts found in places other than their intended location shall be dealt with in accordance with article 5 of the Agreement on the Rescue of Astronauts, the Return of Astronauts and the return of Objects Launched into Outer Space.

3. In the event of an emergency involving a threat to human life, States Parties may use the equipment, vehicles, installations, facilities or supplies of other States Parties on the moon. Prompt notification of such use shall be made to the Secretary-General of the United Nations or the State Party concerned.

Article 13

A State Party which learns of the crash landing, forced landing or other unintended landing on the moon of a space object, or its component parts, that were not launched by it, shall promptly inform the launching State Party and the Secretary-General of the United Nations.

Article 14

1. States Parties to this Agreement shall bear international responsibility for national activities on the moon, whether such activities are carried out by governmental agencies or by non-governmental entities, and for assuring that national activities are carried out in conformity with the provisions of this Agreement. States Parties shall ensure that non-governmental entities under their jurisdiction shall engage in activities on the moon only under the authority and continuing supervision of the appropriate State Party.

2. States Parties recognize that detailed arrangements concerning liability for damage caused on the moon, in addition to the provisions of the Treaty on Principles Governing the Activities of States in the Exploration and Use of Outer Space, including the Moon and Other Celestial Bodies and the Convention on International Liability for Damage Caused by Space Objects, may become necessary as a result of more extensive activities on the moon. Any such arrangements shall be elaborated in accordance with the procedure provided for in article 18 of this Agreement.

Article 15

1. Each State Party may assure itself that the activities of other States Parties in the exploration and use of the moon are compatible with the provisions of this Agreement. To this end, all space vehicles, equipment,

facilities, stations and installations on the moon shall be open to other States Parties. Such States Parties shall give reasonable advance notice of a projected visit, in order that appropriate consultations may be held and that maximum precautions may be taken to assure safety and to avoid interference with normal operations in the facility to be visited. In pursuance of this article, any State Party may act on its own behalf or with the full or partial assistance of any other State Party or through appropriate international procedures within the framework of the United Nations and in accordance with the Charter.

2. A State Party which has reason to believe that another State Party is not fulfilling the obligations incumbent upon it pursuant to this Agreement or that another State Party is interfering with the rights which the former State has under this Agreement may request consultations with that State Party. A State Party receiving such a request shall enter into such consultations without delay. Any other State Party which requests to do so shall be entitled to take part in the consultations. Each State Party participating in such consultations shall seek a mutually acceptable resolution of any controversy and shall bear in mind the rights and interests of all States Parties. The Secretary-General of the United Nations shall be informed of the results of the consultations and shall transmit the information received to all States Parties concerned.

3. If the consultations do not lead to a mutually acceptable settlement which has due regard for the rights and interests of all States Parties, the parties concerned shall take all measures to settle the dispute by other peaceful means of their choice appropriate to the circumstances and the nature of the dispute. If difficulties arise in connexion with the opening of consultations or if consultations do not lead to a mutually acceptable settlement, any State Party may seek the assistance of the Secretary-General, without seeking the consent of any other State Party concerned, in order to resolve the controversy. A State Party which does not maintain diplomatic relations with another State Party concerned shall participate in such consultations, at its choice, either itself or through another State Party or the Secretary-General as intermediary.

Article 16

With the exception of articles 17 to 21, references in this Agreement to States shall be deemed to apply to any international intergovernmental organization which conducts space activities if the organization declared its acceptance of the rights and obligations provided for in this Agreement and if a majority of the States members of the organization are States Parties to this Agreement and to the Treaty on Principles Governing the Activities of States in the Exploration and Use of Outer Space, including the Moon and

Other Celestial Bodies. States members of any such organization which are States Parties to this Agreement shall take all appropriate steps to ensure that the organization makes a declaration in accordance with the provisions of this article.

Article 17

Any State Party to this Agreement may propose amendments to the Agreement. Amendments shall enter into force for each State Party to the Agreement accepting the amendments upon their acceptance by a majority of the States Parties to the Agreement and thereafter for each remaining State Party to the Agreement on the date of acceptance by it.

Article 18

Ten years after the entry into force of this Agreement, the question of the review of the Agreement shall be included in the provisional agenda of the General Assembly of the United Nations in order to consider, in the light of past application of the Agreement, whether it requires revision. However, at any time after the Agreement has been in force for five years, the Secretary-General of the United Nations, as depositary, shall, at the request of one third of the States Parties to the Agreement and with the concurrence of the majority of the States Parties, convene a conference of the States Parties to review this Agreement. A review conference shall also consider the question of the implementation of the provisions of article 11, paragraph 5, on the basis of the principle referred to in paragraph 1 of that article and taking into account in particular any relevant technological developments.

Article 19

1. This Agreement shall be open for signature by all States at United Nations Headquarters in New York.

2. This Agreement shall be subject to ratification by signatory States. Any State which does not sign this Agreement before its entry into force in accordance with paragraph 3 of this article may accede to it at any time. Instruments of ratification or accession shall be deposited with the Secretary-General of the United Nations.

3. This Agreement shall enter into force on the thirtieth day following the day of deposit of the fifth instrument of ratification.

4. For each State depositing its instrument of ratification or accession after the entry into force of this Agreement, it shall enter into force on the thirtieth day following the date of deposit of any such instrument.

5. The Secretary-General shall promptly inform all signatory and acceding States of the date of each signature, the date of deposit of each instrument of ratification or accession to this Agreement, the date of its entry into force and other notices.

Article 20

Any State Party to this Agreement may give notice of its withdrawal from the Agreement one year after its entry into force by written notification to the Secretary-General of the United Nations. Such withdrawal shall take effect one year from the date of receipt of this notification.

Article 21

The original of this Agreement, of which the Arabic, Chinese, English, French, Russian and Spanish texts are equally authentic, shall be deposited with the Secretary-General of the United Nations, who shall send certified copies thereof to all signatory and acceding States.

In Witness Whereof the undersigned, being duly authorized thereto by their respective Governments, have signed this Agreement, opened for signature at New York on 18 December 1979.

II. Parties

As of January 1986, the Moon Agreement of 1979 has accumulated a total of five parties. Of the five permanent members of the United Nations Security Council, none has become a party, that is, not China, France, the United Kingdom, the USA, or the USSR. A list of the five parties to the Agreement as of January 1986, together with the year of joining, follows (information from the Depositary):

Austria (1984), Chile (1984), Netherlands (1984), Philippines (1984), and Uruguay (1984).

Reference

UNGA (United Nations General Assembly). 1979. *Agreement governing the activities of states on the moon and other celestial bodies*. New York: UN General Assembly Resolution No. 34/68 of 5 December 1979, 8 pp.

Index